WHAT THE FOX?!

WHAT THE FOX?!

EDITED BY
Fred Patten

A THURSTON HOWL PUBLICATIONS BOOK

ISBN 9781945247309

WHAT THE FOX?!

Copyright © 2018 by Frederick Walter Patten

Edited by Fred Patten
Book design by Thurston Howl
Cover design by Tabsley
Cover art by Tabsley © 2018
Interior Illustrations by Tabsley and Jeqon © 2018

A Thurston Howl Publications Book
Published by Thurston Howl Publications
thurstonhowlpublications.com
Lansing, MI

To the unknown author of
Batrachomyomachia (*The Battle of Frogs and Mice*)

A comic parody of the *Iliad*, about the epic one-day war between the kingdoms of the frogs and the mice.

Thirsty mouse warrior-prince Psycharpax (Crumb-snatcher) drinks at a lakeside. Frog-king Physignathus (Puff-jaw) offers to take him across the lake on his back, but midway they are attacked by a great water-snake. The frog dives to save himself, and the mouse drowns. A mouse-warrior witnesses this and hurries to report it. The mouse-king declares war upon the frogs in revenge. The mice don armor made of bean pods and nutshells, while the frogs gird themselves with reed spears, plant-leaf shields, and snail-shell helmets. Zeus and the other gods watch them fight, taunting and betting each other to support one side or the other. When the mice start to win, Zeus sends an army of crabs to aid the frogs, to preserve both sides for their future amusement.

This is arguably the earliest known comedy; and anthropomorphic, too. Attributed by the ancients to various authors from Homer himself (ca. 1100 BCE) to about 480 BCE, but by modern scholars to an anonymous poet around the time of Alexander the Great (356 BCE - 323 BCE). Earlier Greek playwrights such as Epicharmus, Magnes, or Chionides were writing comedies (now lost; presumably not with anthropomorphic animals) by ca. 500 BCE to ca. 480 BCE.

CONTENTS

PREFACE

FRED PATTEN

What is furry literature?

The earliest anthropomorphic-animal novel is probably *The Life and Perambulation of a Mouse* by Dorothy Kilner, published in England in April 1784. It is a moral fantasy for children, narrated by Nimble the mouse, who spends his entire life escaping from cats, owls, and especially thoughtless children who consider it fun to torture small animals and birds. Most anthro-animal classics like *The Island of Dr. Moreau* by H. G. Wells, *Animal Farm* by George Orwell, *Watership Down* by Richard Adams, and *Tailchaser's Song* by Tad Williams are hardly a barrel of laughs.

Furry fandom genre literature arguably started with *Mus of Kerbridge* by Paul Kidd (TSR Books, April 1995). It really got going with the appearance of the furry specialty publishers around 2000. Today, books are flowing from FurPlanet Productions, Goal Press, Rabbit Valley Books, Sofawolf Press, Thurston Howl Publications, Weasel Press, and more. Yet, although they feature anthro animals in all genres—crime stories, high fantasy, horror, erotica, science fiction, sports, war stories, and Westerns—they are practically all dramatic fantasies. Despite a few high-profile exceptions, such as "400 Rabbits" by Alice "Huskyteer" Dryden which won both the 2016 Cóyotl and Ursa Major Awards, furry fiction has tended to emphasize the serious.

What the Fox?! is our little bit to correct this imbalance. Here are 24 furry stories that feature a llama barbershop quartet, a postal delivery person who is a werechihuahua, a dog Hollywood script writer, a sweet spider-woman, a cunning dragon, canine superheroes, and more. Some are gentle comedies worth a smile and a chuckle, while others are broad comedies to make you laugh out loud. Whatever your taste is in furry humor, *What the Fox?!* is for you.

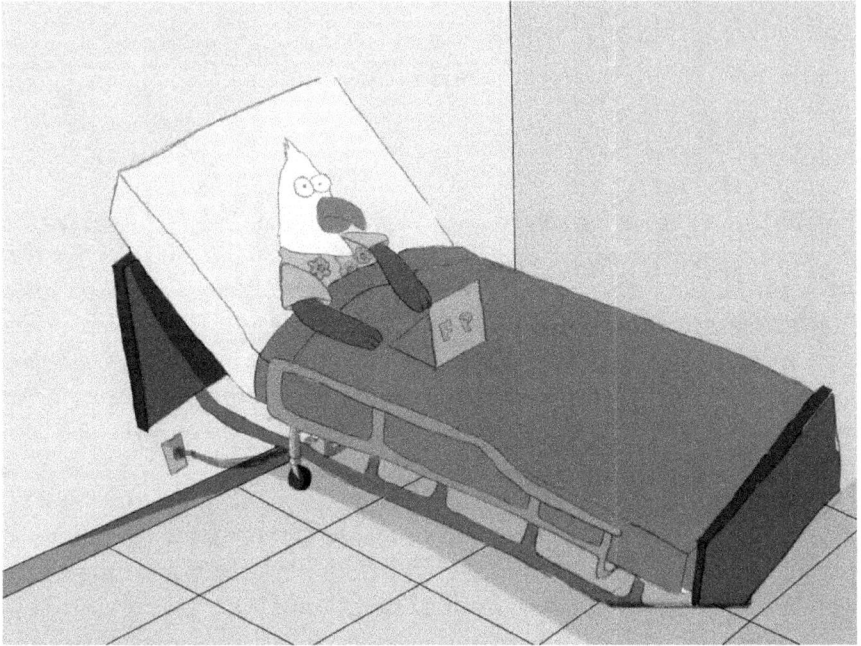

Fred Patten, hard at work reviewing furry literature and
editing anthologies[1]

Each of the pieces in this collection has received complimentary artwork to accompany them. The artists came up with a list of popular comic book, animation, and illustration styles and—roughly—randomly selected stories for each style. They note that this way of illustrating was meant to be "fun," if not always funny. If you're curious about a style, check the Letter from the Artists at the back of the book for the "answer key." This also means that the illustrators took some creative liberty with the pieces, again, to make this a fun anthology.

3

FAPD

SOFOX

Sofox is a game and web developer who hails from Dublin, Ireland. Loving reading from an early age, he's written in many forms over the years but this is his first time to be physically published. On the development side, he developed an app called Algebalance that teaches basic algebra through a fun puzzle game. While loving anthropomorphic cartoons from a young age, he first got introduced to the furry fandom through furry webcomics, which led to the first of many conventions. What he loves about the fandom is the creativity and drive of people to make their own thing that they like.

The briefing room hushed as the Sergeant slithered forward. Several rows of police officers cut their small talk to pay attention to the cobra as he took his position at the front of the room.

"Every day I walk in here and wonder why we're doing this?" the Sergeant began his familiar spiel. "This city's a shithole. The people hate us. No matter what we do, it seems to barely make a tiny dent in the deluge of crime, depravity, and the worst this city has to offer. We're hated by everyone, until the moment they find someone they hate even more; and then they call us to deal with them. Why do we do it? Why do we even try to make a difference? Why do we get out of bed and even try to step outside wearing our uniform? And then I remember...it's because they're paying us."

The room murmured in cynical agreement and nods before the Sergeant quickly moved on to the schedule.

"First up, we have a new officer joining our ranks. Jun Marbles!" A small squirrel in the front row looked up and beamed. "She just graduated from the Academy with completely average grades that are honestly nothing to write home about." The squirrel stopped smiling. "However, she didn't fail or anything, so here she is. Please forgive her fresh Academy naiveté, and try not to immediately destroy her hopes with the soul-crushing reality of what police work is really like before she even leaves the room. Give her until lunchtime, at least." The squirrel was now frowning. "Speaking of soul-crushing, her Field Training Officer will be Sal Nubek." A hippo in the back corner nodded.

"Now for today's roster: Stevens, Segal, you're on patrol. Rhodes, you're on a wild goose chase. That gander has been seen over by the lake district; the first time he's been so close to home since he murdered his family. Kouka, I actually forget what you're meant to be doing, but you never do anything useful, so you can just...not commit crimes for the rest of today. Waterheim, you're on the verge of being suspended for violently assaulting that suspected art thief, so until that happens you can do regular police work. I want you to interview another suspected art thief who claims he was beaten up by a police officer. Nubek? As FTO to Marbles, you'll be training her so she actually knows what she's doing for the rest of her career. Go on patrol, answer the calls, and don't be afraid to throw her into the worst this city has to offer."

"It's all 'the worst.'"

"Who else is there?"

Jun pulled herself into the passenger seat of the cruiser. Sal barely looked at her before starting the engine and pulling out, holding the wheel over her big, bloated stomach.

"You may think you know everything, but you don't. Forget everything you learned at the Academy about procedure, rules, evidence, ethics, morality, and basic hygiene. The Academy is just a bunch of tests and procedures. Here it's reality. You can't just cheat off your neighbor's test, like I did. Out here, there's only one rule: survive and get paid."

Jun nodded, blank-faced.

"Also, watch out for those damn rodents. They're always up to something."

"Erm, squirrels are ro..."

"I meant *rodents* rodents!"

Jun just went silent.

Suddenly, the radio squawked. "We've got a 10-91A, spotted at Lake Drive. Suspect is male, white, arctic fox, believed to be an exile dodger—Ronnie Dodger, who was exiled for multiple infractions. Suspect should be treated as annoying but potentially dangerous."

Sal whipped up the radio receiver. "This is Car 68. You better believe we're on our way." And they were.

The white fox warily crossed the street, only to get slammed in the side by a cruising police car. Sprawled on the street, he agonizingly tried to recover, only to hear the doors of the car open. A big hippopotamus police officer came over to stand over him.

"You know you're not meant to be here."

"I was only trying to...."

The fox grunted in pain as Sal pulled him up, slapped handcuffs on him, and threw him into the back seat of the car. "You have the right to get your ass out of this city forever! Time to head toward the border," and they took off.

The car soon reached a painted white dashed line across the barren ground. Sal stopped the car right in front of it before pulling Ronnie out of the car and pushing him toward it.

"Now CROSS!"

"Oh, I'm sure there's no way I'm going to cross back over," said Ronnie sarcastically.

Sal slammed her large fist right into his stomach, collapsing him.

"You know what, you're right! I'm going to have to make damn sure you can't walk back across. Oh, I know." She pulled out her gun and fired into his leg. He yelled in pain, launching a tirade of expletives.

"This is police brutality!"

"Why does everyone feel they have to point that out?"

"I didn't do anything wrong!"

"You dodged your exile."

"I mean before that. I didn't do anything to deserve being exiled. This one cop just really had it in for me...."

"Well, now you've got two! Now MOVE!" She slammed a kick into his side, moving him infinitesimally toward the border line. Getting the message, he started crawling to close the distance, leaving a streak of blood on the ground behind him.

"Exile dodgers just CANNOT take a hint." They were driving back now, having ensured that every part of the fox's body was on the other side of the line. "They think they're above it all; they can just sneak back in whenever it pleases them. But they just do the same things over and over again, and waste everyone's time. Killing's too good for them. Want a Tic-Tac?"

Jun declined.

"That's how it is. A lot of people running around doing whatever they want and we're the ones that have to put a stop to them. Sure, some of the things we do may not technically be permitted by any legal books or constitutions, but we get results! It's a jungle out there, not a petting zoo. Out there, there are wolves and sheep; and lions, and koalas, and parrots, and...so on. The point is: to catch a wolf you've got to be a wolf, or tiger, or bear, or really any animal with a gun. Firearms really did screw up the whole food chain hierarchy. So keep your weapon on you at all times and fire on anyone that looks even the slightest bit suspicious. Sure you don't want a Tic-Tac?"

Jun refused.

"Seriously, they're not drugged or anything. I keep my Tic-Tacs and drugs separate; learned that one from experience."

Jun refused, emphatically this time.

"Suit yourself....."

Once again the radio squawked to life. "Car 68, could you provide assistance to Detective Shady? He is currently in Northern Hills."

"What's the crime?"

"Possible stolen character."

"Ugh, them criminals never sleep."

"I put so much work into creating that character," Polly Velvatine, a white rabbit, whined from the porch of her house. "His name was Devon. He was navy with purple streaks; always wore these trainers. I was going to have a comic series featuring him in it..."

"It's okay, we'll work this out," the bear detective replied, as the cruiser pulled up. Leaning into the open window, he described the situation. "She's distraught. She spent months with this guy, and now he's gone. We chased leads on this a while ago, but nothing substantial until we just received a tip that someone with that garish color scheme was being walked around here on a leash. The description of the leash-holder matches that of Denise Williams, who, the victim says, regularly sent her creepy messages before Devon disappeared. Of course, creators get sent creepy messages the whole time, so we really only just interviewed Denise. She denied everything, so we just politely asked her not to commit any crimes. This time, I've got a search warrant for her house, so the plan is to knock, ask politely to enter, and if things go south I want you two as backup."

"Ugh, these thefts are the worst. Can't they come up with their own character? Is it that hard to be original? Or even just pay for one?"

"Hey, if everyone was smart, we wouldn't have a job!"

"True."

"Please help me find my Devon." Polly hurried up to the cruiser. "He's so precious to me."

"Is he your first?" asked Jun.

"Well, there was a thing back in high school...but I don't like talking about that...."

"And can you remind me what he looks like?"

Polly enthusiastically burst into a description of her character that was at least three pages long. It was essentially the same as the one she'd just given Shady, only with far more pointless details including talk of his personality, his likes/dislikes, facts about his past, and an intricate breakdown of his fur pattern and preferred clothing.

When Polly drifted into a possible alternate version of Devon who lived in a sci-fi setting, Sal interrupted with a "Thank you" and drove off. They arrived at Denise's house and saw Detective Shady approach the front door.

At the house, Detective Shady knocked several times on the door. A poodle answered, opening the door just a crack and peering out. "Hello, I'm afraid you've caught me at a bad time..."

Shady kicked in the door, throwing the poodle back. With the door open, the detective and the police officers could see Denise was wearing a slick, black, PVC getup. Only, on closer examination, the outfit wasn't exactly...clean...

"Where IS he?" Shady said through gritted teeth, suddenly tense with rage. "Where is Devon?"

"Well, um...Devon is happy...I mean...," she whimpered. A thump was heard coming from downstairs, followed by a muffled yell.

"Of course. Why be original...Come on, officers," he signaled to Sal and Jun. Jun picked up the situation and was actually the first to find the door to the basement. With the three grouped up and Denise handcuffed, they started to descend, Shady first. Shady had the deepest fears about what they would find down there, and every one of them were confirmed. Restraints, ball gags, leashes, whips, bicycle pumps, chains, feathers, handcuffs, diapers, paint, latex, latex paint, branding irons, egg beaters and other tools that Shady didn't want to even imagine the purpose of. And there was Devon, strapped to the ceiling by a hoisted X restraint, an incredibly pained and desperate look in his eyes, a dirty sock stuffed in his mouth. On a platform below him was...well, some things are better not described. There was evidence that pretty much every single item in that room was being used on, in, or with him. Shady threw up, which added to the terrible smells in the room. It was really the one thing Devon hadn't been subjected to at that stage.

"How can you do it?" Shady harangued Denise, now handcuffed in the back seat of the cruiser. Devon was already in an ambulance on the way to get immediate care. "How can you let a stolen character be subjected to...THAT! Why do you people do these things?"

"I just thought it was hot," whined the poodle.

Shady restrained himself. He turned away and walked back to his car, muttering, "There's good out there, there HAS to be..."

"You handled yourself pretty good back there," Sal said.

Jun was taken aback. A genuine compliment? "Well, so did you..."

"Don't turn that compliment back on me. I've been doing this for 12 years. I've seen a lot of shit. Often literally, as you saw today. With that much time, you develop a stomach for it. Except Shady, for some reason. You'd think he'd be used to it by now. He takes everything so personally...Anyway, you went right into that your first time, barely batted an eyelid, handled it like a pro."

"Thanks."

"So...you've seen stuff like that before?"

"I don't want to talk about it." She looked away.

"C'mon, you can tell me...."

"Did you notice anything familiar about Devon?"

"Sorry?"

"The owner. When she was describing Devon, she said Devon was a Lynx-Lion hybrid. She called him a 'Lion' before she corrected herself and called him a 'Lynx,' then corrected herself again and called him a 'Lionx,' which she just about managed to strangle out of her mouth. However when I saw Devon, he seemed more like a Bobcat-Lion, or 'Bion.' It reminded me of something..." Jun leaned forward and tapped on the dashboard computer.

"Hey, did I say you could use the computer? Or start a sentence that trails off?"

Jun leaned back and remained silent. A moment passed.

"Okay, use the damn thing; and finish your sentence."

Jun tapped on the screen again. "...I saw this when I was going over crime reports for this area." She typed a bit more. "There. Dominic Jones. A purple Bion character. Went missing July 1st, presumed stolen. Look familiar?"

Sal almost crashed the car looking at the photo on the screen.

"You mean...?"

"Yep, assuming that my trailed-off sentence was going in the direction I think it was going."

Sal hit the handbrake and threw the car into a violent U Turn. Denise was only lightly slammed against the side door as the car moved onto its new heading and shot off.

"Do the words 'Original Character: Do not steal' not mean anything to you?" Sal towered over the rabbit. She looked nervous, but then anyone who had twice their body height of hippo standing over them would probably act like that.

"W...w...well yes, that's why I called you. How's Devon?"

"Oh, he's fine. Horrifically traumatized beyond all recognition and in desperate need of therapy, but fine. After he checks out of the hospital, he'll be returned to his owner."

"That's great..."

"Which is Terri White! I believe you know her. Went to the same school. Ring any bells? An iguana?"

Polly froze. "Well, I...erm"

"How stupid do you have to be," exploded Sal, "to steal a character and then call the police when your stolen character gets stolen? Do you think we wouldn't have figured it out? Did you really think we'd just hand him back to you? Are you really as stupid as you think we are?"

"Look, it wasn't theft; we had an agreement!"

"An agreement that you'd steal him from Terri while she was buying him an ice cream in the park? An agreement that you'd then repaint him navy with purple stripes and pretend to everyone that he was some made-up, and frankly ludicrous, hybrid with a color scheme that you couldn't even pronounce? An agreement to give him a different name and put him in a comic that, as your filing shows, wasn't even going to credit Terri?"

"I know Terri; we go way back..."

"And she's regretted every moment you've spent with her. Yes, we spoke to her on the way here. She hates you, she never liked you in the first place, or that stupid cow joke you kept telling, which honestly comes across as somewhat racist. You don't have permissions for her character, and with what you've done, I'm not surprised if you get exiled."

Polly's eyes widened "Exiled? But she said I could use her character. She's lying to you. Don't listen to her."

"...I really don't have time for this," and then Sal took out her gun and shot Polly in the leg. "I know that was a bit unprofessional," said Sal to Jun as she got back into her car, "but she was annoying me, and I hadn't shot anyone since this morning. At worst, I'll just pretend that Shady learned the truth, got angry, and shot her. People would believe that; it's the sort of thing he would do. Heck, he may even take credit for it. Just need to dispose of the gun first...or maybe plant it on him. We'll see. Anyway, it's so stupid; stealing someone's character and then calling the police when somebody else steals it. It's like the criminals here believe we're as stupid as they are."

Still handcuffed in the back seat, Denise spoke up. "So...am I still being arrested?"

"Yes," replied Jun and Sal simultaneously.

"Terri's already been in to see Devon...I mean Dominic. She says she plans to put him back to work in trades and prints in order to make money for his therapy bills, but in any event, she says the whole ordeal has really done wonders for his "tragic backstory" vibe. She figures if she just creates the right boyfriend for him, the attention toward him will skyrocket." Sal was giving her report to the Sergeant. There would be paperwork to fill out, but the cobra liked a quick briefing in advance.

"Well, as long as the original creator is happy, that's all that matters!" the Sergeant said. "By the way, you didn't happen to see Ms. Velvatine after you discovered she stole the character, did you?"

"No, we just called it in, and brought Denise to the lockup. We decided not to have them both in the same car."

"Well, when a car arrived on the scene, they saw trails of blood. Apparently Ms. Velvatine had to drag herself to the hospital after being shot in the leg, twice."

"Twice?" asked Sal.

"Twice."

"Oh well, you know how some violent crimes never get solved."

"Do you think there's a danger of that happening here?"

"Well, give the case file to Detective Shady, and we can make sure."

"A solid plan. I will indeed," the cobra then turned to Jun. "So, your first day doing real police work. How did you find it?"

"Unforgettable," replied Jun.

"Good. I was worried you'd give a response that would make me ask for more details. Well, I'm heading home to get drunk and bang the wife, in an order that I've yet to decide upon," and he left the room.

The large but poorly maintained car stopped outside an apartment block. "Thanks for taking me home," Jun called to Sal, both in casual clothes now.

"Hey Jun, you did good today." Jun looked up and beamed. "So you better do just as well tomorrow, or I'll think it was a fluke." Jun stopped smiling.

The car drove off.

Sighing, Jun went into the building, climbed the stairs to her apartment, and went in. Niall was just making dinner as she went in.

"So, how did it go?" he asked.

"Compared to what we were trained for in the Academy? It was nothing. There were only two irresponsible discharges of firearms for the whole day, and I wasn't even asked to clean up a sex dungeon...."

"I just thought it was hot," whined the poodle.

PERFECT HARMONY

JALETA CLEGG

Jaleta Clegg may look human, but she's most likely an alien. It would explain a lot. She usually writes science fiction adventure or fantasy quests or silly horror, but for this anthology, she ventured into the unknown territory of animal barbershop quartets. Yes, llamas DO hum, probably because they never learned the words. And that's what llamas DO. When not writing, Jaleta is usually sprawled on her favorite couch watching bad sci-fi on TV and turning yarn into things like a hedgehog army or ugly afghans. She enjoys cooking weird foods, then inflicting her concoctions on her family. She lives on the dry side of Washington with two elderly dogs, an obese and very large cat who poops demons, a diminishing horde of children, and a very patient husband.

"Where's Geoff?" Melvin whispered as he craned his long llama neck. His bulging eyes blinked, long lashes sweeping his furry cheek. "They're going to call us to the stage soon. We can't perform without Geoff. We'll be eliminated from the competition!"

"Calm, Melvin," Harold answered. He closed his eyes and pinched his footpads together. "Calm…" The word trailed into a musical hum.

Bob joined the hum, two fifths below.

Habit won over nerves. Melvin drew in a breath through his flat nose and joined with the middle note of the chord. The three llamas hummed. The harmony did soothe his jangled senses, even if it lacked the bass note that Geoff should have provided.

"Better?" Bob asked when the chord had faded.

Melvin nodded then replaced his straw boater hat. "Where is Geoff? We can't go on without our bass. I mean, I know he was worried that his jacket wouldn't fit, not after all those workouts he's been doing, but we need him, even without his jacket. It's a quartet, not a trio!"

Harold straightened the collar of Bob's baby blue suit coat. "The colors are so lovely, especially with your dark fleece. I'm glad we chose to go with this one instead of that desert tan the saleslady kept pushing on us."

Melvin nibbled one footpad. "I bet Geoff went and got himself sheared, and he's too embarrassed to show up now. Stupid! How could he ruin our big shot like this? We could go home with the gold, but not without a bass. We've only got two rounds to prove we're the best. We can't do it without our bass. This is barbershop; it's my life! Doesn't Geoff understand that? It's just fun and games to him. This is why I exist!"

Bob adjusted Harold's boater. "Just breathe, Melvin."

They joined in harmony once more, closing their eyes and resting their furry foreheads together.

"Drama Llamas, you're up!" The stage director, a lithe panther, lashed his tail while he checked them off his list. "Way to go, Millie's Madness. Great harmonizing there," he said to the four elephants stepping off the stage.

"Where's Geoff?" Melvin's voice squeaked.

"I see a baby blue suit coat; he's coming. I think." Bob squinted. "That's not Geoff."

The giraffe lumbered, like a crane jerking and bobbing as it moved through lesser construction vehicles.

"He's wearing our suit," Geoff whispered. "Why?"

Bob's phone buzzed. He fished it out of his pocket, stared at the screen, then curled his upper lip. "Geoff says he has laryngitis. He has arranged for a substitute. He should have called us hours ago!" With each statement, his voice grew more shrill.

"Calm," Harold repeated, though his own lip trembled with the urge to curl.

"Drama Llamas! Move it or lose it," the stage manager growled.

"Calm," the three llamas hummed in perfect three-part harmony as they shuffled toward the steps up to the stage.

"That giraffe is headed our way," Melvin whispered. "You don't think he's the substitute Geoff sent, do you?" He blinked his bulging eyes.

The giraffe stopped just outside their circle. They twisted their long necks to stare up toward the high ceiling and the giraffe's head. His knees were on eye level with the llamas. But the suit was the right color, with the black piping and white ruffles on the shirt. The humming chord trailed off into silence.

Melvin's lips worked for a long moment before he could spit the words out. "Who are you?"

"Hey. I'm Dillan. Geoff sent me." The giraffe brushed a hand down the ill-fitting baby blue suit coat. He bent his head under the light beam, twisting his square-spotted neck as he tried to bring his eyes down to their level. He missed by over four feet, but he tried.

"We can't perform like this," Melvin snapped. His bottom lip curled, exposing his square teeth.

"We have to," Bob laid his hand on Melvin's long neck. "The show must go on."

"Now, Drama Llamas!" the stage panther called.

Bob, Harold, and Melvin trotted up the stairs. Their steps were dainty and precise as they took their places on stage. Dillan plopped his too-large feet on the steps. His toe caught the lip of the stage, sending him tumbling into the spotlight in a tangle of long legs and longer neck. The audience gasped, then laughed, as he crashed into the three llamas. All four members sprawled across the stage to more hoots of laughter.

"We are not a comedy act," Melvin muttered. "Get it together, Dillan. Are you certain we can't perform as a trio?"

"Against the rules," Bob whispered.

The three llamas gracefully regained their feet, then stood awkwardly while the giraffe untangled his limbs and scrambled upright. His head bobbed up into the lights above the top of the stage curtains. The audience laughed again. Dillan ducked his head down, curving his neck, then took a long moment straightening his bow tie. Melvin's lips tightened in disapproval. Bob and Harold blinked menacingly.

"We take our music seriously," Melvin whispered once the giraffe stopped his antics.

The judges—two songbirds, a cat, and a hippopotamus—shifted impatiently.

Dillan stopped fidgeting and produced a pitch pipe. He blew a short note.

Bob shook his head and motioned up with his front hoof.

Dillan blew a higher note.

Bob nodded.

The llamas traded looks, then hummed a chord. A high chord.

Harold's face wrinkled with effort. He waved his hand at Dillan.

The giraffe blew a lower note.

The llamas dropped the chord. Harold relaxed into the lower note. The audience laughed.

Melvin waved at Dillan. They needed the bass note to anchor their chord.

The giraffe tooted on the pitch pipe.

The llamas responded with a new chord.

Dillan played another note. The chord slid to a new key. The giraffe bounced between notes faster and faster. The llamas hummed chords, sliding up and down the scale, long necks bobbing to keep up.

The audience guffawed.

Melvin snatched the pitch pipe from the giraffe. He blew a solid C, then tucked the pipe in his coat pocket.

Harold hit a high C. Bob filled in an E below. Melvin hit the G between. All three looked at Dillan, waiting for the low C to complete their harmony. The giraffe froze, staring at the audience. Bob nudged him. Dillan swallowed, long neck jerking. He swayed, then crashed to the stage floor. The audience howled with laughter.

"He's out cold," Bob said.

"What do we do now?" Melvin whispered.

"Final chord, then bow," Harold answered, his long face as calm and unruffled as ever.

They hit a C major, letting their humming trail off into silence. Then the three llamas bowed low. They snagged Dillan's coat and dragged him off stage as quickly as they could manage. The audience cheered and laughed.

The next group, a chorus of seals, flippered their way onto the stage.

The panther laughed and slapped Harold on his shoulder. "Great show, very funny."

The Drama Llamas fled to their dressing room, trailed by the clumsy replacement giraffe. Dillan swayed woozily as he traipsed along corridors too short for his height. Once the door to the room shut, the llamas collapsed on the couches, faces drooping. Dillan awkwardly settled to the floor in the corner, legs splayed out in front of him.

"That was horrible," Melvin moaned. "How can we ever show our faces again?"

"The stage manager said we were great," Harold responded.

"He says that to everyone." Melvin clapped one split hoof over his eyes. "I have never been so humiliated in all my life. It's all Geoff's fault."

"Sorry," Dillan said. His head drooped low over the table. "I just get so nervous in front of an audience. And when I'm nervous, my legs

17

get all mixed up. I thought you wanted an F sharp to start. Then I couldn't find the note and you kept waving your hooves at me so I kept trying different notes—"

Harold shushed the giraffe with a dismissive wave. "I think we just all need to take a deep breath. It isn't the end of the world, after all." He crossed his legs and touched his front toe pads together. "All together now." He hummed a clear note. The other two llamas joined in. All three looked at Dillan.

The giraffe shrugged. "I don't hum."

"Then what do you do, besides fall all over the stage and ruin our performance?" Melvin huffed out an angry snort.

"Melvin," Bob laid a hoof on Melvin's shoulder. "Be kind."

Melvin spit at Bob. Bob retaliated. Gobs of green goo flew back and forth, speckling the baby blue suits and white ruffled shirts.

"Stop it, both of you," Harold snapped, his calm disturbed. "We are here to sing. Let's sing." He hummed a new note.

"I was just trying to help," Bob muttered as he turned away from Melvin. He closed his eyes and added his note.

Melvin turned his angry bug-eyed stare on Dillan. "Where's our bass? We need it to support the harmony." He hummed his note, loud and rough.

Bob and Harold both shook their heads, glaring at Melvin.

Melvin shrank down, his ears flattening in apology. He mellowed his note to match theirs. The harmony blended beautifully. All three llamas looked to the giraffe.

Dillan opened his mouth.

The llamas glared.

He closed his mouth. His lips worked for a long moment. The llamas' chord hummed in the room. The giraffe opened his mouth and belted out the bass note.

Melvin rolled his eyes. Bob sneered. Harold gave a long-suffering sigh.

"What?" Dillan said as the echoes of his note faded. "Was I off-key?"

"No, your note was fine," Harold said, "it's just that we're llamas. We don't sing. We hum."

"I don't know if you've noticed, but I'm not a llama." Dillan gave a giraffish smile. "Notice the lack of a thick fleece, and the greater height, and the knobs on my head."

"And the square brown spots. We noticed," Melvin snapped.

18

"You're a giraffe."

"I don't hum. I sing."

"But we're the Drama *Llamas*. We hum." Melvin lowered his brow and gave Dillan his best glare. At least the best glare a llama could summon. It was mostly pop-eyed brow-wiggling and lip-curling.

"But Geoff is not here, and Dillan is," Harold interrupted. "We have to make do."

"I'll help you teach Geoff his lesson later," Bob promised Melvin. "But I'm still angry at you." He worked his lip to spit.

"Absolutely *no* spitting," Harold said. "We can rise above this."

"But we hum, and we can't hum our chords without Geoff." Melvin folded his forelegs and sulked. "And since our giraffe refuses to hum, we're going to have to forfeit the competition."

A paper slid under their door. Melvin trotted across the floor, stepping with exaggerated caution over the giraffe's splayed legs. He picked up the paper, read it through, frowned, then read it again. "This is terrible!"

"What?" Bob jumped up and trotted over to crowd Melvin as he tried to read over the llama's haunch.

"The judges say we have to sing our next song, not just hum. Sing!" Melvin threw himself into the couch. "We don't know any of the words. We only hum. First Geoff and now this. We're doomed!"

"Maybe not," Dillan said. "I have an idea."

"A giraffe has an idea," Melvin snarked. "I bet it isn't any good."

"We'll never know until we hear it," Harold said. "Now, breathe with me. Calm…"

The chord echoed in the room.

Dillan nodded. "Just hold that chord for a moment, and I'll show you what I have in mind." His grin promised mischief. "And a one, and a two, and a three—"

"Wait," Bob protested. "How is this going to work if you've got stage fright?"

Dillan's lip quivered. "I can sing off-stage. It's only when I see the lights and the audience that I lose it."

"You have to be on-stage to perform," Melvin pointed out, with emphatic hoof motions. "Not falling up the stairs and sprawling on the stage, but standing and," he paused for a breath, "*humming*."

"Singing," Bob corrected. "We have to sing. How are we going to do that? Smarty pants giraffe has a fix for that?"

A giant tear rolled down the giraffe's cheek. "I just wanted to help

19

Geoff out. He's got laryngitis. Can't hum a sound. I'm not a pro like you guys. Do you know how much it means to get to be with you at all? I love the Drama Llamas. And now I blew it for you. I am so sorry."

Melvin's glare melted. A tear to match Dillan's dripped into his cheek fleece. "Really? You love us?"

Dillan nodded. "This meant the world to me, getting to be here with you guys. Humming with you, well, sort of."

Melvin and Bob closed ranks on either side of Dillan, draping their front legs as far as they would reach around the giraffe.

"It isn't over yet," Harold said. "We have one more performance. I just hope they gave us points for comedy on that last performance. But we have to come up with something new."

"I can sing," Dillan said, wiping his nose on his front hoof. "I don't know about humming. If you're okay with humming while I sing, I know the perfect song. All the words and everything."

"This might work," Bob said, his front lip splitting in a grin.

"But what about his stage fright?" Melvin patted Dillan's shoulder.

Harold smiled, a very zen, calm smile. "It's seeing the lights and the audience that scares you?"

Dillan nodded.

"I've got a solution for that. Huddle close, boys, and let me explain. And you, Dillan, tell us what song you have in mind."

"Ladies and Gentlebeasts, welcome to the quarter-final round of the Three Rivers Barbershop Competition!" The announcer's voice boomed, only partly from the speakers. The rhino possessed a truly impressive vocal range.

"I can't wait," Bob said, dancing on his toe tips.

Melvin shivered, head to toe, setting the glitter in his fleece to sparkling. Bob drew in a deep breath.

"Calm," Harold breathed.

"We're going to win this time. All due to Dillan, here." Bob clapped his hand on Dillan's back.

"Just breathe," Harold said.

"Hold my hoof," Dillan stuck one hoof out in front. He adjusted his mirrored shades with the other. "I can't see a thing."

"That's the general idea," Melvin said.

"First up," the rhino said, "Drama Llamas!"

The audience cheered as the three llamas and one giraffe bumbled their way to the stage. Dillan kept a grip on Bob the whole way. They lined up in front of the mics. The audience quieted, waiting.

Bob blew an F.

The three llamas drew in breath, then hummed a perfect F major. They let it slide into minor, then back to major. Bob snapped his fingers for the rhythm. They shifted up to A minor, down to C major, then back to F major.

Bob pointed at Dillan.

The giraffe stayed frozen, smiling off to the left of the stage. His mirrored glasses reflected the spotlight.

The llamas went through the chord progression again, thumping their feet to the bluesy rhythm. This time, Bob thumped Dillan's arm. The llamas paused.

Dillan opened his mouth. The audience waited. The llama trio waited. The judges waited. Dillan drew in his breath.

"Yeah," he sang. The deep notes trembled in the music hall. He let the note hang, drawing it out through a very long breath. He snatched a new breath, then dropped it into the basement. "You know it's all about the neck—" The notes climbed up the scale, then dropped.

The audience gasped. The llamas kicked it into a new humming chord.

"—'Bout my spots, and the face," Dillan belted out. "No sable."

The giraffe gave the song everything he had, his bass voice rumbling the seats on the low notes, reaching and soaring down from the rafters for the high ones. The llama harmony kept pace, sliding through the chord progression with ease.

Halfway through the second chorus, Bob grabbed the mic. He started beatboxing, hissing and thumping into the sound system.

Melvin shot him an outraged glare. Bob shrugged it off and kept going.

Harold grabbed Melvin's ear, pulled him around. The two of them hummed the harmonics.

"You know it's all about the fleece—" Dillan threw his front legs out and his head back. His neck swayed as he sang. His glasses flashed.

A gazelle in the audience swooned into the legs of her date. A trio of raccoon females tossed their masks towards the stage. Other females screamed at his low notes.

"Yeah, my momma she told me don't worry about your height—" Dillan's voice rose, clear and bright through the higher notes. He twirled, his coat flaring out.

The audience went wild.

Bob kept up the beatboxing while he dropped and bounced back up in a slick dance move.

Harold and Melvin swayed, snapping fingers in time. Their humming melodies only bolstered Dillan's magnificent voice.

Dillan's feet flashed as he moonwalked across the stage, his deep voice thundering out the final chorus.

His hoof caught on the edge of the stage. He went over in a tumble of giraffe limbs.

The room went silent. The llamas stared in horror. The audience held its collective breath.

Dillan raised one triumphant hoof.

"'Bout my face!"

The audience shrieked and cheered.

Harold, Bob, and Melvin took multiple bows before helping Dillan out of the orchestra pit that was, thankfully, empty. The cheering reached a fever pitch as he regained his feet. Females of all species screamed the quartet's name as the llamas escorted him off stage.

"Ladies and Gentlebeasts, that was the Drama Llamas!" The rhino's voice sounded weak after Dillan's magnificent performance.

Backstage, Melvin flung his foreleg around Dillan. "I am so sorry for what I said. You can sing with our humming any day. And you, Bob, where did that come from?"

"It's just something about his bass," Bob answered. "Not even Geoff's humming can compare with that voice."

"It's the vocal chords," Dillan said, blushing. "They're so long, see. Harmonics, vibrations, that kind of thing."

"It truly is all about the bass," Harold said. "Whether we win or lose, that was the most fun I've ever had."

The three llamas and the bass giraffe walked out of the concert hall into the night and into legend.

"Ladies and Gentlebeasts, that was the Drama Llamas!"

COUNTER-CURLTURE

TELEVASSI

Televassi writes, naturally, to give his habit of staring off into space some legitimacy, as well as that of routinely frequenting coffee shops to fuel his chai latte "problem." His poetry, prose, and non-fiction have featured publications such as Heat *(Sofawolf Press),* Furries Among Us *(Thurston Howl Publications), and the Ursa Major Award-winning* Gods with Fur *(FurPlanet Productions). Televassi is currently working on a novella that he hopes to finish by the end of next year, but then again he said that to himself the year before. Outside of writing, Televassi likes to rock climb, wander about in the woods, frequent furmeets, and generally be a well-socialized wolf.*

Den-mother was a moon-fearing wolf. She was always bristling her tail about her litter's future; paws perpetually stained with ink from the latest newspaper articles on the troublesome youth. She lifted her ears whenever the balding elders spoke, drinking in their words, tongue twisted against her teeth as they slavered endlessly about their issues.

"They spend their money on avocado on toast, and wear their jeans two inches lower than their parents—rapping rather than howling at the moon! They even have no interest in building dens together!"

And den-mother would nod along with those wolves and mutter to herself, "If their pack mentality isn't curtailed, I dread to think about the future!" Because the first thing you should know about wolves is that pack mentality determines everything. If enough of the pack does it, everyone else follows suit.

They say.

So, instead of spending my Sundays eating sweets and sneaking up on horses with my friends, I was dragged indoors by the scruff of my neck to be told how to be a "proper" wolf. The lessons were on everything a 21st century wolf like me didn't need to know; like the hows, whens, wheres, and whos for holding your tail. Or "traditional language"—that's biting, howling, barking, sniffing. Apparently, it's a dying art because too many of us speak only English these days.

I never experienced a free Sunday as a result; I only knew about them by staring out the window listening to the laughter as the rest of the world skipped on by, unfettered by their heritage.

Today was no different.

The old one-eye stood at the front of the room, tapping his chipped claws against the desk, lecturing a young wolf with faded purple streaks in her otherwise brown mane about how she ought to have memorized the phases of the moon. It's obvious Evie's not listening; it's easy to follow her green eyes as they darted around, counting how many patches of wrinkled skin she can spot as they peered out from underneath that old fool's thinning fur.

Satisfied, the elder snapped his jaws and strode back to the whiteboard, arching his neck as if about to howl.

"Can't you feel it flowing through your veins—don't you feel wild, powerful?" he growled, clawing his fur as he strutted to the back of the classroom. "As beasts, we were feared and admired! We were the first to be uplifted because we were those things to humans, and even later to the rest of modified kind! Yet you pups would rather live without it, abandoning your proud traditions, copying everyone else like an uncultured mongrel!"

I rolled my eyes. Not this again; not the "how can you be a wolf if you've got dyed fur" thing.

I cast my eye back out the window, watching my friends—Blue and Shadow—make faces at the windows as they cycled by. They laughed and shouted, tongues waving in the air like pink ribbons as they sped past. They had it so easy, being dogs.

The old one leapt forward, slapping his paw on my desk—pressing a single, yellowed fang against my neck. I wrinkled my muzzle; his breath stank of rotten meat as he tried that primal method of discipline. If it hadn't fizzled out from our genes generations ago, he might have been able to make me take heed.

"You should remember, you are no dog. A dog obeys. A dog follows. They are the ones who slunk toward the humans' campfires because their pelts were thin. They are the ones who raided prehistoric man's rubbish because they couldn't take down prey themselves." He leaned closer, pressing his withered muzzle against my neck. "If you ever want to be someone, you should never fraternize with dogs," he whispered.

In truth, it was my friends that formed the main reason why den-mother sent me here. She clawed her fur incessantly about it—those loud, noisy huskies. Always barking away—Bark! *Bark!* **Bark!**—"You do it all the time at home, you don't even notice it, you can't control it!" she cried. "And stop curling your tail!"

It never mattered what I argued, to her I clearly didn't know how to behave myself when out with other dens, hiding my disinterest in hunting, or my desire to give up meat. They were things that, she believed, came from some immature desire to copy what non-wolves did, because it was "edgy" and "cool."

"You're doing these classes for your own good!" den-mother snapped. "You'll thank me when you're older!"

And den-father, who at least was still around then, nodded silently at that, his muzzle peering up from the newspaper, wolfish features so stock and same that if I didn't remember his scent, he could have been anyone.

They missed the point. It was about being different. Why be like everyone else when you can be yourself?

I ground my teeth, waiting for the smelly old wolf to finish rambling on, picking at my fur in anger and resentment. He pulled away, going back to strutting down the aisles, holding his thinning tail high like a leafless branch in autumn while I brushed his slobber from my fur with a lavender-scented tissue. "We wolves are the leaders of the uplifted community. Be true to the pack, and you will do your heritage proud," he continued, glaring at me. I made sure our exchange was mutual. I wouldn't let him believe I'd submitted.

I took it as salvation that the bell finally rang.

"Remember, next Sunday, I want a five-page report on the importance and applications of scent-marking!" he howled, swept aside by the tide of fur rushing through the door with clacking claws.

Skidding down the corridors on all fours, I leapt out the door and stood tall, stretching out my arms as I held my paws up to the sun.

Sweet freedom, at last.

Ignoring the rest of the pack as they filtered back to their parents' cars, I raced on ahead, losing sight of them as I weaved past a herd of horses kicking a ball against the red-brick walls, wrinkling my nose at their strong, musty sweat dripping from their manes. Den-mother hadn't arrived yet; she'd texted that she was still stuck in traffic on the freeway, so that gave me precious time to meet my friends.

Despite what the old wolf said, I envied them. Dogs had life easy.

They didn't have a mythical legacy to uphold or anxious parents that forced them to attend stupid classes.

I slunk into the bushes, creeping round the brittle branches, earthy pelt blending in despite the blond highlights Blue had added last time we hung out. Den-mother flipped when she saw them, but there wasn't much she could do but wait for them to fade.

I could hear them laughing and joking quietly ahead, my ears twitching as excitement built. I caught the sweet scent of their deodorant and the smell of cigarettes. Smoking behind the bike sheds—how predictable.

Imitating Mr. Johnson's plodding hooves, I burst out of the bushes, holding my arms above my head, thrashing them about as my "antlers" caught in the branches. His genetics meant he never shed them though—making them horns. It always was a great game to see how loudly you can say that without landing yourself straight into detention.

"Fuck, it's only Straight-Tail!" Blue swore, tongue lolling out of her mouth as she tried to revive his discarded cigarette. "You owe me a new one," she growled, doing her best to hold back the grin twitching at her lips.

"Don't they ever smell the smoke on you?" I asked, wrinkling my nose. I could smell the acrid tang clinging to their fluffy coats; the evidence was obvious enough. "At least I'm careful to roll the scent away before I go," I shrugged, grabbing one from her and lighting up.

"Pff, they teach you that in those stupid wolf-classes?" She huffed, blowing a ring toward me. I poked my muzzle through it like a dog catching a loop, before champing down on it with a flash of my teeth. "It don't matter," Blue continued. "Not even a wolf has their sense of smell half as strong as a feral—and even if they smell something— teacher's got to prove it," she barked, laughing. "If they don't catch it lit in your hand, they can't do nothing," she grinned, wagging her curly tail.

"See, Straight-Tail, despite what your parents say, it's great to have human rules. They might not run on fours or smell a thing, but they've got fair minds." Blue puffed, watching the smoke trail off into the air. "That scent could've gotten from anywhere," she continued, shaking her thick mane in the sun. "Could've just been near someone on the bus, on the train—"

"You're yappering now, Blue. Straight-Tail's a sharp one," Shadow sighed, punching the husky on the arm. "He's not dumb enough to be hoodwinked back to the straight and narrow by some fossil trying to reverse your wayward pack mentality."

Blue grinned, fiddling with her blue highlights and lip piercing, pulling them in mock horror. I absolutely loved how she looked, and I couldn't wait to turn sixteen so I could get a piercing of my own.

"—Best point humans ever thought up, though. They've got this big thing about individualtism."

"In-di-vid-ual-ism, Blue," Shadow corrected. "You've gotta spend more time practicing your English if you want to end up living with them."

"Then don't try an' shut me up when I talk!" Blue snapped, the icy highlights on her hackles standing up as if electrified. "It's easy for you; you already live with 'em."

"Fair point." Shadow sat back, exposing his neck to Blue's teeth. "Humans have got their flaws, don't get me wrong," he continued, turning back to me. "But you know, you shouldn't ignore them because they've got no fur. There's no pack mentality with 'em; it's just about being yourself," Shadow finished, tapping my snout gently.

"—you mean *them*!" Blue barked excitedly, correcting Shadow's mistake.

The black husky frowned, sighing into his paws. *"Just one mistake and—"* he muttered.

"Aw come on, don't strop! Straight-Tail's not got the time for us to be fighting," Blue replied, smacking Shadow on the thigh.

"You do have a point," he relented, fiddling with the blond and green highlights in his mane so they trailed down across his shoulder and muzzle like a human's hair. "We've been thinking about you and us, kid, and we think we've come up with something to show you're one of us—a real 21st century dog."

"Yeah," Blue giggled, squeezing my arm. "We think it's pretty great that you hang out with us—too many wolves get all pointy-nosed about us."

"Ugh, don't get me started on our outdated obsession with being 'wild, noble, and majestic' beasts," I replied, rolling my eyes. They joined in with me.

"Yeah, it's awful they coop you up like a game hen in there all the time—so we've got the perfect prank to get revenge on your teacher."

"After today, I'm more than eager," I muttered, refusing to show enthusiasm or curiosity despite their looks.

"Oh yeah? Anyway, you'll like this," Shadow laughed, rummaging around in his satchel. "It'll serve him right, spewing all that crap about dogs. Don't sweat it if you need more," he said, throwing me a silver jar covered in a couple of scratch-marks and half-peeled stickers.

"Well, we had to take the branding off; otherwise it'd probably get confiscated if they caught you with it," Shadow shrugged, preening his chest fur.

"I didn't realize hair gel was so dangerous," I moaned, rolling my eyes. This was stupid, and wouldn't do anything.

"Not that excited, huh, Straight-Tail?" Blue teased me, catching the unimpressed look on my muzzle as she bit her lip piercing between her teeth.

Shadow shot her mate a scolding look.

"It's about what you can do with it," the husky grinned. "Extra strength, specially formulated for fur. It'll keep the shine in your pelt, it won't glue your fur together; and best yet, it's got no smell, so they won't know you're even wearing it. But here's the thing, if you want rid of it, you've got to wash it off with special formula—otherwise it'll last for weeks!"

"What are you thinking?" I asked them, watching as they curled their tails up tightly behind them, bristling in excitement.

"Well, for one, you're one of us, kid. You don't give in to their pack mentality crap, so we thought it'd be pretty cool to gel you up with a curl, too," Blue smiled, tongue lolling out of her mouth as she leapt over to hug me, working the cigarette smoke and husky scent into my fur. "But Shadow's got a great idea," she continued, tossing me the small blue tub containing the remedy.

"But better yet," Shadow sighed, pulling her off me, "if you use those wolf skills of yours to sneak into your teacher's house—"

"And work this into his tail..." Blue whispered.

Both the huskies nodded, sharing my growing smirk.

"Oh Straight-Tail, this is gonna be more fun than a house on fire."

Den-mother was full of questions as she flipped the indicators on and swerved onto the freeway.

"How was your day? Did you eat a big lunch? What did you learn?"

I had few answers, trying instead to concentrate on stopping my ears from twitching every time we drove over the gaps between the road's concrete slabs.

Thunk *thunk*, **thunk** *thunk*, **thunk** *thunk*.

Even with the radio on, it was loud and irritating.

"How come we're not running home by the river?" That was the quieter alternative, after all, and den-father always went that way when he came to pick me up. Cars were loud, noisy, and left the stink of asphalt in your fur that took days to get rid of.

"I've got to pick up your younger litter-mates from nursery and then get dinner ready," she sighed, combing her claws through her tangled mane.

After den-father had just become father, she'd put less and less effort into keeping up her appearance. I'd overheard their "conversations" the night she came out from the hospital after their small litter. Despite everything, he'd become just a voice at the end of the telephone and a scent I knew once a month.

"It would be nice to hear you answer me about your day," she snapped. She cursed abruptly, sounding her horn at a deer who swerved into the middle lane without indicating. "Too many idiots let loose on the road these days."

Should have taken the river run.

"My day was long. Just more stuff about how to hold your tail, and why you should categorize by scent rather than name."

"Geez, I swear the old coot says one thing useful and then immediately comes back with some rubbish."

My tail twitched.

"Mom, it's *all* rubbish. Shadow says that—"

"For the last time, it's not about them, it's about you," she growled—but not unkindly. "You've got to know how to behave if you want to have any chance of getting on in life."

Den-mother clicked the indicators on again as she turned off under the sign for Stargazer Avenue. The white picket fences didn't divide much here; everything was the same on either side.

"You've got to learn how to make your way among wolf society if you want a bright future. If you turn up to an interview without holding your tail correctly, no one will take you seriously."

"But—"

"I don't expect you to understand now," she said, turning up into the driveway and stopping the engine. I knew it was futile to attempt to argue further.

I spent that evening picking at my chickpeas and lentils while the rest of the pack tucked into rare slabs of meat with abandon—a diet only tolerated because I still kept that oily luster to my fur, thanks to the grooming supplies Shadow smuggled to me. I kept thinking about the pot of hair gel in my backpack. When I finally got dismissed, I rushed up to the shower, unable to keep a firm hold of my tail as it flicked about with delight. I popped the cap open with my claw and reached behind me, rubbing it into my fur, pulling it upward. I waited ten minutes, then let go.

In the mirror, I watched a grin stretch across my face, wider than any before. It didn't just smile for joy, but also for revenge.

Blue snickered like a hyena. Shadow tried in vain to hide his smirk.

"This is gonna be so funny," they both whispered, digging their paws into their sides as they tried to contain themselves. "I can't wait to see the look on his face when he wakes up."

Wolford, for all his talk about being so much like a wolf, slept like a rock. You could hear his snoring from outside his house, night and day, and he woke for little. I remembered this from his very first lesson; a true wolf sleeps lightly and often. That slip was the thing that I seized upon, and I held to that flaw like a torch.

"Serves him right for all this 'true wolf' crap I've had to put up with," I muttered, sneaking closer.

"Yeah, this'll teach that stuffy old fart for forcing you to spend your Sundays cooped up in a classroom rather than hanging out with us," Shadow replied.

"Geez!" Blue gagged. "I can smell him out from here already." She wrinkled her muzzle, pawing at her snout as she rolled her tongue across her nose, trying to wipe away the smell. "Does he ever wash?"

"Not a chance—a true wolf doesn't demean his nature with perfumes," I groaned.

"Is that the crap they have you chant out?" Shadow swore.

"You think that's bad, try reciting the list of foods that a wolf shouldn't eat." I paused. "Chocolate's one of them."

"What? When they made our species they took out that gene-flaw—and even then, they make all chocolate without it anyway!"

"Yeah, what gives?" Blue added, "If it wasn't the case, then I'd have conked it long ago!" The husky fidgeted, paws rummaging around in her wrapper-filled pockets as if to prove a point.

"Yeah, but you can still die from it if you keep eating so much," Shadow teased, even though Blue was as skinny as they come.

"Hey, my parents give it to me because they love me!"

"And keeping up that puppy fat just makes you look so adorable!" Shadow retorted, grabbing the husky's cheeks and making a mock cooing noise. Blue growled and snapped back at him, cursing as she swiped at Shadow's face—but he jumped away, snickering and laughing at his friend.

"Shh! You'll wake him up if you keep at it," I snapped, losing my patience. They never seemed able to stop goofing around.

"Come on," Shadow hollered, "you said yourself he sleeps through anything!"

"Shut up, Straight-Tail's right!" Blue intervened. "If we get this done, then we can all hang out together again, like the good times." Shadow grumbled and bit his lip, fiddling with the blond and green highlights against the black streaks of fur on his forearms.

"So, how're you going to get in there?" Blue asked, cocking her head. "Door's locked, and he's not one to keep a feral and have a dog-flap, is he?"

"I'm surprised he even has a house, considering how much he behaves like a feral," Shadow retorted, still sulking.

Leaving them to bicker, I jogged around the building looking for a way in. The heat of the night was oppressive, forcing me to loll my tongue outside my muzzle and pant; something ill-becoming of a wolf. It kept me cool though.

The temperature had gotten to the old wolf, too, though. Off to the side of the white-picket porch, he'd left a window open; curtains curling outward as they caught the slight breeze. Just to the side of the porch, a rusty, antique drainpipe led upward, close enough that if I climbed up it, I could get on top of the porch, and then I'd just have to reach up and pull myself in through the window.

"No way you can get up that way," Blue shrugged. "You've got paws, kiddo. No way you can grab and haul yourself up that thing." The husky dug into her pockets, whipping out a screwdriver and a set of pliers, snapping them together.

"We're not breaking in!" I snapped.

"But that's exactly what we're doing?" Blue sighed and scratched her head, kicking the grass with her paw as I took hold of the drainpipe. The screws wobbled, but it held firm; the rust crunching underneath my paws. I smirked at Blue as I pulled my way up. I tried to hide the tremor in my legs as I stepped out onto the porch, looking down at the two huskies who stood together, clutching each other's arms, tails curled up behind them. As soon as they caught me looking, they pushed each other back, snapping half-heartedly at each other like it was some sort of mistake. Taking a deep breath, I pushed the

32

window up and slipped inside.

It was dark inside. It stank; the air inside layered like heavy dust, none of the scents flushed out from here in weeks. I took a moment for my eyes to adjust from the moonlight, hoping that the old wolf wouldn't wake upon smelling my scent. He kept on snoring like some old human, tongue caught outside his jaws, sticking out all puffy and dry. He lay on his side, the bed sheets kicked off and rolled up over his ankles; sleeping pills scattered like grains of sand across his bedside table. Creeping forward, I took out the gel, lathering my paws up with it, grinning, remembering the lessons where Wolford had insisted we practice moving silently; "like a true wolf stalks its prey." I bit my lip, trying to keep my hands from trembling as my excitement built, working the thick gel into his ragged tail, curling it backward. The urge to shout, to declare some victory crept up my throat, but I stayed silent, listening to the growing patter of raindrops outside.

When I slid back down the drainpipe, Blue and Shadow were sprinting back and forth, trying to vent their excitement. I joined them, pumping my legs, paws clawing and taking out chunks of turf as I outstripped them, laughing as the growing rain washed away our scents—not that anyone these days had the nose to notice.

The next day passed in agitation, seconds stubbornly bending away like the hairs of a cat on edge. We spent the day sprinting through fields and tangled undergrowth—even ducking out of my last class to spend the hour with Blue and Shadow behind the bike sheds stuffing our muzzles full of chocolate.

When den-mother picked me up, muddy-pelted and reeking of sweat, all wildness in my eyes, she made a fervent prayer through gritted fangs that I'd learn some manners in class tomorrow, else I'd be the one scrubbing the floors clean. The look on her face was priceless when we bumped into James, a deer who lived next door to Wolford.

"Gotta say, my mom's relieved. For the first time ever, he was silent last night—and the one before! About time he stopped waking everyone up with all his damn howling, even if he is that ill!" he said as he went about scraping the velveteen off his antlers.

Den-mother flinched when he said that. She didn't ask me about the lessons that day.

The next day all the wolves found ourselves corralled into the classroom by Emerson the head teacher, a white-pelted moose with lofty antlers. The scent of excitement lingered in the air, subtle but electric, enough to get some hackles standing on edge—the instinct to follow tingling in my tail.

"You may not be aware that Mr. Wolford has been faring poorly for the last few days; however, he has insisted on coming in today for your lesson today. I hope you'll show him due respect for his commitment to your education," he finished, muzzle falling back into his trademark squat, grumpy shape as he walked out the door.

Wolford limped through the held door, holding himself without any of his usual demeanor. He was hunched over, sullen-eyed, defensive; keeping his back to the door at all times—crossing over to his desk by sidestepping like a crab. Instead of standing, he sat, resting his gaunt arms upon the desk, propping up his skeletal frame with his thinning paws. It was plain to see that he reeked of worry. His eyelids were haggard and seemed to scrape across his eyes whenever he blinked.

Instead of launching into his usual tirade, he just sat there, staring back out at the class as the class stared back at him.

"It's hard being an old wolf," he murmured, forcing the room's ears to point and lean forward. "We don't tend to age well. In the old days, I would have met my end in the hunt as soon as the cold started to creep into my bones."

He paused, running his tongue across his gums, nostrils flaring.

"But it's against our spirit to lie down and give up," he said. "Now, please get out your essays I set you last week," he commanded, standing up and in doing so, revealing his curled tail.

In unison, the entire front row of the class cocked their heads.

"Sir, that's not how you hold your tail!" Stevie, a young arctic wolf, barked.

Wolford stood still. He gritted his teeth, tendons visibly straining on his bald patches, as he tried—and failed—to straighten his tail.

"No," he growled, glaring at the pup, "but as you age your body changes—"

"But that's a dog's tail!" The white wolf bit his tongue, confused.

"Will my tail curl when I get older?" Evie, Stevie's sister, cried out, clutching her tail.

"It could happen to anyone!" Fred barked, laughing as the younger wolves fretted at themselves with their paws.

"Emerson said you were sick! What if I get sick?" Tom leapt back, his chair clattering on the floor—and with it, the pin dropped.

34

A rumination of excitement rippled through the wolves. The scent of it rose throughout the room, stifling all others.

I felt my heart lurch. My toes curled, claws scraping against the floor. I bit my tongue, but my muzzle twitched.

Pack mentality kicked in. That old, venerable wolf who had set the standard of what made a wolf was here with his tail bent back like a common dog.

And everyone followed.

All behind the desks, poking out from behind their chairs, the pack's tails rose, bristling—pulled back, as if drawn taut by invisible strings.

The class no longer looked like wolves, but an entire chaos of huskies. They laughed and cried and shouted as he tried to instill order, but they were infected now, and no matter how loudly he growled or bared his teeth, they scrapped about with each other like sled-dogs fighting to get free of the traces.

Then, they broke out, sprinting along the corridors with their ridiculous tails bobbing about behind them, shrieking out for their parents as they cried about the contagion.

It was a beautiful ruckus.

Blue and Shadow ran in to join me, howling like wolves in their laughter, holding their hands over their faces as we jumped up and down, struggling to vent the excitement that flowed through us, watching as the younger wolves rushed toward their parents who still hadn't yet left the school.

Den-mother spotted me, barking loudly, ears pricked upright in alarm.

"What happened?" she questioned, shaking me while the other parents bickered.

"He infected our children!"

"He taught them how to act like a dog!"

"Absolutely despicable! I'm not letting my litter near him again!"

Den-mother sighed, biting her lip, folding her ears. She grabbed hold of me, patting me down, whispering to me. She reached back, cautiously patting my tail—which in spite of it all, remained straight.

"I should have trusted you when you said you knew how to behave," she apologized, shoulders sagging. "It's just been hard without your father."

I said nothing, catching Shadow stamping down on Blue's foot before she opened her mouth and ruined it.

"Does this mean you won't send me to those classes anymore?" I asked. "I know how to behave," I replied, edging her on.

She pulled back, frowning.

"As long as you continue to behave," she smiled, taking my paw. I took that moment to hold my tail high in triumph—just like a proper wolf.

As we drove home, my phone buzzed as Shadow texted me.

"How did you know to gel your tail straight?"

I smiled, but I didn't reply. A good wolf always has a plan. It was one of Wolford's rules, after all.

A good wolf always has a plan.

THE CARROT IS MIGHTIER THAN THE SWORD

NIDHI SINGH

After attending American International School, Kabul, Nidhi did her BA English Honors at Delhi University. Currently, she lives with her husband in Yol, a picturesque cantonment, which was a British POW camp housing German and Italian soldiers during the World Wars.

More than fifty *of her short stories have appeared internationally in the magazines or from the publishers* A Lonely Riot, Mirror Dance, Body Parts Magazine, Military Experience and the Arts, *Grey Wolfe Publishing,* Expanded Horizons, *Vagabondage Press,* Rigorous, The Qualitative Report, SPR, Fantasia Divinity, Fiction on the Web, Storyteller, TWJ Magazine, *Indie Authors Press,* Flyleaf Journal, Liquid Imagination, *Digital Fiction Publishing Co.,* The Los Angeles Review of Los Angeles, *Flame Tree Publishing,* Four Ties Lit Review, The Insignia Series, *Inwood Indiana, Bards and Sages Publishing,* Scarlet Leaf Review, Bewildering Stories, Down in the Dirt, Mulberry Fork Review, *tNY Press,* Fabula Argentea, Aerogram, Fiction Magazines, *The Flash Fiction Press,* The Dirty Pool, Asvamegha, *Thurston Howl Publications, etc. She has also authored several translations of the Sikh Holy Scriptures.*

A great rustling swept over the treeless tracts as droves of furry hares, kestrel-eyed and keen, lanky-legged and tough, fanned out to munch on sedge and dwarf shrub. They rested and foraged in turns, leaping and lolloping across the heather and the bent, as the cold wind, bemoaning the winter just departed, passed with a sigh over the yellowing grasses and fire thorns crouching low. Some, in spring frenzy chased one another, sparring with their paws. Leverets, with long ears and black markings, rubbed their eyes; sleeking their furs with well-licked paws, they raced the sun with eyes cocked to the sky, where peewits, with their slow wings squeaking, and golden plovers, with reedy whistles piping, circled.

By the pool with gray reeds at its rim, King Carrotta, warm as an oven loaf in his brilliant white coat, surveyed the soggy realm with satisfaction; twirling his whiskers, he drew a straw to suck from a pitcher plant. As he hummed, and slurped in tandem with the concerts of nature, another sound, that didn't quite agree with the general sunshine, rang in: the slow weeps of a creature, proud, ashamed of his pain.

King Carrotta, with many a winter past him, knew well to mind his own business; the craft of surviving in the bitter, wild white was a tricky one. So, he chucked the straw and bounded away in large merry leaps, and found spike rush to whiten his teeth upon. But the cries, like misty wreaths fluttering, wheeling about over the moss and heath, followed him, and he could no longer shut his ears to them. Unhappily, he tossed over his shoulder a juicy blue-black bearberry, and contrary to his good sense, bounded across the bog to see what ailed this poor soul.

There, near a frozen tarn, at the mouth of the barren cavern, lay a giant fire-breathing dinosaur, writhing and worrying, grieving and growling, raging and raving, howling and heating, and turning and twisting, around and around, with endless rebound. He could barely spit fire, and smoke wisped out his damp nostrils. He had an arrow ripped through his wing, which he beat weakly. Drenched in tears of shame, but not of his own making, his eyes, big, black, fearful, and staggering, implored for help.

"Whatever happened to you, silly bird," asked the King, staying a safe distance behind an alder brush—just in case. "Who are you?"

"Doesn't anyone even know? I am Terex—the fire breather—arch of the alpine forest!" Scooping air into his lungs, he exhaled with force—a tiny cloud of vapor popped out of his face, lingering briefly in the bracing cold, before vanishing. The arch firebomber hung his head in shame.

"What in blazes!" Carrotta scurried a little closer. "What brings you so far up north?"

"I used to feast upon veggie Sauropods that mow the earth like cows. Not long ago, some crazy Nenets, not content with hunting Caribous, shot me down with an arrow when I was only minding my own business—flying low, hugging the treetops, looking for some warm, succulent meat to dig my teeth into. Why, I wasn't even firing up when these looting, lust-dieted lowlifes shot me down just for sport—for I have armor on my back, club on my tail, fire in my entrails and dung in my horns—what use are these in any hearth? I flew as far and away as I could, my wing bleeding, till I could no more, and crawled into this hollow to die."

"Why the howling, the tossing and turning then, mate? Spring doesn't last here forever—you're disturbing the peace. Do what you have to, and keep it low, okay?" The King crouched on his powerful hind legs and made to spring off.

"Hey, wait…err…umm…I could do with a little…" mumbled Terex, his dark face blanched with pain and blood loss, all of his six monstrous eyes downcast in humiliation.

"Oh, so the mighty Tyrannosaurus needs help from a humble bonnybunny then?"

"Must you… really speak aloud…" the dinosaur darted glances left and right.

"Right-ho then—keep tight." The Bonnybunny hopped close to the mauled wing, and hummed and hawed. "Nothing the sharp cogs of a drove will not set right. Wait here for me," said he and leaped across the marsh to marshal his marshals.

Soon, a vast oinking and honking advanced over the mellowing permafrost, and in no time the Bigwigs, the Cottontails, the Flopsies, and the Pookas had chewed through the hardwood shaft and elk sinew of the arrow, and pulled it out.

Dr. Jack Quack, the local on-call GP, boiled some carrots in a geyser and rubbed the mashed taproot on the wound. "You'll be good to go in no time," he said, stepping back to admire his handiwork.

"What's that," the monster wailed, all his six eyebrows shooting up, when the does brought before him a sumptuous spread of liverworts, carrots, lichens, and caribou mosses. "Where is the meat?"

"Eat your veggies; it's low fat and won't clog your arteries," the doctor firmly declared. "The carrots might even help you see in the dark."

"Only wabbits eat carrots," the proud predator moaned.

"Watching too much television, has our sickly boy been? It's not your Bugs Bunny show, Mr. Raptor—eat 'em."

And so the raptor soon recovered; a dark flush once again suffused his handsome fiendish looks, and he was able to flap his wings without wincing. When he could take short flights over the bog and take his pickings from the Caribou and Musk Ox, the lapins knew it was time to let the visitor head back to his forests down south. The brief spring was already waning, and the coldhearted dusk was beginning to close in like a slow trap of ice.

So one morning, by the long creek, on mist-blurred grass, Carrotta shook his visitor's claw, and bid him adieu. "Can't say I'm sorry to see you go, though—you know, with bunnies—they get a little hot under the collar with all those blazes and flames. They got better tricks to keep the old gal hot." He winked as the raptor flapped his mighty wings, and soared away in a wake of soot and ash.

As early as the next winter, on a dark frozen night, Terex was back in the rabbit kingdom. This time, he had company—more winged, taloned, horned and fire-spitting beasts following him—each more desperate than the other. Word skids fast on the frozen swampland, and the hares were on the ready with a reception.

"What brings you back?" King Carrotta slammed a parsnip-tipped spear against his iron breastplate, and signaled the uninvited guests, creatures that left a bloody and blazing brume in their wake, to halt at the gates of his realm.

"A massive rock has hit the earth. Almost the entire population of our non-avians has been wiped out. I liked what I saw here the last time. We come in peace, brother—to take over new territories and advance our race. We were friends once; remember me—you hosted me last spring as well?" Terex flapped his wings, large as the sails of a galleon, and hovered over the king and his assembled guard, his nostrils seething and smoking.

"You come in peace, yet you slash and burn our lands?"

"That's what fire-breathing dinosaurs do, brother—breathe fire."

"Well, it doesn't suit us. It thaws the permafrost, and burns the food on the table, not to mention the greenhouse gases that discharge because of all the warming. I ask that you spend the night here, and return to your Taiga in the morning. When you were sick, we took you in, and now that you've returned to your previous fiery splendor, we don't want your dark blood-gouts of flame and phlegm scaring the kits."

"I mean no harm to the cupcakes—see, we don't eat no wabbits. Who wants to be coughing up fur for days afterwards?"

"We are no cupcakes or bunnies to you, Mister Terminator—we are Hares." Carrotta drew up to his full fuzzy height and raised his lance aloft.

"So, are you going to stop us with a handful of pink carrots and doll faces?" asked a smirking dragon minion. Sweeping his spiked tail, he sent the hare's entire front line scrambling into disarray.

Worthy King Carrotta, having proved himself in many a battle with marauding weasels, ripping white foxes and squawking harlequin ducks, on seeing his battle formation in a state of near-rout at the very first feinting enemy maneuver, turned to his soldiers, and lifting his big voice, shouted, "Hooold! Rrready for battle!"

On cue, his guard brought up its banners and sounded the giant bugle. In a flash, as the dinosaurs blinked, an army of a hundred thousand assembled in battle formation on the vast fields of tufted saxifrages and foliose lichens. The front lines were made of several 32-hare-deep phalanxes that locked their shields together and thrust their spears; behind them were yeoman archers and stalwart redcoats at the ready; on the flanks, infantrybucks, with shakos raised on muskets; lastly, chariots of toboggans pulled by grays and piloted by martial lemmings brought up the fighting rear.

Well-armed with both bucklers and steel, the gathered army felled the affront of the air, as a growing tempest vexed the skies. "Dex Aie," "Out out;" war cries pierced the air; impatient steeds of war stamped their angry hooves on the trembling land; and such a blasting and noise with their horns and drums, and flapping of pennons and screeching of Saracens, and stomping of hobnailed boots they made that it seemed all the great devils of hell had descended there.

"Forward!" commanded their leader, and the army began to march in step, slowly gathering pace and momentum. "Halt!" the King shouted, as his frontlines advanced within thrust and parry range of the enemy. The lines turned a quarter right, and muskets were brought to the ready.

The ardor of the monsters seemed to abate a bit; the sounds weighed heavily on their spirits, and they became chary of being put furiously to the slaughter. A knave and a cad quivering in the rear did make a lame attempt at spitting a flame, but such an accurate volley of carrot-tipped arrows descended that it seemed thunderbolts were falling from the heavens.

Clutching a bleeding eye, seeing his rank and file descending into disorderly rout already, Terex, the arch talon of the woods, made a wise decision to stay alive for battle on another day. "O mighty King," he said, "you're taking this a tad too seriously. We are inclined to accept your generous offer of staying the night, and returning peaceful and vacant possession of your lands at the first break of light. Peace, brother!" Spreading his giant armor-plated flanks, he slowly took a step back.

"Return then, beyond frozen lakes yonder, and do not bother to say goodbye in the morn," King Carrotta raised a paw, and pointed their way out. The visitors flapped their leathery wings, and meekly retreated to lick their wounds, and count their losses.

In the hare's camp, the elders gathered in council, some heady with victory of the day, some drunk on carrot wine, most waiting for a sign from their meditating King to disperse to their warm forms and waiting does—for spring was waning, spent, and the desire rousing, unspent.

"Hark ye all," spoke the monarch at long last, after much reflection. "I don't expect the raptors leaving us so easily in peace. Master Hedwit, the wise owl, brings word that the Pangaea is indeed breaking up, and a massive rock has crashed into our world, snuffing out entire species. These are dark times indeed, when we must keep the faith. Let us do our bit to preserve this biome, home to our ancestors, and legacy to our children. We must rally the white bear and the gray fox—even the flapping swamp geese and the hardline hawk to save this planet, and if…"

"What if, if?" asked of him Roger R. Rector, head priest and chief savant.

"If only man was on our side—rapacious, ravenous, ruthless, ruinous man. Or if he became the enemy of our enemy, the battle would be easily won."

"Look around you, sire. We are a million strong, and growing; what devil may not we easily vanquish?" asked General March.

"True—our strength in numbers—but as the first beams of sunlight glance across the fenlands, he will return, in greater numbers, better organized. Today, we took him by surprise; tomorrow, we need another trick up our sleeve," said the wily Hare Monarch.

"What do you suggest we do?" asked his general.

"I want you to take four divisions of our finest infantry, battle-scarred, and war-worthy, and steal the carrots from man's farms."

"Carrots, me lord? Only bugs-bunnies eat them on television," reminded the sage.

"It's not for eating, O wise one. We have enough food—for now. When the village finds its carrots plucked, vamoosed from its fields, barren, like the pleasures the rake seeks, it will fetch its hounds, and come after us. At that moment, I expect to be joined in battle with the raptors unrepentant, and once man arrives on the bent, his badgers and fleabags on the scent, his kettledrums and whistles in a torment, and his temper and thrill on ascent, we shall beat a hasty, well-organized retreat, and let one felon deal with another, to their heart's malcontent."

"A wonderful idea, me Regent!"

"To the village then, my Braves; hasten, before the night's dark veil lifts on our fortunes and intent."

On the morrow, as Carrotta had predicted, the Godzillas returned, perched on the willow, ready to heap burning coals upon their heads. His armies too, out in full heraldry and badges, shouldering muskets and pikes, had assembled ready for the sparring. Pavisiers and cross-bowers oiled their wares and cracked their knuckles, and gunners winched down catapult beams, carrying bushels loaded with carrots, slate, and magma. The cavalry commanders, wearing orange surcoats and blue helmets with coronets, their mounts in caparisons decorated with the national vegetable, the carrot, hoisted the colors. The Tribunes, ever and anon, blew their olifants to summon retribution; and solemn the misery pipes wailed. The hares took defenses behind a long line of iron ties joining blocks of stones together. Once the paeans had been sung, the frontlines began to march unwaveringly into combat. The monsters hissed and seethed, and battle was joined.

Flying arrows carpeted the sky; the silver sun blacked out completely; mounts leaped and scurried, and flames in the winds of death shivered incessantly. The armies marched, the fires blazed; the armies fell, the lusters died. Again the glows returned, the lands burned, and down the red-hot valleys the armies marching went. Embers blinked and lives crumbled in hell's furnaces; bodies shone and dusked in fitful glows; red tongues darted and snaked in the smoky air, fields and hills lay black—one could taste the burning grass. Next season's bud was roasted, her larvae toasted, the lichen cooked brown, soot on its stem, writhing half-dead.

In the pandemonium, the leftmost flank began to sound their bugle, and Carrotta knew the enemy of his enemy had arrived. Upon his order to the guards, a trusty messenger streaked through the battle order, barking his king's command to the captains and commanders. The rearguard turned about, hoisted its colors, and began to march in orderly retreat. Slowly, the flanks opened up, letting hollering man and feisty dog into the heart of battle, till only the frontlines in contact remained to face certain death.

Along with them, many a man, taken aback with the violence and mayhem, perished, but not before many an enemy had been shot to the blazing ground. Valiant Carrotta, himself wounded badly, made away with most of his army, while the monsters lost most of theirs.

The men would return, he knew, with many more, for retribution, and that would be the end of the invaders. Many lives had to be lost, but land would be restored to its pristine glory.

In the Hare's camp, the war council, joined by the bear, the gray, the goose, the owl, and the weasel, and many more, had gathered again, huddled in dialogue. The silent King lay in agony, his end near.

"What is to be done next, King dear?" asked General March.

"You did well today, my general. I leave a proud man." He beckoned the general with a painful paw, bandaged in moss and carrot mash. The general walked over to his bed, and held his hand to his wrenching heart; tears welled up in every eye.

"I leave this kingdom in your able charge, General March; lead our brethren, every living soul that walks the earth, or swims in its waters, or flies in its skies, every blade of grass and leaf and fruit that sustains life, unto everlasting peace; this I command, nay implore you, will be your holy grail, the reason for you to prevail."

"No, my king, come morning, and you will be upon your paws, proud and doughty, showing us the way," the General cried.

"Promise me this," the King clasped his General's hand, and implored him with dimming eyes, "promise me now!"

"I promise, my Lord."

But ere Carrotta breathed his last, the curtains of the royal tent flapped and a messenger stepped in. "Hail the king! My Lord, a most unlikely visitor has appeared at the gates—we have him detained at the tower. He asks your audience."

"And who might this intruder be—an informant...a spy...a laggard...an envoy—who dares to vex when we are in council?" asked the head priest.

"It is he—T-T-Terex—in p-person!" the messenger bowed.

"It's a trick!"

"Knavery!"

"A double-dealing treachery!" The assembly roared. "Dispatch him at the gates—finish the lying villain."

"Wait," the King rasped. "Take me to him." He waved aside the protests and howls and bade his guards to carry his palanquin to the tower.

Terex, his feet chained to a turret, sat crestfallen on the ground, his shoulders hunched, his wide plume spiritless and flagged.

"How do you want me to treat you?" asked Carrotta.

"The way one king treats another," said Terex.

"Free him at once," Carrotta commanded. "What is it—what trickery assails your manner now?" he asked when the raptor had risen on his feet.

"I know I'm not worthy of your trust, mighty Hare, but like you, I was only saving my kind. Alas, that strange insertion of man and his wily ways into the fracas did us in. As I look back, I see friend and foe, family and fellowship, perished. I repent mocking you—what valor, what sacrifice, what discipline your ranks showed today—I salute you and this land. I am at a crossroads: my troops have no more stomach for battle; I know man will return tomorrow and annihilate us with his devices—tell me, O king, what must I do?" he wailed, his giant frame wracked with sobs.

"Return to your forest, raptor, save the last living of your kind. Shrink, sprout wings, change into a bird or something; adapt, learn patience, and you will be fine."

The raptor nodded; he knew change was upon them, and they had to learn. "Hail! Take care, good friend," he said, and fluttered away.

"What should we do now, my lord?" asked General March.

"Return to the old ways. What man or hound could ever catch a fast hare?" he winked. "Man has a short memory—he will never have any dearth of hunt and sport as long as this land lives. Till then, good runnings, my friend."

His general nodded in agreement, and gazed up at the skies. The freezing stars had begun to twinkle again, as the smoke and haze of battle started to clear. It was quite some time before he realized his king's hand had gone cold and lifeless in his grasp.

"At that moment, I expect to be joined in battle with the raptors unrepentant, and once man arrives on the bent, his badgers and fleabags on the scent, his kettledrums and whistles in a torment, and his temper and thrill on ascent, we shall beat a hasty, well-organized retreat, and let one felon deal with another, to their heart's malcontent."

A WEB OF TRUTHS

JAMES HUDSON

James Hudson is a fiction writer from Sheffield, England, whose stories usually feature talking animals in one form or another. His love for anthropomorphic animal characters began at an early age when he became aware of them in cartoons, books, and video games. Discovering the furry fandom as a teen opened up a whole world of anthropomorphic content to him, and he is still very much obsessed with the wealth of varied and high-quality content the fandom creates. Having experienced the fandom from the sidelines for many years, he now aims to contribute to it with his writing, and hopefully make a few new friends along the way.

The wait had been excruciating, and yet its end brought Gerald no relief. Even as he grasped the cold metal of the door-handle, fully accepting the inevitability of turning it, he consciously longed to simply ignore the persistent chiming of the bell and the muffled mutterings coming from outside his apartment. He wished he could just disappear into the alluring safety of his living-room and drink a nice cup of tea. Why, of all the people in the world, had he decided to invite his parents around? Why not Steve from work? Admittedly, Steve didn't smell great, and there had been that incident with the steak knife, but at least it didn't matter what Steve thought about anything. Steve would have been a lot safer than *them.*

Of course, Gerald knew why he'd asked his parents to be the first to see his apartment, and its eight-limbed secret, and knew why he was so reluctant to open the door to them now. The reasons were one and the same; because his parents' opinions mattered to him. He needed their approval, and so did Cecilia.

"Gerald Thompson, what's the bloody hold-up?" his father's voice came, slicing through the door with the subtlety of a chainsaw.

Suddenly feeling nine years old again, Gerald turned the door-handle almost instinctively, not wanting to anger his father any further, as if he might be punished for being mischievous if he didn't do as he was told.

"Sorry, Dad," he said with a nervous laugh as he flung the door open. "Hi Mum," he added, noticing that puzzlement, concern, and relief seemed to be doing battle for supremacy on her face. It seemed as though concern had the upper hand.

"Is everything alright, Gerry?" she said in a voice more heavily accented than her more traveled son's. It was a kind voice that matched her kind face, and Gerald grimaced at the thought of having deceived her. He knew, however, that she might have refused to visit had he mentioned Cecilia, if she had believed him.

"Yes, absolutely. I'm just so happy to see you both. So happy..."

"Are you going to let us in then, son?" his father said brusquely, but with enough of a smile to soften the impact.

In his agitated state, Gerald hadn't been aware that he was still standing in the doorway, blocking his parents' path. It was with some degree of inner conflict that he slowly stepped aside and finally opened the door fully to them.

"It's not *that* messy in here, is it?" his mother asked as she stepped across the boundary.

"No, not *messy*," Gerald said with a nervous laugh. "*That's* not the problem."

"*That's* not the problem?" his mother repeated.

"I mean, that's *not* a problem. There is no problem. Certainly not a spider, if that's what you mean," he said, hoping he'd covered his tracks successfully, but somehow thinking he hadn't. He probably shouldn't have said anything about a spider. His parents definitely looked suspicious.

"A spider?" his father asked quizzically.

"I don't like spiders, Gerry," his mother added worriedly.

Cursing himself initially for his slip-up, Gerald then decided he'd actually done himself a favor. They would, after all, have to know soon enough anyway. "Okay, right, actually there *is* a spider," he admitted.

His father smiled and rolled his sleeves up in a show of masculinity. "Right, get me a rolled-up newspaper. I'll get rid of the hairy little devil in no time."

"She's a girl," Gerald said quickly, alarmed by his father's murderous intent.

"Who is?"

"The spider. Her name is Cecilia."

There was a moment of silent confusion before Gerald's mother spoke. "You haven't got yourself a pet spider, have you? You know I don't like spiders," she said.

"No! She's not a pet. She was here when I moved in. *I* didn't name her," he said honestly.

Now, the confusion had become almost palpable, like a thick fog in the hallway. "Well, who..." His mother's question went mercifully unfinished. It was obvious what she had intended to ask, and yet the three of them somehow knew there was no obvious answer, so there the question hung, in limbo, never to be completed.

Things were going better than Gerald had expected. He had told his parents about Cecilia, and even that she had lived with him from the beginning. Certainly, they were confused, but he'd known they would be until they met her. If only he knew what was going to happen when they did.

"Look," he said, starting to feel as though his parents were ready. "I think it might be best if I just show you. She's in the living room. That's where her web is."

Unsure glances were exchanged between Mr. and Mrs. Thompson, followed by nods of wary approval.

"Okay," his father said in a low voice.

"Okay," Gerald replied as he led his parents, who were now rather quiet, through the hallway in the direction of the living-room. Had the hallway always been so long? He wasn't sure.

Before he opened the door to the room of greatest importance, Gerald turned to his parents and tried to reassure them a little more. The last thing he wanted was for them to panic or get upset.

"Look, when you go into the living-room, you might panic or get upset. Please don't. I can understand why you might find Cecilia frightening, but she's never harmed me, and believe me she could if she wanted to. I mean, she's bigger than me for one thing, and her fangs have got to be two inches long...but, erm, just forget I said anything."

He pushed open the door and stepped into the living-room, bracing himself for what he suspected would be a barrage of criticism.

Noticing that his parents were not in fact following him through the door, Gerald turned to see them huddled in the hallway, apparently afraid to enter. Something about the scene felt very silly to him, and he laughed, not at his parents as such, but at their irrational fear. Hadn't he tried to reassure them?

"Oh, you!" his mother suddenly exclaimed. "You were playing a trick on us, weren't you!"

Starting to laugh heartily, his father added, "Good one, boy. You had us going there for a second. A spider indeed!"

They walked through the doorway shaking their heads merrily, happy in the belief that their son had shown great imagination and wit in fooling them so successfully.

What followed was extremely disappointing for Gerald. His mother's screaming and subsequent collapse helped distract his father for a few moments, but only long enough for him to invent a new and unrepeatable word which Gerald knew, instinctively, meant something along the lines of, *What in God's name is that thing in the corner of the room, oh god he wasn't joking,* before he added to the number of unconscious parents on the living-room floor.

A single soft, russet hair; the last hint of Cecilia's assistance in moving Gerald's unconscious parents from the floor to the couch, removed carefully by guilt-shaken hands. Gerald suspected his parents would be too distracted by Cecilia's mere presence to realize that their son could not possibly have moved them onto the couch without the assistance of Cecilia's eight strong limbs.

"Thank you," he mouthed up at her as she repositioned herself on the web in the corner of the room.

"You're welcome," she whispered back, her mouth not possessing lips suitable for mouthing words intelligibly. Her smile was unmistakable, however.

Even to Gerald, who had lived with her for several months, Cecilia seemed a little odd. That is not to say that there was anything questionable about her personality or manner, for she was extremely personable, but her appearance still caused him the occasional moment of wonder. If Cecilia had been merely a giant, albeit talking, spider, then Gerald felt he could perhaps have passed her off as a hallucination, or even the product of some sort of mutation or experiment. Cecilia was, however, no mere linguistically-blessed giant arachnid. What Gerald saw, and presumed his parents had seen before their brains had decided to disconnect them from what he hoped was reality, was an undoubtedly feminine creature with bodily features belonging to those of both a spider and a human woman.

The core of Cecilia's body was clearly that of a human woman, albeit one covered in soft, brown fluff which Gerald had since learned many spiders possessed, but her limbs were eight-fold and she used them to cling dexterously to the thick white strands of her web. Of course, it barely needs saying that the required orifices for web-production were also present on her body, placed in a small, tail-like protrusion on her lower back.

Then there was Cecilia's face. Gerald found himself staring in wonder at Cecilia's face even now, when he should have been preparing for his parent's return to the land of the living. Her face was both human and arachnid, like the rest of her body, and yet such a description was woefully inadequate. Her eyes were multi-faceted and dark like skillfully cut jet, and, if you looked carefully enough, you could see that she possessed more than the human norm of one pair, the others being positioned higher up on her head. The largeness and position of what could be called her *main* eyes was sufficient to give the impression of binocular ocularity, however, and Gerald tended to look into those eyes as if they were the only ones she possessed. The structure of her skull was not so different from that of a human woman either, and a delicately proportioned one at that, albeit her skin was covered by the same brown fur-like hair that grew across her entire body. No nose could be found on her face, but her mouth was small and dainty, and quite capable of expression. The result of Cecilia's peculiar features was a face that Gerald had always found quite appealing, and had since come to think of as beautiful in a strange sort of way.

"Gerald! What the hell is that thing!? Get away from there!"

The cry from the couch alarmed Gerald, and he spun round rapidly to see his father pointlessly pointing in the direction of Cecilia, who he had apparently misinterpreted as dangerous. The distressed Mr. Thompson then began frantically beckoning Gerald toward him, as if proximity to Cecilia might in some way be endangering his life.

With a sigh, Gerald moved slowly over to the couch. "It's really alright. I tried to explain before you saw her, but she's really not going to hurt anyone." He sat next to his father on the now rather crowded couch, and saw that his mother had not yet rejoined them in what they seemed to agree was consciousness.

"Gerry," Gerald's father began, with an expression which seemed to question his son's sanity, "that's no spider. That's a bloody monster." He was talking in hushed tones now, as if he didn't want the spider to hear him.

Cecilia giggled. "I'm not a monster, Mr. Thompson. I'm Cecilia."

There was a tense silence in the room, and Gerald watched his father carefully. When Gerald had first noticed Cecilia, sitting as she was now, in the corner of his new living-room, he had not reacted with quite such aversion as his parents, but it had certainly taken him a few seconds to come to terms with her existence. He watched his father now for signs of the same.

"It can talk! The monster can talk, Gerry!" He was pointing again, and looked almost as if he might leap up from the couch at any moment. "That thing can talk! It sounds like a bloody woman, Gerry!"

"She *is* a woman, dad," Gerald insisted, knowing that he might take some convincing on the idea. He watched his father's eyes darting between Cecilia and himself as if trying to find visual evidence for his assertion.

"Like hell she is! That's a monster and no mistake. Women don't have that many legs, son. Your mother, for example, has only two legs. Look," he pointed at his wife's legs.

There was a stirring from the end of the couch. "That's right, dear, but what..." Her sentence ended in a sort of strangled scream as she remembered why she had lost consciousness in the first place. "Why are we just sitting here?!" she hissed.

Nodding, Mr. Thompson grabbed his son's arm. "Too right. We're all getting out of here, and then I'm calling the police or...pest control or something. Actually, a priest!" he tugged his son's arm. "Come on, son, we're going to find a priest!"

There was a loud and quite unexpected sound as Gerald's palm met his father's stubbly cheek with more force than he'd intended. His remorse came instantly. "Oh, God, Dad, I'm sorry. That was completely unnecessary, wasn't it?"

Open-mouthed in shock for a moment once more, and with Mrs. Thompson clinging to his arm and mirroring his expression, Mr. Thompson then closed his mouth, and began to think.

"No, I needed that. I've gone insane, haven't I?" he said after a few moments' contemplation.

"What? No, I don't think so."

"Well, I think there's some sort of spider-person thing in the corner of your living-room so I think I *must* have gone insane."

"Cecilia," said Cecilia. "I'm not a thing, I'm Cecilia."

"You see, I even thought I heard the thing say that its name's Cecilia. What kind of a name is that for a monster? I must have gone mad. That's the only answer." He turned to his wife. "I'm truly sorry, dear. I suppose I best call the doctor and have myself committed." He paused a moment in contemplation before settling on something. "If they can't cure me, I will understand if you re-marry," he said, at which Mrs. Thompson began to sob.

Seeing that things were not going quite as well as he'd hoped, but about as well as he'd feared, Gerald stood from the couch and walked back over to Cecilia. He stood beside and slightly below her, facing his parents.

"Right. Listen to me, both of you. Cecilia here," he pointed up at her, making her grin, "is not a monster. She's Cecilia. You've not gone insane; she's as real as anything I've ever known in this world." By now his parents were listening intently, their shock and fear numbed by a more agreeable sense of unreality. "She lives here with me, and we get along just fine. She's never once hurt me. In fact, she's been very good to me, so why don't you start acting like adults and be a bit more...nice?"

"Thank you, Gerald. That was lovely," Cecilia said in a voice that was pleasantly feminine and yet not quite human.

Mr. Thompson exhaled so deeply that it sent a slight quiver through the web across the room. "Okay," he said in a way that suggested he was beyond trying to comprehend the situation and had resigned himself to the mutual madness he was a part of. "Okay, whatever you say, son. I don't even know what to think anymore."

Mrs. Thompson said nothing and looked at everyone in the room as if they were speaking a foreign language.

"Good, okay, that's good, I suppose," Gerald said, looking up at Cecilia with what he hoped was a smile.

With what was unmistakably a smile, Cecilia nodded and began addressing Gerald's parents. "Thank you, Mr. Thompson, you really have taken this much better than either of us expected. You too, Mrs. Thompson."

She offered no detectable response.

"As you know, my name's Cecilia. I think you've noticed that I'm a spider-morph so let's not dwell on that." She giggled, causing Gerald to do the same. "I live in my web in the corner of your son's apartment and I'm very happy here. I think Gerald is, too." She smiled down at him.

"Yes, of course," Gerald replied enthusiastically.

"Wait a second," Mr. Thompson interjected, pointing accusingly, once again, at Cecilia.

Waiting to hear what his father's objection was, he just hoped that, whatever it was, he wouldn't use the word "monster" again.

"What legal right do you have to live in my son's apartment? He rents this place, and I know for a fact that he can't legally sub-let it to another tenant, certainly not without the landlord's permission anyway. Well, son, do you have permission to sub-let your apartment to a monst...to Cecilia? Well?"

The legal query had caught everyone off guard, but Gerald and Cecilia smiled at one another, realizing that Mr. Thompson had made an effort not to offend; and he was asking a reasonable question, too.

It was Cecilia who answered. "The landlord knows about me. Actually, I've been here longer than Gerald so there's really nothing to worry about."

"Nothing to worry about?!" The shrill rhetorical question came from Mrs. Thompson. "I mean...you're not...What do you even eat?"

This was an even more unexpected question. At first, it seemed an odd thing to ask, but the implication of it became clearer the longer the question hung in the air.

"Giant flies," Cecilia answered with a straight face, giving Mrs. Thompson the reply she and Gerald had realized was expected.

"Oh good lord!" came the cry from the disgusted mother. Mr. Thompson put a hand to his mouth as if he was about to be sick. Gerald rolled his eyes.

"Not the best joke, apparently," Cecilia said almost apologetically.

Mr. and Mrs. Thompson looked up at her in disbelief.

"I usually eat whatever Gerald makes. He's quite the cook. You must have taught him well."

The looks of disbelief on the faces of Gerald's parents did not diminish, despite the misconception having been corrected, but in fact were merely redirected from Cecilia to Gerald.

"You cook for it, erm, her?" his father asked.

He paused, considering his answer but seeing no reason not to be truthful. "Yes."

Mr. Thompson furrowed his brow, deeply considering what he had heard. "So do you stick slices of pizza and cake to her web then, or what?"

The laughter that resulted from Mr. Thompson's absurd suggestion baffled its originator. Mrs. Thompson also failed to see the funny side.

"My web isn't for catching prey, Mr. Thompson. It is more like the couch you are sitting on now. I find it comforting."

It was clear from the downward glances of the Thompsons that they were now imagining sitting in a giant web. They shuffled uncomfortably. "Oh," Mr. Thompson concluded insightfully.

"So where do you eat?" Mrs. Thompson said, addressing both Cecilia and her son. "Do you eat together? I don't see a dining table..."

The questions raised further questions, and Gerald wasn't keen for them to be answered yet. He looked up at Cecilia imploringly. She seemed to understand.

"Well, actually, I do eat up here in my web, just not quite how you imagined it. Gerald..."

Gerald was thankful that Cecilia hadn't finished her sentence, but realized *he* would have to say something instead. If he said nothing, his mother might read between the lines; or the threads. He was starting to panic again, and spoke before he had really considered what he was going to say. "Mice!" he said suddenly, much louder than he'd intended.

"What?" Mrs. Thompson replied, slightly alarmed.

"What?" Gerald parroted, hoping his mother hadn't heard him say "mice."

"Mice. You said mice."

"Why would I say mice?" Gerald asked, knowing very well why he'd said mice. Cecilia was looking at him with a kindly smile and a twinkle to her black eyes that told of suppressed laughter.

"I don't know, but you did," his mother persisted.

Gerald sighed. At least he didn't have to tell his parents that he ate his meals with Cecilia in her web. "We have mice in the apartment," he admitted.

"I told you we should have called pest control," Mr. Thompson added with a smug grin. He was glad to have been right about something, even though he was in fact wrong.

"It's not as simple as that, Dad."

"Of course it is. I know it seems cruel, but they need to be exterminated. It's not hygienic to have mice living in your apartment. They aren't people, Gerry. They won't suffer."

With those words came a distinct rustling from somewhere behind the couch, followed by an alarmed squeak and a general sense of foreboding.

"What was that!?" Mrs. Thompson shouted, lifting her feet off the ground.

"Oh dear," Gerald said quietly. "I shouldn't have mentioned the mice. They told me not to mention them. Now, they'll be upset."

Before Gerald's parents had registered what their son had said, there was a patter of tiny shoes from behind the couch, followed by the timid appearance of the apartment's smallest residents.

Standing roughly two-feet in height on two legs, and dressed in neat, improbable clothes, the two mice emerged from behind the couch, not wanting to be seen and yet needing to be in case they were exterminated if they were not.

One mouse was dressed in a smart little suit, and the other in a delightful summer dress that looked like something a doll might wear. Not only were they clearly a married couple, but they seemed a more convincing model of the concept than the humans sitting rigidly on the couch.

"Please don't exterminate us, sir. We don't mean any harm," the mouse in the suit begged.

The high-pitched and heart-felt plea was met by open-mouthed incredulity from the Thompsons.

"Don't worry, Peter, no-one's going to exterminate you," Cecilia offered by way of reassurance.

"No, of course not!" Gerald added.

"Stop it!" Mr. Thompson bellowed. "I've had enough of this! It's madness, I tell you! Madness!"

The mice cowered at the thunderous sound of Mr. Thompson's protest, and Cecilia's web practically rippled as the sound waves impacted with it.

"Dad, I know it's difficult to understand at first, but if you look past..."

"They're the wrong size!" Mr. Thompson yelled, pointing accusingly at the mice.

Gerald raised his hands in surrender. "I know, they are a little big for mice, but..."

"Big? What are you talking about, boy? They're far too small!"

Now all eyes were on Mr. Thompson, with everyone expecting an explanation to his bizarre assertion, but not immediately receiving one.

"What do you mean, Dad?"

"Mice are bigger than spiders," he said, beginning to explain his logic. "I can accept the talking, but not this. Cecilia is a spider. Why is she bigger than the mice?"

"Actually," Cecilia began calmly, "many species of spider are larger than the average mouse. The goliath bird-eating spider for example is known to eat prey the size of..."

"We're not in the jungle, young lady! This is my son's apartment, and I'll be damned if there's any giant bird-spiders within a thousand miles of here. This isn't bloody Australia! Why are those mice so small? Answer me that!"

"Erm..." Cecilia was lost for words for the first time in her life.

"Dad, don't you think you're missing the point?"

"What? What do you mean?"

At this point, Mrs. Thompson tugged on her husband's sleeve and looked at him with eyes that implored him to stop making things worse than they already were. "He's right, dear. There are talking mice over there, and you're worried about whether they're to scale with the talking spider-thing?"

"She's right, mister," the female mouse added. "You're not looking at this right at all. You should listen to your wife."

"Thank you," Mrs. Thompson said softly to the mouse, but then paused. "Wait a minute..."

A general sense of unease fell upon Gerald as he watched the last trace of his mother's sanity ebb away.

"You're wearing clothes!" she declared at last.

"You only just noticed? You need glasses, lady!" the mouse replied rudely.

"Susan!" Peter exclaimed, before turning to Mrs. Thompson. "I'm so sorry. Please don't listen to my wife. She's always like this. And, again, please don't exterminate us. We only just started couple's therapy. We..."

"No, you don't understand!" Mrs. Thompson interrupted. "Of course I noticed your clothes, but why do talking mice wear clothes if talking spiders don't?" She turned to Cecilia. "Oh my God! You're naked! Son, look away from that woman, or spider, or whatever it is!"

"Mother!" Gerald exclaimed, but then thought for a second and turned to Cecilia, who was trying not to laugh again. "Actually, why don't you wear clothes? I mean, everyone can see your...womanly parts."

There was a spluttering as Cecilia failed to suppress her laughter any longer. "Because I don't *like* wearing clothes. My fluff makes me itchy if I do. Anyway, you've never complained about seeing my womanly parts before."

"What?!" Mr. Thompson exclaimed, leaping from the couch and causing the mice to flee in terror. "Right, that's it, we *are* leaving this time," he yelled, pulling Mrs. Thompson to her feet. "Talking spiders

58

and ridiculously tiny mice are one thing, or two things even, but I won't stand for smutty insinuations about my boy!"

"Dad! She was just joking, for heaven's sake." Gerald looked to Cecilia for support, but she just shrugged the part of her that could most accurately be described as her shoulders apologetically.

In a flurry of huffing and head-shaking, Mr. Thompson dragged Mrs. Thompson to the living room door and turned to deliver what seemed as though it might be a verdict of some sort. "Son, we'll talk about this on the telephone," was all he said.

As she was being dragged away, Mrs. Thompson managed to look at Cecilia and say, "Perhaps just underwear?"

"Hm," Cecilia replied non-committally. Perhaps she would have to make a compromise.

Gerald followed hastily after his parents, not wanting their visit to end on a sour note. "It was lovely to see you both. You're welcome any time," he said, as if nothing out of the ordinary had occurred.

"Perhaps *you* could visit *us* next time, eh son?" his dad said before pausing to look his son in the eye sternly. He nodded without saying anything further and made to leave with Mrs. Thompson but then stopped suddenly. "Son. This might sound odd but...in your living room, erm, was there..."

"A giant spider-lady called Cecilia?"

"Yes."

"Yes, there was Dad. You're not crazy."

"And the mice too?" Mrs. Thompson asked, prompting a look of admiration from Mr. Thompson, who hadn't thought to ask about the mice.

"Yes, they're real, too," Gerald said, genuinely reassuring his parents for once.

"Oh, good. That's ok then."

Gerald smiled. "Yes, it is." he said as his parents left him in peace.

With his parents gone, Gerald was able to carefully clamber up Cecilia's web in a manner he was still not entirely confident about, and was relieved when he felt eight fluffy limbs embrace him, allowing him to relax at last. "I think that went quite well," he said to the pretty, brown-furred face next to him.

"That's such a cliché," she replied light-heartedly. "And a lie. But I admit it could have gone worse. They didn't call a priest anyway. Your parents seem like nice people."

"Now, I think *you* must be lying. They called you a monster and threatened to exterminate Peter and Susan."

"Don't be silly, Gerald. We both knew it wouldn't be easy for them. We've changed their understanding of reality a little bit."

Gerald laughed. "More than a little bit, I think. But all for the better in the long run, I hope. Anyway, they'll have to accept you, or they'll lose me."

The webs trembled as Cecilia caressed Gerald's skin with her ticklish fur. "Don't say that. They'll understand. And I'll be there to help them understand."

He sighed deeply. "I love you, Cecilia."

"I love you too, Gerald."

A thought then caused Gerald's smile to become slightly crooked, although none the less genuine. "I have to say though, even if they accept *us*, I'm not so sure they'll accept...you know..."

"Oh, *that*." She giggled happily.

"Yeah, *that*. Just how many babies did you say we're expecting?"

The result of Cecilia's peculiar features was a face that Gerald had always found quite appealing, and had since come to think of as beautiful in a strange sort of way.

SUDDENLY, CHIHUAHUA

Madison Keller

Madison Keller is owned by two rowdy Chihuahua mixes, who are gracious enough to allow her to live in their home. She transcribed this story at their behest, since they could not type it up themselves without thumbs. With her owners' permission, Madison has written and published numerous short stories and novels, one of which was a finalist for a 2016 Cóyotl Award for Best Novel. When not chaperoning her Chihuahuas to the dog park or writing, Madison likes to ride her bicycle and play tabletop role-playing games despite her owners' objection to the fact that they cannot participate.

The dog came tearing out of a cat flap set into the front door and was gnawing on my ankle before I'd barely registered its presence. He was the ugliest thing I've ever seen. The tan Chihuahua had an under-bite, so that his lower teeth stuck out beyond his lip, making him look like a bulldog; his nose was slightly off center; and one eye was milky white. On top of that, his head was comically larger than his spindly body.

I leaned over and grabbed the tiny thing by the back of the neck, trying to pull it away. It growled low in its throat and didn't let go. I tugged harder, and my pants gave way with a sharp ripping sound.

Unfamiliar routes were my bane. If I'd known this house had a crazy Chihuahua, I would have been on guard sooner. I'd seen the flap in the door, but, based on the size, I had thought it was for cats.

"Nugget! Chicken Nugget! You bad dog," a feminine voice scolded. A woman, probably in her early twenties, came out of the front door of the house the little monster had come from.

I lifted Nugget and held him out toward the woman. A scrap of blue fabric from my pants hung from the Chihuahua's mismatched teeth.

"Oh, thank you," the woman said as she took him from me. "I'm so sorry about that. He is such a terror. I thought for sure I'd locked the flap, but somehow this little devil always manages to get out anyway." She shook her head and glared at the little dog. There was some warmth in her look, but underneath it was a glimmer of real exasperation.

Anger welled up in me over my ruined pants. But my supervisor had been clear that one more outburst at a postal "customer," and I would be fired, so I gritted my teeth and did my best to keep my voice even as I replied, "I'm fine, thanks."

The woman shrugged at me, clearly dismissing my presence, before disappearing back into the house.

Back in my mail truck after completing my circuit, I pulled up my leg to examine the damage to my slacks. A big chunk had been torn off all the way up the calf.

Even worse, Nugget's bite had caught my skin. Blood had soaked into the cuff of my white sock. I didn't bother to pull out the first aid kit since it had already scabbed over.

A fresh surge of anger ran through me, and I pounded on the steering wheel hard enough to bruise my palms. A new pair of pants was *not* in the budget for this month, or any month really.

I made it home without further incident, but the wound on my ankle itched furiously as I began slicing the veggies and frying the steak strips for fajitas.

At five-thirty, exactly, the front door banged open.

"Dinner's almost ready," I yelled. If I left the stove now, my shells would burn.

"Not staying, darling," Kirby, my husband, called from the front room. "Bowling league tonight."

"But—" I started to protest.

"No time to chat." He stepped into the kitchen, pecked me on the cheek, and then was gone, the front door slamming closed behind him.

I stood, frozen in the act of flipping a fajita shell until the heat burned my thumb. I yelped and jumped away.

The clock was edging up toward six, so where were my kids? I dug through my purse for my cell phone.

"Where r u?" I typed, eyes narrowing to glare at my daughter's picture on the screen, as if I could send my glare through the phone along with the words. "Dinner getting cold."

"At Brianna's," came the terse reply from my oldest, Maria.

"Studying for a test tomorrow. Home late. Had pizza. Love you."

Taya, my youngest, replied a few minutes later. "On way home now. Already ate at Staci's house."

The mounds of food I'd spent the last hour preparing stared back at me from the table. I growled and got the Tupperware, slamming the cupboards closed.

My hands shook with anger as I began scooping the food into the plastic containers. The shaking grew worse, and my trembling fingers dropped the serving spoon. It fell into a container I'd already filled, tipping it over and dumping fajita mix off the table and all over the floor.

"¡Qué putada!" I screamed, frustrated, hungry, and exhausted. One more thing to clean up.

I moved to get a rag, but my whole body began to shake hard enough to make my teeth chatter as if I was freezing.

Without warning, the whole kitchen seemed to expand around me; the walls becoming farther apart, the table and then the chair bottoms rising above my head.

A moment later, soft navy fabric fell over my entire body, blocking my vision. I struggled out of the mound of clothes with difficulty. My fingers didn't seem to be working properly, and I couldn't get a grip on the fabric to lift it. I thrashed my way free and tried to stand, but my legs were shaky. What was going on?

I fell to all fours, a strangely comfortable position, and glanced around. The colors of the kitchen washed out, reds becoming pale brown and yellow, and the navy of my uniform faded to pale blue. My whole body tingled oddly. I twisted my head to look down at myself, trying to figure out what was wrong.

Soft brown fur came into view, along with a thin tail that curled above my back. The tail wagged back and forth, and I realized that I could feel it there on my butt.

Suddenly, somehow, I'd become a Chihuahua.

After a few moments of balancing on my spindly back legs and craning my neck, I spotted where I'd left my cell phone on the kitchen counter, next to my purse.

I backed up and charged. My claws scrabbled for purchase on the linoleum, but I managed to build up some speed even in the tiny kitchen. I jumped as hard and high as I could, only to smack headfirst into the drawers, not even halfway up.

I stumbled around dazed. Above me, my phone chimed, and

buzzed with an incoming text message, the vibration moving the phone until a corner peeked out over the edge. The phone might as well have been on the moon for all the good it did me down on the floor.

The front door creaked, and a girl's voice called.

"Mom, I'm home!"

"Thank heaven!" I trotted out into the living room. "Taya, you have to help me."

Taya blinked down at me in surprise and shut the door behind her, shedding her muddy tennis shoes and backpack onto the floor.

"Young lady, you know better than that. Put your shoes on the porch and pick up your backpack," I snapped at her, stomping one little Chihuahua foot.

"Mom, are you home?" Taya said as if I hadn't spoken. She peered around in bewilderment. "Where are you? And when did we get a dog?"

"What?" My whole body began shaking again. "I'm right in front of you!"

"Man, this thing barks a lot," Taya muttered to herself.

"I'm not barking. I'm talking!" I jumped around at her legs, but it was no use. From her comment, it was obvious all her daughter heard when I spoke was the barking of an excited dog.

Taya walked into the kitchen, groaned at the mess, and began to clean up. "Dad's gonna be pissed."

One by one, my family got home, each commenting on my absence, the pile of clothes in the kitchen, and speculating on the strange dog. I continued to yell pleas for help, but, like Taya, they heard only barks.

Finally, they went to bed, shutting me into a bathroom alone. I curled up on the rug and whined myself to sleep.

I woke up the next morning stiff, sore, and naked, but thankfully human again. The hardwood floor was cold on my bare feet as I tip-toed my way into the bedroom, put on pajamas, and slipped into bed.

Kirby rolled over as I tugged the covers up, throwing his arm around me. A few moments later, he yawned and opened his eyes. "Juana? Where've you been?" he mumbled sleepily.

"Friend emergency. Thanks for watching her dog for me while I was out." I'd had a lot of time to think up an excuse while locked in the bathroom overnight.

"Without your purse? Or pho—"

My alarm buzzed, cutting him off. I slapped it off, pecked him on the cheek, and rolled out of bed, rushing into the bathroom to forestall further questions. By the time I got out, he was fast asleep again.

After picking up my truck full of mail, I parked in the same place as yesterday and began delivering letters.

"Hey, hey! Go away! My house!" A low voice growled.

I stopped, startled, as I hadn't seen anyone around. A big black lab growled at me from behind a chain link fence.

The black lab opened its mouth. "Stop! Don't come any closer, you intruder!" the dog barked.

I froze, startled, and stared at the dog. "What? Did you just *speak* to me?"

"Yes I did!" the dog barked. "I told you to stay away from my yard, you stranger."

"I won't go into your yard, I promise." My face heated with embarrassment.

"See that you don't." The dog sniffed and sat, watching me warily through the fence as I passed.

I stopped again with my hand reaching for the mailbox and looked at the dog. Feeling a bit silly, I said, "Don't be startled. I'm just going to deliver these letters and be on my way."

The black lab huffed and didn't reply. I took that as assent, popping the letters into the box before speed walking away.

Had that dog really *talked* to me? Was I going crazy? I pulled out my cell phone.

"About yesterday," I texted to Taya. I sent the text, but then hesitated. Taya had been the one to get home and find me, but I had no idea how to word my question without sounding crazy. While I was thinking, I dropped mail off at the next house. My phone pinged before I figured it out.

"NP. Dad explained. RU ok?" Taya texted back.

"Fine. Everything is fine now."

"Gr8. Wish we could keep the dog. So cute." Taya followed up with a slew of emoticon hearts and kisses, then another ping. "What's the dog's name?"

How to respond to that? I chewed on my lip, staring at the phone. What if this happened again?

"Bella," I texted back with a smile. If I was to be a dog, I might as well constantly be told I was pretty. "We'll be dog-sitting her in the future, whenever my friend needs us to." I tucked the phone away.

"Hey, you! Stay away! This is my dead squirrel," a dog barked at me from behind a white picket fence.

"I don't want your dead squirrel," I answered absently, focused as I was on my bag and gathering the mail for the next house.

A man walking toward me on the sidewalk, stopped, and gawked. "Lady, what is your problem?" he yelled, crossing the street to avoid me.

Nugget's house was coming up next. He was a Chihuahua, and I'd turned into one yesterday after he'd bit me; I hoped he was home, so I could ask him about it. The connection was tenuous, but it was the only explanation I could come up with.

I took a deep breath to steady my pounding heart, opened the gate, and started up the walk. Their mailbox was mounted on the wall next to the front door, and yesterday Nugget had come after me only after I'd turned my back.

The pet flap squeaked. I turned and crouched, catching Nugget by his collar just as he lunged for my ankle, again.

"Got ya," I crowed, lifting the little dog.

Nugget blinked at me in surprise, and then barked in a high-pitched voice while squirming wildly. "Put me down so I can kill you properly, invader."

"Not until you've answered a few questions." The collar dug into his throat, so I shifted my grip to encompass the scruff of skin on the back of his neck.

"Intruder!" Nugget screamed, continuing to squirm and snap.

The same woman came out the door, giving Nugget an exasperated glare. "Thank you for catching him. He's such a handful!" She held out her hands.

"Just a sec." I pulled the thrashing Nugget close, struggling to keep hold of him and the heavy bag of mail. "What did you do to me yesterday?"

"The bite was a warning to never come back!" Nugget was almost foaming at the mouth now, he was so frantically barking and flailing. "Obviously, stupid human."

"Tell me how to break the curse," I hissed, anger making my voice tight. A tingling tightness ran over my skin, and I could feel myself beginning to shake.

"Curse? I don't know what you are talking about! Get out of my territory." Nugget twisted free, leaping for the ground, but the woman from the house caught him before he landed.

"Bad Chicken Nugget," she scolded, sweeping away into the house, not even giving me a backward glance.

I staggered away, trembling so violently I could barely work the catch on the gate. It finally popped open, and I lurched onto the sidewalk.

My bag of mail felt as if someone was filling it full of rocks, getting heavier and heavier with each step. My vision narrowed to a strip, the colors fading and dulling. I managed two steps more and collapsed into the bushes.

When I thrashed free of my clothing, I found myself once again a dog. I lifted my muzzle and screamed at the sky in frustration.

Once I calmed down a bit, I sat in the dirt and tried to figure out what to do. My mail truck was parked just one block over, but there was no way I would be able to get the door open. It wasn't just the problem of my paws not being able to manipulate things, but, as a Chihuahua, I was just too short. Plus, I didn't dare leave my bag and clothes just sitting here under a bush, for anyone to steal. Thinking about my clothes made me remember my pockets, and my cell phone.

After a few minutes of nosing around at my pants, I managed to get my muzzle into the pocket. As delicately as I could I took the edge of the phone in my teeth and tugged it free. The screen was dark and sleeping. I tapped it with my paw and the lock screen flickered into view, prompting me to "Draw your Pattern." A 3x3 block of dots filled the screen underneath.

"¡*Mierda*!" I cursed. I'd forgotten about that, since I usually unlocked it using the fingerprint reader on the back.

I tried to draw my pattern, but even my tiny Chihuahua paw was just too big. The phone misinterpreted my touch, losing the line or connecting the wrong dots.

As I worked, cars buzzed by in the street, and a few people walked by on the sidewalk, but no one noticed me or stopped to investigate.

My trembling had subsided while I worked on the phone. I lay there, head resting on my outstretched paws, trying to decide what to do. I wasn't sure what triggered it, but my skin tingled, and my fur began to recede.

Branches scratched at my bare skin and tangled in my hair as I grew in size until I sat naked in the dirt, only partially concealed by the remains of the broken bush I'd been hiding under.

A car screeched to halt on the road next to me, a shocked young couple sitting in the front seats staring at me open-mouthed. I smiled, gave them a little wave, and began dressing as inconspicuously as a naked woman could on a public street. A second car pulled up behind the staring couple and honked loudly several times, which jolted the couple out of their reverie. The car lurched away, although not without several backward glances by the couple.

The car behind them roared off without incident. By that time, I'd gotten my pants and shirt on, so all they'd seen was a disheveled woman awkwardly putting on shoes. I stuffed my underwear and bra in my mailbag. It would have taken too long to put them on, and I needed to get out of here, before that couple called the cops.

I picked up my phone, wiping the dirt I'd smeared on the screen with my paws, and called my supervisor to let her know I couldn't finish the rest of my shift, making up an excuse about being violently ill. Which was true, in a way.

The next morning, I called in sick, promising my livid supervisor I'd bring a doctor's note with me when I returned.

After Kirby and the kids had left for the day, I turned on the computer.

I stared at the blinking cursor in the search bar. I'd had a grand plan this morning that a quick Google search would solve all my problems, but now that I was here, I realized I had no idea what to search *for*. I leaned back in my chair, drumming my fingers on the desk.

My mind flicked back to the old monster movies I'd used to watch as a kid on late-night television. Zombies, ghosts, mummies, swamp creatures, demons, devils, and, of course, werewolves. I shook my head.

I most assuredly wasn't a werewolf. I'd seen the movies. Not only did I not turn into anything close to a wolf, but I also wasn't violent, bloodthirsty, or out-of-control. Plus, most importantly, I wasn't turning on a full moon. But, what was I then? The werewolf shapeshifted. *I* shapeshifted. And a dog was kinda like a wolf, right?

At a loss, I typed "werewolf" into the search bar and clicked "search."

The first result was, of course, Wikipedia, but scrolling through didn't yield any useful information. I clicked the Back button.

The rest of the page's results were from various games and movies, so I clicked over to the second page.

"Werewolf World News" and "Cryptid Hunters" webpages made me give a startled laugh, until I remembered why I was here.

Another two hours of research brought me no closer to an answer. I tried searching for "curses," "witches," "magic," and even "lycanthropy" after reading the Cryptid Hunters webpage out of desperation. Nothing.

I slammed the mouse down in frustration and rested my head in my hands. My hands began to shake, and then my whole body vibrated. I barely had time to register what was happening before I found myself on the floor engulfed in swathes of fabric.

I dug my way out and then sat on top of my clothing with a litany of curse words, thinking of what had just happened.

A pattern had begun to emerge. Each time I'd changed I'd been angry and only changed back after calming down.

With that in mind, I hopped back up into the chair and then onto the desk. The computer was still on, with Internet Explorer showing the Google homepage.

It took some trial and error of tapping on the keyboard with my paws and moving the mouse around with my nose, but soon enough I managed to get the cursor back up into the search bar and typed in "calming exercises" by pressing the keys delicately with a claw.

Half an hour of progressive muscle relaxation later found me back in human form, naked and sprawled on the couch. After I got dressed, I printed posts on calming techniques until the printer ran out of ink.

I wasn't yet confident in my ability to remain calm, in-control, and, most importantly, *human* for the entire working day. However, the bills wouldn't pay themselves.

I repeated my mantra meditation exercise that I'd practiced—*a mal tiempo, buena cara*—and headed for work.

The black lab barked at me again, but a quick reassurance that I would respect his territory boundary mollified him. He barked goodbye to me as I left.

That made me stop and smile. The dog had been more polite than most of the humans I'd had to deal with during my years of delivering mail.

Rather than ignoring the next dog on my route, I stopped, introduced myself, and explained that I was delivering mail to her owners and would leave as soon as I was done. I felt a bit silly, talking to the fluffy, white, basketball-sized poof that passed for a dog at this house, but I left the mailbox with a smile and the feeling that I'd just made the little dog's day.

By lunch time, I'd actually started to enjoy myself, but then I got to Nugget's house. I scowled down at the pile of letters in my hand, debating with myself on what would happen if I just tossed them over the gate and went on with my route.

However, I didn't think, "Sorry, ma'am, I didn't deliver their mail because they have a tiny, ugly Chihuahua that bit me, and now I turn into a dog when I get upset," would fly with my supervisor.

No sounds came from the house, but that didn't mean anything. My eyes never left the dog door as I opened the mailbox by feel, slipping the letters inside.

I backed down the walk, but nothing happened. The house was still as a tomb.

Only after the gate was latched firmly behind me did I relax with a sigh. I twisted my hands together, realizing they were shaking, so I settled down cross-legged on the sidewalk and did breathing exercises until I felt settled enough to continue on with my route.

I passed by an alley, and a stray poked his head out from between two trash-cans and growled a warning at me.

"Hi there," I said, stopping, but not looking directly at the dog.

The dog's head vanished from view. I shrugged and continued on. I couldn't do anything if a dog didn't want to talk to me.

I caught sight of the stray again a few blocks away. I recognized the distinctive white spot around his eye, so I knew it was the same dog. He shadowed me for several blocks before slinking away.

My bag was empty, so I headed back to my mail truck for another load. I unlocked the door and swung the empty bag inside before climbing up after it.

"Ouch," a squeaky growl came from where the bag hit the floor.

Halfway inside already, I twisted and leaned over to grab the canvas, flinging it away to reveal Chicken Nugget crouched between the seats. I barely had time to wonder how he'd gotten inside before he lunged.

"Charge!" he howled, leaping at my face with his fangs bared.

I yelped and flinched back, flinging up my arms to protect my face from Nugget's snapping teeth. Teeth grazed my arm, and he bounced off to land on the driver's side seat. The hit jolted me back, and my feet slipped on the edge of the door frame. I tried to grab the seat, but my hands slid right off the slick plastic covering.

My arms windmilled as I fell backward out the door, screaming in surprise. I landed hard on my ass on the sidewalk with my arms flung behind me. My right wrist gave a popping crack as I hit, and I gasped, the shock of it sending sparks of pain all the way up my back.

I stood, but a growl from behind me made me whirl around. Four dogs advanced on me in a ragged semi-circle. I recognized two of them; the tiny, white poof-ball and the shy stray with the spot over one eye.

My inner-Chihuahua reared up, telling me not to show weakness to the pack, but I couldn't help but back away until I hit the side of the truck.

Nugget appeared in the corner of my eye. He jumped out with a hop that was at once graceless and delicate. His four legs flailed through the air yet he landed lightly, like a dandelion seed buffeted by the wind, both out of control and light as a feather.

"Nugget, call off your dogs. I have nothing against you," I said, growling and showing my teeth in my best imitation of a dogs.

"Then, why keep coming to all our territories, invader?" Nugget sniffed. "And then you accuse me of *cursing* you? This is to give you a lesson."

Without any further warning, all five dogs advanced. *A mal tiempo, buena cara,* I chanted, trying to calm myself down. If I changed while the pack was on me, I wouldn't stand a chance.

"I'm just delivering things to your humans," I said, slowly and firmly.

The white fluff-ball halted. "She *was* nice to me, Nugget. Most of the humans don't even interact with me."

The stray cocked his head. "Fifi has a point. This human talked nicely to me earlier. We shouldn't attack her." He looked hopefully at me, tail starting to wag slowly.

The two dogs stopped and looked at Nugget, who was trembling violently, ears pinned back to his head and growling.

"But she humiliated me!" he barked.

I kept my expression serious, but inside I was smiling. The energy was leaking out of the pack. "I apologize, Nugget. I've had a bad week, but I shouldn't have tried to blame you for it."

All four dogs turned their attention toward Nugget, so I took the opportunity to sidle toward the truck door. I knew somewhere inside it would be a bad idea to turn my back on the pack, defused energy or not. I reached back, feeling out the edge of the driver's seat and then running my hand down until I felt my lunch bag.

A few quick tugs got it free. My injured wrist throbbed, but I ignored the pain as I unzipped the bag and pulled out the baby carrots I always kept as a snack.

"Here you go," I said, tossing a fat carrot in the air. The stray caught it with a happy bounce in his jaws. Then, I went around the ring of dogs, tossing one to each of them. They all began gnawing on the treats except for Nugget.

"I'll bring better snacks for each of you tomorrow," I said, suppressing a smile. "Consider them payment for allowing me brief access to your territory."

The stray finished his first. He cocked his head at me, lifting one ear, and then at Nugget. "Consider it done."

Fifi and then the other two dogs barked their agreement. Nugget snarled, clearly unhappy, turned up his nose at his uneaten carrot, and went racing off. The stray lunged forward and snapped up Nugget's carrot with a single crunch.

"More tomorrow?" the stray asked after he finished crunching the last carrot.

"Yes, more tomorrow," I assured him.

Fifi and the other two dogs wagged their tails, satisfied, and trotted off after Nugget. The stray came up with his ears pricked forward and sniffed me gingerly before following them.

Once I was sure they were gone, I turned and stared at the truck, contemplating how I was going to finish my route with a sprained wrist.

"Wow, that was something," someone said.

The speaker was close, but huffing for breath as if they'd been jogging. I turned and looked down, but didn't see any dogs. The sidewalk in either direction was clear as well. A person cleared their throat near the hood of my truck and I jumped, looking up.

"Excuse me." A man stood at the front of the truck. He raised his arm and gave me a brief wave. He was sweating and breathing hard as if he'd just gone for a jog, although he was wearing slacks and a button-up shirt.

"Didn't mean to interrupt, but I saw how you handled that pack of dogs. I was quite impressed."

I blushed scarlet and faced him, embarrassed that I'd been so focused on looking for a dog that I'd missed him standing so close.

"Oh, well, thank you. But it was no big deal. I know most of those dogs from my route, so I already had a rapport with them," I said.

"Still," he said and shook his head. "I thought you were going to get mauled. It's why I ran over here to help, but, by the time I got here, you had things well in hand." He smiled and stuck out a hand. "My name's Rob."

"Hi Rob, I'm Juana." I shook hands with him, and only as he pumped my arm up and down did I realize I'd unconsciously given him my injured one to shake, yet my wrist didn't hurt at all.

I glanced down at my arm, where Nugget had nipped me during his surprise attack. The scratches he had left were already gone; all that remained of the wounds were two thin lines of drying blood. In the movies, the werewolves always had amazing powers of regeneration. I resolved to reread the Cryptid website about the werewolves when I got home.

Rob was talking again, and I tore my attention away from my miraculously healed arm and back to what he was saying in time to hear. "Would you consider freelance dog training?"

I blinked at him in surprise. "Dog training?"

"Yes." Rob blew out a breath. "You took those dogs from aggression to tail-wagging to eating treats out of your hand in less than a minute. I've tried everything to train my dog without success, but after watching that display, I'm willing to give it one more try."

"I'm sorry, I'm not—"

"I'll pay you two hundred dollars." He pulled out his wallet and showed me a wad of bills.

"I get off work in thirty minutes," I said, trying not to boggle at the amount.

The Humane Society building was a big gray, concrete building sitting out in the industrial neighborhood, squashed between warehouses and factories. My husband and I trailed behind the girls, who pushed excitedly through the glass doors ahead of us.

"Maria, Taya, slow down," I called, but they were already pelting through the lobby toward the dog viewing area.

"I'm still not sold on this," Kirby grumbled.

I smiled sweetly at him. "The girls have already promised to help, and I'll be around during the day to keep the dog out of trouble. I can even take it with me when I visit clients. You won't have to lift a finger."

"About that. I can't complain about all the extra money you're bringing in or how much calmer you've become, but," Kirby eyed her. "Where did this sudden inspiration to become a dog psychic come from, anyway?"

I shrugged. "I told you. I just discovered I had this way with dogs, and the rest fell into place. Now, hurry up, before the girls pick out a Great Dane or something."

We passed through the lobby and entered the area with adoptable dogs. The girls stood two kennels down from the door, cooing over a big, fluffy Husky mix.

The dogs' plaintive cries for help tugged at my heart strings and I wanted to take them all home. I did my best to tune them out.

"Remember, girls, small dogs only! We don't want to scare Bella when she comes to visit."

I shooed them away from the big, fluffy dog. They moved a few kennels down and stopped.

"Wow, who's going to adopt that hideous thing?" Maria giggled, pointing at the dog further back in the cage.

"O.M.G., it's looking at me." Taya wrinkled her nose. "C'mon, let's go." She grabbed her sister, and they moved off down the aisle.

I drifted over, curious to see the dog they'd so quickly rejected. A small tan Chihuahua was curled up in a tight ball against the back of the cage. It looked up as my shadow fell over it, revealing an off-center nose, an under-bite, and a comically large head with bulbous eyes.

"Chicken Nugget?" I said with a gasp. "What are you doing here?"

"Go away, human, don't taunt me about the loss of my family," he growled half-heartedly at me, the fire gone from his voice. He got up and shifted, so his back was to the front of the kennel before lying back down.

Tears pricked at my eyes. All the little dog had wanted to do was protect his family and they'd thrown him out. "I'm not here to taunt you."

"Juana, who are you talking to?" Kirby said. I jumped and fell into the chain link front of the kennel. I'd been so focused on Nugget that I'd forgotten Kirby beside me.

"I was talking to the dog," I admitted, blushing. My heart had begun to beat rapidly, and I could feel the tingling tightness in my skin. I reached out and wrapped my fingers through the metal diamonds, closed my eyes, and chanted. "*A mal tiempo, buena cara. A mal tiempo, buena cara.*"

"Is something wrong, Juana? You know I don't speak Spanish." Kirby knelt down beside me and gently touched my hand.

His touch helped me relax further. "It's an idiom. Literally, it is 'when things go wrong, keep smiling.' In English, I guess it is close to 'turn lemons into lemonade.'"

To my surprise, I felt the touch of a cold nose on my fingers. I'd shifted to look at Kirby while I explained my meditation mantra, and, when I glanced back, I saw that Nugget had come over and was looking up at me with big, soulful puppy-dog eyes.

"I'm sorry that I lashed out at you." Nugget stared up at me. "I only ever wanted to protect my family."

"It's alright, Nugget," I said. I was tempted to reach a finger through to pet the end of his muzzle that still rested against my hand, but I didn't want to disrupt the fragile peace between us. "I shouldn't have tried to blame you for my problems."

Kirby snorted, and I knew he'd just rolled his eyes, although I kept my gaze fixed on Nugget. "Juana, honey, the dogs are not talking to you. Save your act for your clients, ok?"

I ignored him and kept talking to Nugget. "Chicken Nugget, please accept my sincere apology for any trouble I caused you."

Nugget pricked his ears forward and wagged his tail. "I forgive you, Juana."

I suppressed a smile. He was forgiving me.

"Thank you, Nugget," I said instead.

"You are welcome, dog-human," Nugget said.

I spun on Kirby, who'd been watching me with a put-upon expression. I pointed at Nugget. "We're adopting this one."

"What?" Kirby and Nugget both responded in unison and both wrinkling their nose in distaste.

"You heard me," I said, replying to them both. "We're going to be one big, happy family."

I tried to draw my pattern, but even my tiny Chihuahua paw was just too big. The phone misinterpreted my touch, losing the line or connecting the wrong dots.

KENYAK'S SAGA

MIKASIWOLF

With Wordcraft as his sword, and Fursona as his shield, MikasiWolf had been fighting through the War of the Slush since 2007. Despite the evil forces of Lethargy and Writersblock, he's determined to keep their forces at bay. He hopes to someday experience the Publication, a spiritual uplifting of novels previously left in the dust. Several conquests to his name include FurPlanet Productions' The Furry Future *(2015),* Gods With Fur *(2016),* Dogs of War *and* Dogs of War II *(both 2017), Jaffa Books'* Claw the Way to Victory *(2016), and the VancouFurs 2015 Conbook, What The Fur 2015 Conbook, and Anthrocon 2015 Conbook.*

MikasiWolf's alter ego is a Design Engineer who wishes he could spend his workday designing tales and sagas rather than car audio parts. Some things aren't for the faint of heart. He currently hides in the following addresses: twitter.com/MikasiWolf and furaffinity.net/user/mikasiwolf. Feel free to DM him with any comments you may have! Or if you just wanna talk. He doesn't bite...yet.

We had first set out to the vast seas of our world, not knowing what the turbulent waters of Ægir would bring. Nomads in our own way, always wandering; always searching. Some say that we fair wolves of the Northern Coasts were born of the ice floes themselves, and as such were destined to be carried away by the immemorial roads of the sea. Yet others say that we sail the seas merely in search for new lands to call our own, lands we drift upon the shores of. That the reason we conquer and pillage is to obtain what riches of the land we lacked, with every settlement's destruction our gain. For as hardy as my people were, the lands of our birth were much too harsh for any kind of existence. Some even called us the Terror of the North. I admit that a number of us were fighters at heart; but allow me to explain why I, Kenyak the Unproven, am sailing the Seven Seas with but a pawful of companions. Not in a longship, but in a fishing skiff we pilfered just as our own village fell to its invaders.

Vikings being invaded? What a laugh, I hear you growl. Har-bloody-har-har. Thanks, but no thanks. It's presumptuous of you or anyone else to assume that the fiercest of warriors would never be routed from their lands. After all, for every powerful civilization, there exists many others happy to see it fall. One reason why no one truly knew why we saw fit to invade the lands of others was that our endless pride and honor refused explanation. On that note, it was also far more pleasing and awe-inspiring to speak of having to leave due to poor agricultural conditions, than to let slip that our good neighbors had decided to take up arms against us. That said, there was only so long we could stay before their realizing there were so many more of them than us. One didn't have to be a skald or chieftain to weigh those odds.

Surely, we weren't the best of guests when we had first arrived, pillaging their villages and killing their kings. But that was all in the past. Besides, my father's father and his men did it, not Father Dear. So it was highly uncalled-for when the local Picts charged into Rarkshirg as we were drinking our health to Odin. While we were being good hosts to our guests from the Thaneship of Skerrig, with a storm raging outside the hall, the cervine Picts set upon us with antlers and spears. Were it not for the fact that I was in a storehouse swiving away with two gals my buddy and I had the good fortune to get to know better, we would not have lived to swive another night. I had always told Rorik he never fully concentrated on whatever he did, and so it was he who stopped us in the midst of our private merrymaking. "Kenyak!" he'd whined. "We're being attacked!" My leggings came back up faster than they ever had, unless you counted that one time alone in the armory when Father almost caught me.

Now, the *Jarl* and his warriors were in no shape for any counterattack. It was as much fear as poor combat skills that drove Rorik and me along with our two beauties to the nearest boat. I had heard that casting off during a full-on gale was a far worse way to die than in battle, but just you try thinking straight with one paw on your leggings, and an unfinished tankard of bloodmead in the other. Not to mention the war cries of our attackers to give impetus. It wasn't often that I had the best of Sherrig bloodmead to drink, so you'll excuse me if I didn't get my priorities straight.

That was the last time I had any mead to drink. I regret nothing.

Rorik and I cast off just as the attackers came round the storehouse and spotted us, and it was as much as the force of the gale as our own doing that set our boat at the mercy of Ægir, almighty *Jötunn* of the seas. I was never much of a sailor, fighting between the sails and the tiller, but believe me when I tell you that sailing a boat with little experience was exhausting, not to mention backbreaking. This, along with the fatigue of our prior activities, led us all to sleep the night through, leaving us at the mercy of the storm.

Father had decreed that, someday, I should travel far beyond the reach of our current expeditions, alongside the best of his warriors. I was to be the first to board, and the first to stake our claim upon new lands. But he never could have imagined his son setting out on his first voyage in a fishing skiff. With the most unseeming of companions, no less.

First up, Rorik the Bewildered, the Thaneship's slow-wit. There was little point in calling him a warrior; we all were, like it or not. He could spend the entire day learning how to master a simple sword swing, only to slice through his own footpaw. Till today, he lacked the foresight to wear paw protectors. But the females seemed to like him for some reason, and his easygoing nature was one of the reasons why we were such good friends. For every suggestion I made, he would nod with a dazed, fangy smile.

On his left, beside the rotting fishnet, was Velka Good-Swallow, daughter of a high-ranking thane from Skerrig. A she-wolf whose name bespoke either a calm demeanor, outspokenness, or skills best left unmentioned. Greda the Slow was the only other survivor of our village, and was one of the few bear *Karls* in our settlement. She was also Rorik's preferred companion on nights such as yesterday's. It was either through weary attrition, or the impossibility of getting him paired with the other wolves, that the Thaneship let it be. Not unheard of, but every warrior was expected to sire cubs nonetheless. Just like Rorik, she was similarly slow-witted; yet another example of birds of a feather flocking together.

Loki's beard! It was no picnic when we awoke to the sight of the featureless sea all around us. Even if it were night, my rudimentary knowledge of astro-navigation, addled by the best of blooded mead, wouldn't help in finding our way back. Besides, we all knew the Thaneship was lost when our delightful neighbors paid a visit.

"By Odin's eye, Kenyak, we've got to get to Skerrig!" rilled Velka.

"My people need to know what happened! Only they can right this affront on our honor! We have to sail back at once."

I cast a half-lidded amber eye at her. "And how do you propose we do that, sweetie?" I asked, gesturing at the open expanse of sea. There was no visible land around, as far as the eye could see. The only indicator of direction was the sun, already halfway to the apex. It's all very good to know where the East was, but it meant little if we were off the coast of somewhere we hadn't been.

Velka folded her arms and huffed in true Viking fashion, her tail flicking agitatedly. Did I ever say I found that cute? Especially when it kept doing that in the storehouse last night…

"Besides, with the way our luck's going, your people may already be food for the crows," I said as I flapped my arms. Velka glared. "It's not likely the Picts would have beef with *just* my Thaneship. We're all carnivores, after all. Just stating the facts, sweetheart." I waggled my ears at her.

"Kenyak, there're gulls that way," spluttered Rorik, pointing his paw behind me. "Maybe we aren't so far from the Thaneship after all! We're saved!" He laughed in relief, throwing himself into the wide arms and ample bosom of Greda's.

Oh, well. Looks like my fantasy of sailing into the uncharted lands of Those Who Dare were dashed. I bit back a scowl as Rorik and I set about maneuvering the sails and tiller in the right direction. A more difficult task than it looked, with my best friend doing mostly the opposite of whatever I was doing. The girls weren't of much help, naturally, what with their merry dance that rocked the boat from side to side. A longship, this wasn't. In my heart, I was more worried about what awaited us back on land. But did we really want to spend the rest of our lives on this tub? Granted, we had two beauties on board, but even the most outgoing of sailors needed food and mead every now and then. And as embarrassing as it was to admit, a lot more variety. I couldn't fish that well, anyway, and Rorik didn't have even a shred of my competence. Besides, that net looked like it could come apart at any moment.

Our arms and backs were sore by the time we beached, and I stepped out gingerly onto the coast. There was no telling how far we had landed from our recently-razed Thaneship. From the shape and appearance of the trees in the nearby forest, I could tell that we'd never been to these parts. Besides, the air smelt way different, though I couldn't pick up any other scents. It wasn't much colder than my old home was, so our clothes and fur were still good enough to keep the draft out.

"Where in Valhalla are we?" I muttered. The thing about trees was their universal appearance. No matter where you went, they looked much the same; green and brown. It wasn't like I knew my plants; foraging and lumber-gathering weren't my strong points.

"Kenyak?" said Rorik, his voice quavering. "I don't think we're alone."

Fenrir's arse, I almost capsized the boat in my haste to get back inside. "Whatever do you mean?" I hissed, eyes scanning the trees, one footpaw out in case we needed to push off. Velka and Greda had their ears up, quivering where they crouched. As far as I could tell, neither feral nor biped could be seen. And given our recent fracas, either one could prove dangerous.

"There's something moving in the trees. And I don't think we're anywhere near home."

Well done, genius. To prove his point, a group of figures burst out of the trees, axes and spears in paw. They also gave a long drawn-out whooping as they did, which sent the fur all the way down from my neck to tail fluffing out. I made to push the boat off, but then noticed something about the warriors dashing toward us.

Unlike the native people back home, these were wolves. Very feminine, unabashed wolves, if their bare rippling chests were anything to go by. As far as I knew, my Thaneship didn't have any women in our shield wall. There were sagas that spoke of "shieldmaidens," females who took up arms, but I had always figured out those sagas as a kind of comic relief. But even they tended to don some form of armor or clothing. Not that I was complaining, with my eyes taking in the wonderful sights before me.

The problem was this contributed to the delay in my pushing off, and the attackers quickly had us surrounded. Velka and Greda screamed as two of the of the wolves pulled them to shore, my ears flattening as they landed muzzle-first into the sand. I reached for my waistband, only to realize just then that we were seriously unarmed. Weapons tended to get in the way of what we had planned last night. The wolves forced us into kneeling positions, spears pressed against our backs. I couldn't help but risk a glance over to the ones holding us, and realized their grins meant ill intent. Rorik, Velka, and Greda shivered where they knelt.

One of the wolves stepped forward. From her loincloth, she drew a knife, and though it was of stone, I had no doubt it did its job well enough. She took a long look at each and every one of us, then pulled me upright by the front of my tunic. I got a good look at her whatchamacallits, right until I felt the edge of her blade against my neck.

She looked to the rest of her clansfolk, and muttered a string of syllables of a language I didn't recognize. It didn't sound anything like the language the natives back home spoke, but then, they looked nothing like them as well. With fur of a tawny hue, and paint markings of reddish ochre, this was unlike the blue woad that the Picts preferred. Several of the natives shrugged or otherwise replied, and one of them stepped forth.

Despite the fact that she'd got to be far older than any of the others, with grizzled fur around her neck and ears, she carried a certain grace and authority for her stature. Her tail was raised higher than the rest, and the markings upon her fur were far more elaborate. The wolfess holding me stepped away from me as her Chief(?) approached. To my great surprise, she pulled Rorik upright as well, and otherwise paid Velka and Greda no heed.

The Chief walked around me and my friend, who looked more curious than scared. That's Rorik for you. The Chief sniffed us each and every other way, and it was all I could do not to giggle when it started to get ticklish. Velka stared at this aghast, and all I could do was give her a "What did you expect?" expression. After what felt like a long while, the Chief stood up, licking her lips. She barked several commands to her people, and as one, they surged forth. They grabbed us by the arms and pulled, and I was about to defend myself when I realized they were all smiles, with their tails a-wagging. I looked back and saw that Velka and Greda were also being likewise led away, though their captors didn't afford them more than a second glance. The way that several of my captors ran their paws down my and Rorik's bodies made me realize what lay in store for us.

"Kenyak, what's going to happen to us?" asked Rorik, clueless as ever.

"It's gonna be fun, my friend! Just wait and see!" I barked back. One of the females drew her fingers through my ruff and growled.

As could be expected, that day turned out to be a fun and fulfilling experience. When we got to the village, which consisted of skin huts nestled around a stream, I had my first misgivings about our living conditions. All of us were used to sleeping in properly constructed wood and stone houses, which gave reasonable warmth if they had a properly-lit hearth and everything. None of these huts had any fireplaces within, but it was soon apparent that there would be no shortage of warmth to be had. As soon as we arrived and the other villagers heard what their grinning chief had to say, the wolves were practically fighting to get me and Rorik into their own tents. I couldn't say I didn't expect that, what with my good looks and all; but what they saw in Rorik was anyone's guess. It was only after the flap of a tent belonging to a group of sisters closed that I wondered why we haven't seen any male natives so far. All thoughts of that were soon forgotten as they practically tackled me to the floor of the tent.

If this was how the natives treated their newcomers, I felt very welcome indeed.

The first month was exceptionally enjoyable for Rorik and me. Velka and Greda were delegated to another part of the camp, where they helped the villagefolk with whatever needed to be done, such as preparing recently-caught game for the fire. I saw them occasionally, in between sleepovers with different villagers. The villagers were far from negligent; in fact, they kept Rorik and me well-fed. Over time, we learned some semblance of their tongue. Not that it was required during sleepovers; that by itself seemed to have a language of its own that transcended cultural boundaries.

"Willow, why are there no other men around?" I asked my latest conquest, after we were done. Flexing-Willow claimed to be no more than about my age, though she smelled far older. She had several war scars of her own, but I hadn't really noticed them in the heat of the moment. No pun intended.

"Our men are no more. They went to fight the enemy of our People, and did not return," Willow snuffed into my ear. "But the women of the Ruikuk can fight on our own. You and your friend are our men now." She bared her fangs in what could have been a playful gesture, and nipped me on the nose.

I was flattered, but I was too tired by then to reciprocate in kind. Then she left, and the next in line came in. I mentally shrugged. If Rorik and I were all that were left to take good care of them, then that's what we'd do.

By the third month, I was exhausted. I suspected that Rorik was too, though he didn't admit it. Even the brews by their local healer couldn't keep up my strength. At least the females weren't as demanding as they had been during the first two months. I sat warming my paws by the fire, and just then, Rorik came up.

"Having fun, Rorik?" I asked tiredly. Rorik seemed surprised at that statement, as if he hadn't just come out of the Chief's tent. In our three months here, not once had she invited me to her bedroll. Again, what anyone saw in Rorik I didn't know, but there's really no accounting for taste.

"Fun? It's exhausting! So many people insist on me moving much more vigorously," replied Rorik. He sat at the fire, bringing his head near to warm his ears. I gave up warning him not to do that after the first fifteen times back at the Thaneship, and the charred fur of his ruffs were testimony to undying habits.

"Aye, Rorik. It feels much better that way. Well, for the other party, at least." I replied.

"What I was doing was meant to be fun?" wondered Rorik.

I opened my mouth to reply that, yes, the main reason why anyone did what we were doing was for fun. Then, I realized that explaining would do as much good as the last fifty times, so I kept silent. We sat in companionable silence, the only sound being the crackling of the flames, tinged with the scent of burnt fur. Lately, fewer and fewer of the villagefolk were doing hunting, or any of their other duties; but I figured they already had a lot of food stored up.

"The villagers are all getting fatter," commented Rorik. "They had seemed so slim when we first arrived. Did their diet change?"

"No, Rorik. Ours' did," I replied. I spied several of the wolfen beauties walking toward the healer's tent, bellies swollen through our efforts. "It appears that you and I are going to be fathers. Or rather, fathers of many. I always wondered what parenting would be like."

"I always wondered where the cubs came from." Rorik's left ruff was sufficiently singed, so he angled his right ruff closer to the flames.

"I don't wonder, Rorik. I know."

A great commotion could be heard at the Chief's tent. It appeared that a crowd had gathered outside. Not having anything better to do, I dragged a smoking Rorik to where the crowd was. Velka and Greda were already there. On seeing Rorik, Greda hugged him as if they didn't already see each other every day. Velka narrowed her eyes at me before turning away with a huff.

"Nice to see you too, my love." I said to her. Velka had been green with envy ever since my suitors dragged me into their tents on Day One, so I tried making it up to her a couple of weeks later. To my great surprise, she resisted my good looks and charm, something the people in this fine village couldn't seem to get enough of. You could chalk it up to cultural differences if you like, but it had me wondering if she'd felt left out. But it wasn't like the Ruikuk were giving me much time or energy left to let her in on the action, so I felt that she would have to wait her turn.

Or at least after we found out what the Chief had to say. I'm sure we could find an empty tent soon enough.

Chief Gushing Water stood at the mouth to her tent, her paws resting upon the bulge of her belly. She carried a smile as she spoke, her voice carrying across even in the open air.

"The Healer has wonderful news to share with me," said Chief Water. "Ever since our menfolk had traveled across The Great Water to right an affront to our people, and failed to return, we had been beset with a dilemma over how to continue our lineage. For it is our duty as the People to carry on what had been started by She Who Births All, our Guide and Creator. Just as She had created The People, so shall we create our children to carry forth her legacy.

"Just as The Great Water took our menfolk away, so did it give us a blessing of two fine specimens in our image. Through that, our People can carry on with our lives, not worrying that we are unable to fulfill our duty in creating those who must come after. The Healer has confirmed that all womenfolk are now with cub."

"Honored to be of service, Chief!" I spoke. But Chief Water carried on like I hadn't spoken.

"But as a People, we have to be independent, lest external influences threaten our way of life," said Chief Water. "Just as we had found greater freedom when our menfolk oppressed us no longer, we now have to cast off the shackles that would bind us to the point of reliance. Within your bellies lies the key to your future. Our future." The Chief's eyes narrowed, her jaw set in a smile. "Just as She Who Births All had sent her emissaries through the sea, so shall we return them to it. Enforce Her will!"

"Enforce Her will!" roared the Ruikuk womenfolk. Their axes and knives appeared in their paws, and it was all I could do to turn tail and flee.

We found ourselves back on the tub in which we had come to this land. If it wasn't for the Ruikuk's courtesy in giving us a head start, we might not have gotten that far. For people who were pregnant, they still ran amazingly fast. The boat was just where we had left it, complete with rotten fishing net. Once we were well out of bow and throwing-spear range, the four of us sat on the deck in silence.

"Great plan, O Unproven One," snarled Velka. "Are you happy now? Have your aching loins been thus far satisfied? Or do you need another month or more?"

"I don't mind going back." confirmed Rorik. "The Chief showed me things I didn't know before."

"Listen, Velka," I said. "Stop trying to blame me for everything that happened. If anything, you should all be thanking me instead."

"Thank you, Kenyak." said Rorik and Greda together. I gave a little bow.

"Thank you? By the Arse of the Serpent, what exactly have you done for us?" spat Velka.

"If I hadn't rushed us out of that storehouse to the boat, the Picts would have gotten us," I began. "They don't play nice, not with the way they use their antlers to gut their foes. Do you deny I saved your tails then?"

Velka frowned deeper. "No, but—"

"And when we arrived on whatever Gods-forsaken land that was," here, I jabbed a claw toward where the Ruikuk was, "do you deny that the Ruikuk were going to stick us? Do you deny that if it wasn't for my good looks and charm, along with that of Rorik's, they would have thrown us back into the sea? These people thought we had been sent to alleviate their menfolk problems, and I did my best to play the part. The fact that they didn't have us skinned and roasted means that my performance was more than satisfactory. Admit it."

Velka glared back. "Admit that you're something of a bed warrior? There's no doubt about that."

"Velka, Kenyak did his best. As did Rorik," spoke Greda. "Sure, he might have thought with his dick, but you have to admit that his actions have saved us all. The Ruikuk have their cubs, while we still have our lives. We were little more than prisoners, but we're now free."

And she speaks! That had to be the longest sentence Greda had ever uttered. Not unless you counted a long drawn-out moan, but that likely counted as a single word. The bear was never one for speaking, and I had always attributed it to her general slowness. Why else would she be called Greda the Slow?

Velka's eyes wavered. "Right. But what do we do now?" she finally said.

"Stake it out on our own. Live like a true Viking," I answered with a puff of my chest. "There are so many things I could show you."

"I've seen it all. Been there, done that," Velka snapped back. A growl built up in the depths of my throat as I stepped forward, and who should bar my way but Greda, her arms crossed.

"We're far from our lands, Kenyak. We'll never survive by ourselves," Velka commented. "We need to go to where other people are, and see if they'll let us move in with them. But we're going to have to earn our keep."

"Nothing easier."

"No offense, Kenyak, but it's not likely your assets are going to be of much use. I'm thinking more of helping out with their chores like Greda and I had. Something you and Rorik have yet to do."

I bristled, while Rorik whined pitifully, but again it was Greda who spoke.

"I heard one of the villagers mentioning there were other tribes to the west of here," said the bear. "I've taken note of where the sun set each day, so we just have to go in that direction." She gestured with a paw to an area past the land mass from which we had just been evicted. A strip of land loomed far ahead.

"So we're sailing with no direction and purpose, exactly like our maiden voyage?" I asked. "Why am I not surprised?"

"It's worth a try."

"Suppose we've got nothing better to do."

Needless to say, it was exhausting trying to maneuver the boat toward the land mass which I sincerely hoped would be the end of our journeying. We had already been evicted from two homes in the space of little more than three months, long enough for me to get less-than-comfortable over getting milked dry. All told, it had been rather enjoyable. The healer fed me and Rorik copious amounts of herbal tonics to keep our strength up. But the fact of the matter was that I, like every other Viking, needed to sheath his sword once in a while. As a famous warrior once said, "An overused sword will never hold a keen edge." Rorik would likely fight on even if he was totally out of it, but I believe you don't need me to explain why that was hardly a good benchmark for my thoughts.

It was late evening by the time we were about 200 feet off the coast of where Greda had said that people lived. People who hopefully wouldn't take advantage of two young males in need of tender loving care, after having others forced upon them with nary a choice. Don't get me wrong, I had tried seeking out conquests of my own choosing back in the Ruikuk village, but either an over-domineering streak or continuous bad timing gave the females cause to reject me more than once. I was thus satisfied with whatever tail I got, even if it was with someone who might have been twenty years my senior.

The four of us brave Vikings huddled together in the center of the boat, the unfastened sail acting like a blanket on this cold night. In our haste to leave, we were unable to bring little more than the clothes on our persons, which for Rorik and I, were nothing more than leggings. The Ruikuk could be pretty impatient, you understand, so we usually didn't bother with tunics. I made to get cozy with Velka—to show her I was sorry, you understand—but a growl and a quick jab down below told me it would be best proposed another night. We didn't have any food with us, though Rorik had ripped a haunch of meat off a spit when we ran, so there was little we could do except hope that we could find some berries or roots tomorrow. Somehow, I doubted my ability to hunt feral prey with little more than my bare paws.

Falling asleep on a boat at night had taken on an almost familiar feeling. Strange, really, given that this was only the second time it had happened.

I awoke not to the morning sun, but to a strange scent that my nostrils picked up even through the fabric of the sail. For a moment, I thought Rorik was going at it with Greda after finally being reunited for more than a few minutes, but then I would have recognized that tang anywhere. I gave a deep yawn as I lifted the sail away from my head, my eyes creasing as Sól cast her rays upon me.

And stopped right in mid yawn.

Before me were several faces peering over the hull of our boat, their eyes bright and curious. Their fur was of a dark brown, with small round ears that could barely be seen on the short fur that graced their round heads.

I gave a yell as I sprang backward, waking my companions in my haste. When they too looked around and saw the newcomers, screams and yells permeated the air. The newcomers looked startled, pointing their spears uncertainly forward, and it was then I realized there were two boats adjacent to ours, each carrying four natives apiece.

These guys wouldn't understand any Norse, so I switched to the only native language I understood. "We mean you no harm. We sailor men. Not poke us with spears!" I blabbered in broken Native.

This only seemed to infuriate the newcomers further, and in turn, they jabbered back in a language none of us understood. They rowed their boats closer. Sooner or later, it was going to have to be all paws on deck. And by paws, I meant me alone. Velka and Greda had started shaking against each other, and Rorik was whimpering worse than the first time he set his tail on fire.

"Oh, Sweet Odin! Good Freki and Geri!" spluttered Rorik, his ears flattened as he too huddled against the girls. "Fenrir, protect us from the evil that befalls us—"

"You speak Norse?" asked one of the newcomers, his spear wavering as he did. The four of us froze. I then realized I was clutching Velka to myself, not that she seemed to be complaining just yet. I took what I could get.

"*Já*, so we do." I replied after a pause. I didn't wish for the newcomers to mistake our silence for rudeness, not when they were armed and we weren't. "How's tricks? Is the fishing any good here?"

Velka turned to me with a snarl. "Is that the best you can think of? 'How's tricks'?"

The newcomer who had spoken smiled. "Girl, you have to admit your mate's got balls to remain cool with spears pointed right at him. You better hang on to this one."

"We're not mates!" Velka seemed to realize my hands were now where they shouldn't be, and smacked them hard enough for me to take them away with a wince.

"Riiiight." The otter looked at her for another second before turning to me. "So what are the whole lot of you doing? Our fishermen spotted this boat of yours, and our chief sent us eight to take a look. Granted, this is the sea, but the older otters would say our tribe holds the sole fishing rights to it."

Otters. Of course! Our sagas told of a people that were equally at home on Land or Sea. It was said that it was from otters that we wolves of the North learned the ways of the sea, and later became the feared fighters that others would know us as. We must look like pretty sorry Vikings right now, without our weapons and gear, and in the case of Rorik and me, without upper garments.

"We aren't fishing here. We were chased out of our homes and thought we could find someplace else we would be welcome," I said, neglecting to add that it was twice that it happened.

The otter brightened, and with a wave of his paw, made his companions lower their spears.

"Come with us to our chief. There is much for us to discuss," said the otter with a twitch of his whiskers. "We'll tow your boat with us. I'm Two-Fishes, a hunter of my tribe. You are?"

"Kenyak, Rorik, Velka, and Greda. Our honorifics are of no consequence."

"If you say so. You people have such funny names!"

It appeared that things were looking up. When we landed on the coast, I half-expected to have my and Rorik's assets checked out, but that didn't happen even as Two-Fishes walked us through the village square. But it could be the fact that we weren't exactly species-compatible. Unlike the Ruikuk settlement, the village of the otters was built right over the water. There were spaces between the planking for otters to quickly surface or submerge themselves, as a means of travel or to search for prey. They were a lively people, with a chittering that permeated the air, the sound of the waves mixing with the splashes of their lithe bodies through water. What would be pathways in an otherwise conventional village were boardwalks. I noticed that here, the females were doing the same roles that the males were, whether be it building, fishing, or maintaining the boardwalks. I must have been staring too long, because one of Two-Fishes' companions caught hold of my arm right before I walked through a gap in the boardwalk.

"This way," said Two-Fishes, leading us across the wooden path that led into a seaside cave. The cave was cavernous, by otter standards, meaning two wolves needed to stand on top of each otter to reach the ceiling. I couldn't see any chiselmarks on the surface of the stone, however, so the cave had to have been formed naturally.

Two otters sat by the light of what I would know as an oil lamp, running their fingers through the entrails of what could only be fish. Unlike the others, these two had paint markings of blood and crushed earth. I wondered how often they had to reapply them whenever they decided to take a dip.

Two-Fishes stepped up to the larger of the otters and whispered to him. The Chief turned toward us, his eyes lighting up. There was something about otters that made you feeling like prancing about in joy; be it in the way they walked, as well as their other mannerisms. In the Thaneships, and the tribe we had briefly been guests of, leaders tended to carry a certain stature apart from the other folk, almost as if behaving the way others did was a crime. But this Chief had none of those frills.

"Norsemen? Come here, come here!" The otter opened his arms in a hug and embraced us in turn. Despite his size, his head barely came up to my chest level. Velka looked sharply at him, but the other otter at the table, a female, came up and accorded Velka and Greda the same greeting, which alleviated her discomfort.

"Well met, well met," said the Chief. His Norse was impeccable, which made me wonder how fluently it was spoken here. "I'm Chief Wallei of the Whalehunter Tribe, and this is my wife, Chieftess Mattri." A nod and a smile from the female otter. "I lead the men, and she leads the women. An arrangement that keeps everyone happy."

"That's good to know." I gave a glance at Velka, but she otherwise ignored me.

"So, Norsemen. I understand that you had been driven from your homes?" Wallei's whiskers skewed in questioning.

Velka and Rorik made to speak, but I, the spokeswolf for our motley array, cut in. "I wouldn't say that. We left because the conditions of our home suited us no longer. It was, for lack of a better word, getting rather *tense*."

"Two couples eloping after their parents discovered their love for each other! Of course I understand!" Chief Wallei beamed. I raised my eyebrow. "What, you think we haven't heard of your sagas? How else do you think we can speak your tongue?"

"Pardon me, Chief, but how did your people first get to know of it?" I asked, starting to get a little confused. Maybe the four of us had died out at sea after all, only to drift into some Valhalla or Fólkvangr where the natives could speak Norse. Somehow, I doubted that.

"Tell me," Chief Wallei paced about the cave, brushing off the remnants of whatever he had been handling off his paws. "Have you heard of a place called Vinland?"

Vinland. Vin-land. Of course. I remembered one of the countless sagas my people had this habit of telling. Given that it was usually recounted after a bellyful of mead or wine, no one actually took the tales seriously. One of the sagas told of my people traveling to a place far to the west after having been blown off course. Through the grapes and berries they found there—all the better to make wine with—they named the place Vinland, "Vin" being an allusion to wine. But the details of my people leaving the place was shrouded in mystery, a mystery drinkers in the mead hall weren't all too inclined to solve.

"You might have to enlighten me on that," I said. "And my companions, too."

Chief Wallei gave a knowing smile and led us deeper into the cave. Here, the roar of the sea was louder, such that I had to flatten my ears to keep them in working order. Chieftess Mattri held up a lit oil lamp which Wallei took. Here, the light illuminated the paintings on the walls. They had been painted in natural colors, such as white, brown, and red.

"About twenty summers ago, we found your people sailing off the coast of our land," said Chief Wallei, gesturing toward a scene. In it, what could have been several longships drawn by a six-year-old cub could be seen, though I didn't comment on the artistic style. "They were wolves, but not the same as the ones further inland. We were curious about them, and it was some time later that we started trading.

"Then, your people settled in an area. There, we continued trade, and even learned of their ways. They were skilled fighters, that much was for sure, and many of us wished to learn the ways of war from them. But it was not to be so."

Now, Chief Wallei looked grave as he moved on to the next scene. Here, a painting depicted eight figures lying stiffly upon the ground.

"One of the People reported that the Norsemen slew eight of their number, and only he survived to carry on the tale. It was thus without question that my ancestors decided your people do not belong here." I turned to the next scene, and bit back a whine. Several figures, wearing the unmistakable pattern of chainmail could be seen running away from several figures brandishing spears, their swords and kite shields abandoned as they fled. Their arms were thrown up in fear, tails curled between their legs.

"This looks familiar," confirmed Rorik.

"I can explain—" I began, but Chief Wallei raised a paw.

"There's no need. It was poor judgement on our part. Shortly after those Norsemen fled, another tribe sent their warriors to seize our lands and fishing grounds. They were wolves, far stronger than any two otters, and it was only when our females fought alongside the males that our enemies were defeated, but not without great loss. We then knew that should the Norsemen have been here, they would have been able to counter this threat to our people."

Rorik looked about to inquire if the enemy tribe was the one that had so recently kicked us out, but I didn't want him ruining our chances just yet.

"You could be right, Chief." I said, but Chief Wallei hadn't finished.

"It is said that prophecies are best found in prey that has traveled throughout the world, and fish is no different. I had read the entrails of many fish, and they told us that someday, men from the direction of the setting sun will come to these lands. The four of you have been sent to train us in the ways of war that your people are legendary for! And to repopulate these lands with warriors worthy of your people!"

"Train us, Norsemen," asked Chieftess Mattri urgently. "Train us, and you'll always have a place with our people."

I opened my mouth to deny us being warrior material, then realized this could be our chance to start a new life. After all, I did have some basic training in spears, axes, and shields, the first two of which the otters would be able to provide. Velka had been a daughter of a Thane, and so would have learned some of the basics. As for Rorik...

We're just going to have to keep his incompetence a secret.

"But of course, Chief and Chieftess." I said with my most winning smile. A smile that had gotten me out of trouble, and into bed with many. Not that I was trying to bed these two; it would be a scandal even among the most open of peoples. "When do we start?"

Eight years later...

I sat upon a log that overlooked the Whalehunter village, rubbing my hands over the fire as I took in the sight before me. In the years since we'd arrived, the otters had been more than welcoming. It helped that they found my basic weapon skills satisfactory enough to incorporate into their training regime. To my initial horror, they insisted that Rorik get involved as an instructor. As luck would have it, Rorik's impression of a drunken warrior convinced the Chief it would be of great use especially after one entered a trancelike state. Something that could be easily achieved ever since I showed the otters how to make wine.

As for Velka and me, we got along fine. She knew that for all my efforts to repopulate the Ruikuk, I was only trying to do what I thought best, and we settled down in a house we built together on a cliff that overlooked the village. She could never stand the smell of fish guts. Rorik and Greda lived nearby as well, and it would be remiss of me to say that his house would never have been complete were it not for the help of me and a couple of outgoing villagers. A builder he wasn't, but then, there were few things Rorik was.

I looked up at the sound of rustling grass, and right on time, Rorik approached. He had just completed a bout with several of the warriors. Were it not for his inherent lack of judgement, he would have quit a long time ago. Fresh bandages and salves could have been seen on his brow and limbs.

"What's up, Rorik?" I greeted.

"Up?" As usual, Rorik turned his head to the heavens. "Looks like a sunny day, Kenyak."

"Good. I hope it stays that way."

Excited barking came from behind me, and as a pack, my four cubs crowded around Rorik, leaping and prancing all about him. Rorik gave a half-smile as he patted them, which was much harder than it looked.

"Uncle Rorik! Uncle Rorik! When is Greda going to have cubs?" asked Kayak, one of my own. I had named him partly off my own name, but it was only a year later that I discovered I had also named him after a type of native boat. The native sensibilities must have rubbed off on me.

"I don't know, Kayak. Greda and I have been wondering for the last eight years now," replied Rorik.

I shook my head at this. Despite my and Velka's efforts, we could never convince Rorik that wolves and bears were just not biologically compatible. Not that there was a lack of trying.

"Cubs! Leave Uncle Rorik be! He's still exhausted from training! Go play somewhere else!" barked Velka. The cubs growled and whined, and soon they were all over me, trying to see who could nip my tail and get away with it. "Rorik, remember to get those dressings changed tomorrow, alright?"

"As I always have," Rorik nodded, heading back to his hut.

"Good day, husband." said Velka, coming up to stand beside me. I turned quickly to her. The years had been kind to her, in more ways than one. Of all the wolves I would find myself on a boat with, there were few I would rather have with me. She had a sharp tongue, but was also a good wife and mother, which was more than anyone like me deserved. Within her belly was what would be my fifth cub. After Velka caught me in bed with one of my otter students, she had thundered if she wasn't good enough for me. What she didn't understand was that good students had to be rewarded accordingly. I made it up to her, however, with the cub in her belly as proof of that. The native's lifestyle and diet had kept me in good health.

"Good day, Velka." I answered. I turned my gaze back to what I had been gazing upon.

"What are you thinking about, Kenyak?" asked Velka. "Every afternoon, I see you gazing at the sea. Were you thinking about your home? Or about how it was through it that we first arrived here?"

I nodded. "We Vikings are always connected to the sea. Our lives flow upon it like the ice floes of the north. Just as the sea was our means of escape from the Picts and the Ruikuk, it was also the means by which we found a new place we could call home. A place that my wife and family can grow up healthy and safe." I raised my muzzle and gave her a nuzzle.

Velka gave me a lick. "I love you, Kenyak."

"I love you too, sweetie." Velka went back to the cubs, who had by now engrossed themselves in who could knock all the others down. Just like their father, they were warriors through and through. When I first started out on this odyssey, I had been known as Kenyak the Unproven, purveyor of uncharted lands down below. But so much had happened since then. The flight from the Picts. My gift of many future warriors to the Ruikuk. Our invitation to train the Whalehunters in the fighting arts. My marriage to Velka, with the occasional tryst to keep me sane.

But with all my deeds and successes abounding, I'm sure that I'm now deserving of my new title. Kenyak the Proven, He who Trained and Conquered.

Down on the beach next to the Whalehunters' village, several female otters lay sunbathing upon their backs, a tradition I had brought to the community. Whenever time permitted, I always made an effort to gaze upon this glorious sight; a sight worth traveling across the world for.

We had first set out to the vast seas of our world, not knowing what the turbulent waters of Ægir would bring. Nomads in our own way, always wandering; always searching.

RAPSCALLIONS

MARY E. LOWD

Mary E. Lowd lives in a crashed spaceship, disguised as a house and hidden behind a rose garden in Oregon. The derelict vessel is crewed by a team of cats, dogs, the occasional fish, a reclusive professor, and several of Mary's own genetic progeny. In this chaotic environment, Mary writes fiction. She's had more than one hundred short stories published so far, and her novels include the Otters In Space *trilogy and* In a Dog's World. *Her fiction has won an Ursa Major Award and two Cóyotl Awards. Until her canine and feline crew make her vessel space-worthy again, Mary will continue writing. Without a working spaceship, it's the best way she can find to explore the universe. Learn more at www.marylowd.com. Read more of her stories at www.deepskyanchor.com.*

Lieutenant Libby Unari, a black cat and science officer with a focus on botany, had a tray of biology samples in her lap—cuttings and sprouts, planted in soil samples—taken from a forest moon. The moon itself hung like a green star in the rear window of the shuttle craft, receding into the distance as they flew away.

"That was a very peaceful away mission," Captain Pierre Jacques meowed. The pink-skinned Sphynx cat didn't usually accompany away teams down to previously unexplored planets, but he'd made an exception for this forest moon. "Why, I don't think I've felt that relaxed since I was a kitten! I should get off the bridge of the *Initiative* more often."

Lt. Unari's black triangular ears skewed. "I don't think it was just the break from your daily routine... There's something very strange about some of these plants. One of them has an almost catnip-like quality." She'd been feeling inexplicably euphoric during the away mission as well. "And some of them are even stranger." She narrowed her eyes at the sprout with bell-like flowers again. She hadn't been able to make any sense of the unimeter's reading on it.

"Catnip-like qualities?" the captain meowed. He nudged the yellow Labrador Retriever piloting the shuttle. "Did you feel... I don't know, unusually invigorated down there in that forest?"

Lieutenant Natalie Vonn shrugged. "I always feel invigorated in a forest. Dogs love their walkies," she woofed.

Lt. Unari looked up from her tray of plant samples to see the starship *Initiative* looming on the main viewscreen—a beautiful silver behemoth with graceful curves and thousands of sparkling windows, alight with the life inside. They were almost home.

Suddenly, the shuttle craft rocked violently and dirt spilled from several of the plants in Lt. Unari's sample tray. A second ship appeared on the viewscreen from behind the familiar, comforting bulk of the *Initiative*. This ship was a gaudy gold; much smaller than the *Initiative*, but armed to the teeth with electron torpedo turrets and blazor guns. It looked overburdened with weaponry, like it should fall right over. Except it was in space and had nowhere to fall.

"What the hell!" Capt. Jacques hissed. "Was that ship firing at us?!" The gaudy gold ship answered with a bright red bolt of blazor energy, and the shuttle rocked violently again.

"We need to get docked right away," Lt. Unari meowed, trying to scoop up dirt from the shuttle's floor with her paws and put it back into the sample cups.

"Too late," Lt. Vonn woofed, working the shuttle controls frantically. "We took a direct hit to the power core. We won't make it. The shuttle's gonna blow!"

Capt. Jacques hit the comm-pin on his navy uniform's lapel, calling the teleportation bay on the *Initiative*, and meowed, "Three to teleport aboard! Immediately!"

The Sphynx cat, black cat clutching her tray of plants, and yellow lab glimmered with quantum energy as the shuttle exploded around them; their atoms dispersed and bounced freely through the universe like ping pong balls in a lottery tumbler, until the siren call of the teleporter summoned them back together inside the *Initiative*. Each atom snapped into place like a block in a kitten's Lego set, exactly like they were supposed to.

Each of the three officers had teleported a thousand times in the past, but this time, *something was wrong*. Lt. Unari's black tail swished, and her ears flattened as she stood on the teleporter pad. She looked up at the White Highland Terrier behind the teleporter console. Usually, he was the same height as Lt. Unari—he was not a big dog.

But now, he looked huge. His bearded face loomed high above hers.

The teleporter console looked unusually large, too.

"I feel strange," Lt. Unari mewed, and her voice came out oddly high-pitched. She looked at the tray of plants in her paws and gasped to see the sample cups were all empty—bare dirt, no plants.

"What in the name of uplift is going on here?!" the captain spat. Except, when Lt. Unari looked over at him—he wasn't the captain. He was a tiny pink-skinned Sphynx kitten wearing a uniform that dripped off of him like he was wearing his parent's clothes.

A yellow lab puppy who looked a lot like Lt. Vonn laughed and pointed at them. "You're both teeny-tiny kittens!" she woofed. Then, she slapped her paws across her muzzle, surprised by the puppyish tone of her voice. Next, she noticed the way her own uniform bagged out over her newly tiny limbs. Lt. Vonn tried to straighten the fabric out, but there was too much of it. The uniform was far too big for her puppy body and wouldn't lie flat, no matter how she twisted or pulled at it. Soon, she was simply chasing her tail, turning circle after circle, pulling on the baggy fabric.

"Uh... Doctor," the White Highland Terrier woofed into his comm-pin, "I think you'd better get down here. There's been a teleporter accident."

The doctor's voice answered over his comm-pin, sounding weary: "Again?"

By and large, the teleportation was a very reliable technology, and much of the Tri-Galactic Navy's exploration of the three galaxies depended on it. *However...*

Sometimes, things went wrong.

Doctor Waverly Keller, an Irish Setter with long wavy red-furred ears, had seen some incredible things done by malfunctioning teleporters. She'd seen the *Initiative*'s first officer accidentally copied, so that they had to deal with two of those shaggy collie dogs barging around, trying to herd everyone on the ship. She'd been transported into a parallel universe where all the dogs were cats and the cats were dogs—her own doppelganger had been a lovely Abyssinian cat with red fur that perfectly matched her own. Why, Dr. Keller had even dealt with Ensign Mewly when the teleporter had beamed him back out of phase with the rest of the ship, and he'd thought he was seeing ghosts everywhere. Mewly was a naturally paranoid cat, and that had not been helpful for his paranoia.

Dr. Keller thought she had seen everything. But she had not seen the teleporter turn adult officers into kittens and puppies before. She looked over her three patients—yellow puppy, black kitten, and pink-skinned kitten—sitting on their medical bay beds, changing into more appropriately-sized clothing. All three full of the exuberance and impatience of kittens and puppies.

"Doctor!" the Sphynx kitten who fancied himself the captain spat, as soon as his tunic was in place. His furless tail swished angrily. "My ship is under attack, and I'm needed on the bridge!"

"Pierre," Dr. Keller woofed as gently as she could, though she feared it came out condescending. "I can't clear you for duty—we don't know how this transformation has affected your intellectual abilities. Besides, do you really want the bridge crew distracted by whether they should take orders from a *kitten* while the ship is being fired upon?"

The Sphynx kitten snarled and grumbled and tugged on the collar of the tunic he'd changed into, borrowed from some officer's kitten, no doubt. It fit him better, but it wasn't his uniform. He wanted his uniform. He wanted to be on the bridge.

On the bridge, Commander Bill Wilker barked commands and rushed from one station to the next, leaning over the officers and encouraging them as only a collie dog could. Under his command, the *Initiative* swerved to dodge electron torpedoes, reversed the polarity of its shields to ricochet bolts of blazor energy back at the attacking vessel, and even tried bouncing off the nearest planet's atmosphere to throw the gold vessel off their tail. Nothing worked. And the herd dog found himself herded into a corner. Well, a dead end. Backed up against a wall? Fighting without a paw to stand on?

Metaphors be damned. If Cmdr. Wilker couldn't save the ship, he would at least save the crew. "Open a video channel to our assailant," the collie barked.

The calico cat at the helm answered: "Channel open, Sir."

The panoramic view of the nearest planet—a dusty red ball clouded by purple storms—and the glittering stars around it on the main viewscreen flickered out. The scene was replaced by the sneering beak and feathered face of an avian alien, staring at them with dark, beady eyes. The alien's yellow and white feathers ruffled out behind its head like large ears, and a wattle of purple-blue skin on its neck wagged, riddled with piercings, as it spoke. "You will surrender, bock!"

The rows of gold hoops on its wattle clinked together. "We will board your ship, bock!"

"I have some conditions!" Cmdr. Wilker barked.

"No conditions! Bock! We will teleport all able-bodied individuals to the surface to mine for hyper-diamonds, bock. Everyone else stays onboard." The chicken-like creature preened its feathers, smoothing the ear-like fluffs back down. "Hostages, bock."

Cmdr. Wilker wound his white paw in the long sable fur of his mane, trying to think quickly. He needed a way to steal the ship back from these aliens after turning it over. That meant keeping some of the crew onboard. "We have children on this ship."

"They'll be kept safe, bock. As long as the adults work hard."

"And our computers are very complicated," Cmdr. Wilker woofed. "Are your crewmembers capable of handling a..." He hoped these space chickens weren't too smart and risked rambling off a string of techno-babble. "...*quintuple induction eigenvector cooling quantum charm operating system?*"

"Bock what?" The tufts of feathers on either side of the alien's head fluffed back out again, giving the bird a startled expression. But it quickly recomposed itself. "Of course, we can learn any operating system, bock. Heating, cooling; charming, off-putting. I mean, we're very smart, bock. But maybe we'll keep you onboard, just in case. Bock. It'll be faster than adapting to an entirely new...quantum operating system without help. Bock bock."

"If you insist," Cmdr. Wilker woofed mildly. On the inside, the collie grinned wolfishly.

All over the Tri-Galactic Navy vessel *Initiative*, giant turkey-chickens appeared in bursts of gold-and-green quantum sparkles, bulbous blasters grasped in their feathery wing-hands and sneers plastered across their hooked beaks.

The alien birds marched canine and feline officers at blaster point to the teleporter bay and beamed them down to the harsh planet's surface.

Two chicken-aliens teleported into the medical bay. One pointed a blaster at Dr. Keller and gobbled, "Come with me."

The other spread its wings wide, as if trying to look welcoming, and bocked at the seeming-children: "You three like games? Bock?"

Dr. Keller barked angrily, "These children are my patients! They need me!"

But the chicken was having none of it and waved its blaster menacingly. "They look fine, bock. They won't look fine if you make me shoot them."

Dr. Keller snarled but acquiesced. As the chicken guided her out of the medical bay, the Irish Setter arranged to pass by the kitten captain. She leaned down and woofed into his tiny pink-skinned ear, "My daughter is in the schoolroom—she can help you." Then, the chicken-alien jabbed Dr. Keller in her ribs with the nose of its blaster, and she hurried on her way, long red brush of a tail tucked between her legs.

The second chicken-alien bobbed its head and bocked, "See? Fun game—all adults go away, and fledglings can play."

The captain and Lt. Unari exchanged a look, pink-skinned kitten and black-furred kitten with their ears skewed. Lt. Vonn watched the look that passed between them and sensed that now was not the time to fight back. It went against the security chief's instincts, but she wasn't a full-sized yellow lab right now. She was a tiny puppy with huge feet.

The chicken-alien was easily four times Lt. Vonn's current size, and even if the puppy could knock away its blaster, those talons and beak looked fierce.

The giant chicken swept the seeming-kittens and puppy toward the medical bay door with its wings, but Lt. Unari scurried under the curtain of feathers. She darted over to where she'd left her tray of plant samples, now a tray of cups filled with dirt.

"What's that, bock?"

"Uh...toys?" Lt. Unari meowed. "We need them for our... games?"

"Mammals are weird, bock." The chicken shrugged. "But you can bring them. Bock. Now come along."

Once in the corridor, the chicken guided the captain and lieutenants the opposite direction of Dr. Keller. Away from the teleportation bay and toward the schoolroom.

As a long-term exploration vessel, the *Initiative* had a number of families onboard. Personally, Capt. Jacques didn't understand it. He didn't understand bringing kittens or puppies aboard a starship. He didn't understand choosing to have kittens or puppies at all. He'd been a wild little rapscallion as a kitten, and he would never want to deal with a whole litter of little hellions like himself.

He flexed his tiny crescent claws and hoped these space chickens wouldn't like dealing with him either.

The schoolroom was equipped with computers and laboratory equipment—not full-sized equipment, but child-proofed versions for the kittens and puppies to learn on. So, as soon as the chicken-alien turned the captain and two lieutenants loose with the crowd of real children, they set straight to work.

The chicken-alien guarded the door, wings crossed and yellow feathers puffed out impressively. The hordes of kittens and puppies chased each other, climbing right over banks of computer consoles, tumbling and wrestling, barking and yowling, and raising the sort of ruckus that generally wasn't allowed. The chicken didn't care. As long as they stayed inside the schoolroom.

Capt. Jacques' pink ears flattened tight against his skull, and he meowed at his lieutenants, "We need a plan—and we're going to have to figure it out in this horrid chaos."

A small red-furred Irish Setter, a true puppy unlike Lt. Vonn, edged into the group and woofed, "Be glad for the chaos. Without it, that guard would notice right away that you're up to something."

Capt. Jacques looked the puppy up and down—with those long, curly, red-furred ears, Leslie Keller looked almost exactly like a miniature version of her mother. She was the brightest and best behaved puppy that the captain had ever met. The only puppy that the captain had ever been able to stand.

"Leslie, we need weapons to take back the ship," the captain meowed. "Is there anything in here that we could use?"

The Irish Setter puppy laughed, but the captain kept staring at her levelly. Deadly serious.

"You mean, like something sharp or dangerous?" Leslie woofed.

"Exactly," the captain meowed, glancing around the room furtively. He looked extremely devious as a kitten with his furless pink skin and oversized triangular ears. "Where can we find something like that?"

"You can't, Captain," Leslie woofed. "Adults keep things like that *away* from children."

Lt. Unari held forth her tray of dirt cups. "What about a bio-scanner?" she mewed. "Is there anything like that?"

"Oh, sure," Leslie barked.

The Irish Setter puppy led the black kitten with her tray of dirt cups to an aquamarine and pink machine. It was bulkier and more brightly colored than the bio-scanner in the actual science labs; all of the angles and corners had been smoothed and rounded. But it was a bio-scanner. Well, close enough. The display screen was lower resolution than Lt. Unari would have liked, and the computer processer much, much slower...but it would have to do for now.

"You have an idea?" the captain meowed at Lt. Unari, but the black kitten was too busy with the bio-scanner to answer.

While waiting for Lt. Unari's response, the captain watched his other lieutenant, Natalie Vonn, drift casually away, edging a few steps at a time farther from the bio-scanner, as if she weren't up to anything—until another puppy bumped into her, and then the yellow lab puppy was off and running. Tumbling and barking with all the others, as if she were nothing more than a puppy and not the ship's chief of security in a bizarre teleporter-related predicament.

Capt. Jacques decided to charitably assume that Lt. Vonn was trying to protect their cover. Though it looked an awful lot like she was just *playing*.

The captain scowled. "What are you working on?" he snapped at Lt. Unari, losing his patience. He had not been patient as a kitten. That was a virtue he'd developed over many years, and he wasn't sure that it had stayed with him when the teleporter had shrunk him back to kitten-sized.

Lt. Unari's black ears skewed, and she gave the captain an appraising look, cool beyond the years that her kitten-body displayed. "It's just as I thought, captain. The plant samples that I brought back from the forest moon—they're all seeds now. That's why the sample cups look empty, except for dirt."

"Seeds?" the captain meowed. "The teleporter de-aged them too?"

"Yes."

"Why?"

"I'm still working on that..." Lt. Unari took one of the sample cups—it looked the same as all of the others—and held it up for the captain and Leslie Keller to see. "But I think this plant is the culprit."

"Is it the catnip one?" Capt. Jacques asked.

Leslie Keller stifled a laugh. "Is that what officers do on away missions? *Get high on catnip?*"

The Irish Setter puppy got quiet real fast when both kittens—actual adult officers in disguise—glared at her.

"Actually, captain," Lt. Unari meowed, "that one was a yellow grass. This one had purple bell-shaped flowers."

"That's very interesting," the captain said in a way that made it perfectly clear he wasn't interested at all. "But is there any way we can use this information? Possibly to get ourselves back to normal again?"

He glanced into the crowd of cavorting children where Lt. Vonn had a dachshund puppy in some sort of wrestling head-lock. If you asked the captain, the yellow lab was having entirely too good of a time as a puppy. "We need to get the *Initiative* freed from the talons of these bird aliens. And I can't do that as a doggarned kitten!"

"Uh...actually..." Leslie Keller looked very nervous about talking back to the ship's captain, even if he was smaller than her for the time being.

"What is it?" the captain meowed. "Spit it out."

"Well, if you go back to normal, those chickens are going to teleport you down to the surface with my mom and the other adults." Leslie pawed at the floor and avoided the captain's eyes. The gesture was genuinely young and endearing; it reminded the captain that this was a puppy separated from her mother.

Capt. Jacques tried to be gentle as he said, "We have to do something."

"But do it as kittens!" Leslie barked. "They won't expect it. Besides, if that plant did this to you, couldn't you use it to do the same thing to all the chickens?"

Capt. Jacques began to object that it was the teleporter which had done this to him, but Lt. Unari meowed, "You mean, turn the intruders into fledglings?" The black kitten phrased her words like a question, but before anyone could answer her, she was already busy running more scans on the plants, muttering to herself and deep in thought.

Meanwhile, the chicken guarding the schoolroom started flapping its wings and squawking, "Settle down! Bock! Don't you fledglings ever rest!" The noise and chaos had finally gotten to it.

The chicken alien's exasperated exclamation was met with titters of laughter from the marauding puppies and kittens. Instead of settling down, one of the puppies and two of the kittens took the chicken's flapping wings as an invitation to draw the guard into their games. The puppy jumped around the chicken in circles, wiggling and woofing. The kittens batted at the chicken's long pinion feathers at the tip of each wing.

The chicken squawked louder. The puppies and kittens laughed harder. It was all getting out of hand, and the captain worried about how far the chicken's patience could stretch before it remembered the blaster holstered at its side and decided that a couple fewer hostages would still be quite enough.

"We need to get the children under control," Capt. Jacques

breathed under his whiskers. If he were full size and wearing his uniform, he'd have simply ordered them to behave. Though while that worked fine on officers, he wasn't sure how well it would work on *officers' children*. Probably not well. Honestly, he sympathized with the flustered flapping chicken. "This is going to end very badly."

"We need the Galactic Culture Tutor," Leslie barked.

"The what?"

"It's a lumo-graphic projection that teaches us about different societies and cultures." Leslie got knocked aside by a pair of large St. Bernard puppies wrestling, but she recovered her balance quickly. She was such a subdued and serious puppy. "Everyone loves it, but the teacher only runs the GCT every couple of weeks. Says it's more entertaining than educational, and we're better off reading."

"That sounds extremely wise and reasonable of your teacher. There is no better way to learn than from hardbound books," Capt. Jacques meowed. "However, in this case, I think some entertainment may be warranted. Would you turn it on?"

Leslie lifted a paw to her brow in a salute and woofed, "At your service, Captain!" Then, she scurried off to the corner of the large room—dodging other puppies and kittens at play—to where a lumo-projector was mounted. At the push of a few buttons, the projector powered up and fired several dancing blue beams of low-intensity laser light into the center of the room. The blue lines of light traced out increasingly complicated geometrical shapes until suddenly coalescing into the form of a tall deer-like creature with a wide rack of antlers sprouting from its head and dressed in a flowing toga.

Blam, blam! Two blazes of red light shot right through the unfazed deer and exploded one of the computer consoles on the far side of the room. Puppies and kittens ducked and shrieked. The chicken—who'd fired the two blasts—held out its blaster and stared at it like it had turned out to be an eggplant instead of a weapon.

"Excuse me," the captain meowed, raising his voice above the din, "But the lumo-projected individual is not a threat to you. Merely a diversion for the children."

Leslie elbowed the captain aside and stood in front of him, blocking him from the chicken's view with her larger body. "It's a game," she woofed. "Just a game." Then, to the captain, she whispered, *"Be careful—it'll realize you're not one of us."*

The chicken re-holstered its blaster and tilted its head, examining the lumo-projection. "Game, bock?"

"Hello!" the deer said brightly. "I'm the Galactic Culture Tutor. You can call me the GCT! What culture would you like to learn about today?"

Like magic, all of the puppies and kittens in the room settled down and formed a circle, sitting on the floor at the GCT's feet. Even Lt. Vonn followed along. Being a puppy came far too naturally to her.

A terrier girl called out, "I want to learn about Cetazoids!"

In response, the deer morphed into a green-furred long-spined otteroid and said, "The otter-like peoples of Cetazed are not only telepaths; they're actually flora instead of fauna! The chlorophyll in their fur is what makes them green." The green otter began dancing, long spine swaying hypnotically. "This is a traditional Cetazed dance, done when all three of the world's moons are in conjunction."

Somewhere, flute-like music played. Many of the kittens and puppies swayed along to the dance, but they all stayed demurely in their places. Captain Jacques could see why the teacher didn't want to use the GCT too often. Its magic might get used up, and this sort of power was invaluable.

A kitten called out another species, and the GCT transformed into a giant cockroach who taught them about democratic duelocracies. Then a puppy called out another, and the cockroach transformed into a purple giraffe.

After a few more iterations, Lt. Unari edged up to the captain. The black kitten whispered, "I've isolated the effects of the plant with the bell-shaped flowers. It releases a telomeric transform wave."

The captain nodded, realizing that he'd been watching the GCT for easily an hour by now. "Go on."

"The wave encourages growth in nearby telomeres. The shortening of telomeres over time causes aging, so re-growing them...causes the opposite."

The captain whispered in awe, "We've found the plant version of a fountain of youth."

"I believe that the teleportation beam massively amplified the telomeric transform waves' effect."

"Can we duplicate it?" the captain asked in a rush.

"Yes," Lt. Unari said. "But not from here. We'll need to get to the bridge or a teleporter bay."

The captain put a paw out and laid it on Lt. Unari's shoulder. "Even more importantly, *can we reverse it*? I don't want to stay a kitten." The Sphynx kitten looked tired. He had to be bone-weary to worry

108

about himself at all while his ship was still in danger.

"Unfortunately, that's a question for Doctor Keller, not me."

"Well, then, let's get Doctor Keller back." The captain had Lt. Unari explain all of her research to him, everything he'd need to do if he got to the bridge or a teleporter bay. Then, he threw himself on the floor, rolling and kicking, hissing and spitting, yowling as if in pain. "Ooho whoa, pain, so much pain!" he yowled, shaking as if he were having some sort of seizure or fit.

Skeptically, the chicken strutted over.

"You have to help him!" Lt. Unari meowed.

"He needs a doctor!" Leslie woofed.

Even Lt. Vonn pulled herself away from the circle of puppies and kittens watching the GCT—now a bulgy frog creature, slick and shiny with wet amphibious skin.

The yellow lab puppy woofed at the chicken, "The doctor told you we were her patients!" Lt. Vonn looked genuinely worried. She hadn't been paying attention to Capt. Jacques' and Lt. Unari's scheming and thought the captain might be in real pain. Perhaps a side-effect of the teleporter accident. "You have to do something! Now! This is the captain—" Lt. Vonn's black lips pulled back in a grimace as she realized her mistake, but she fixed it. "—'s son! The captain's son! The captain will destroy *all of you* if you let his son die!"

"The captain?" the chicken bocked. "That big fluffy thing is this scrawny pink thing's father?"

Lt. Unari and Lt. Vonn looked at each other, as if trying to synchronize their plans. Since they weren't telepathic like Cetazoids, the synchronization utterly failed. At the same time, Lt. Unari meowed, "He's adopted," and Lt. Vonn woofed, "He's *really* sick."

The chicken alien flapped its wings in a gesture of resignation. The intensity of the yellow lab puppy's urgency had bowled it over. "I'll get someone down here, bock, to take this mewling mess up to the fluffy one on the bridge."

The pink-skinned kitten kept rocking and yowling, throwing a hissy fit, but when the chicken looked away, he winked at his fellow officers.

On the bridge, Cmdr. Bill Wilker patiently explained how the *Initiative*'s computer system worked to a flabbergasted pair of chickens for the fifth time. Each time, he changed the explanation slightly, throwing in random words he remembered from quantum physics and chemical engineering courses back at the Tri-Galactic Naval Academy. He hadn't been much of a student back in those days—too busy chasing cats. But he remembered enough to confuse these avians.

While the collie pointed at buttons and display panels with one paw, he discreetly typed out codes with the other paw, making sure the chickens didn't notice. He wanted to help the crew members on the surface directly, but so far all he'd been able to do was beef up the power of the computers in the schoolroom, relaying their processors out to other faster computers. It wasn't enough, and with every minute that passed, he worried more about all the cats and dogs on the planet being subjected to dangerous mining bock. No, mining work. These chickens were getting to him.

Little did the commander know, without his silent help from the bridge, Lt. Unari's research on the bio-scanner would have taken days rather than an hour. Right now, the schoolroom was the most powerful room on the entire ship. But it didn't have access to the teleporters. No matter how beefy the schoolroom computers got, they simply weren't connected to the teleporters. Most of the time that made sense. Kittens and puppies shouldn't be accidentally teleporting themselves all over the ship. Or out into space. But today, that safety precaution was keeping the chickens in charge.

The doors to the bridge slid open, and Cmdr. Wilker looked up to see a ruffled chicken standing over a tiny version of the captain who was doubled over, clutching his stomach, moaning and yowling in pain.

As soon as the Sphynx kitten saw the collie, though, he rushed over, threw his tiny arms around the big dog, and buried his pink-skinned face in the collie's overflowing beard. "Dad!" he meowed.

"Uh...yes...Son, how are you?" the collie fumbled. He was surprised the chickens were buying this, but he wasn't about to inform them of the biological differences between cats and dogs.

The captain looked up at his first officer with wide kitten eyes, doing a surprisingly good job of playing the role of an innocent child. "Much better now that I've seen you!" he meowed. "But my friends...Libby and Natalie...we're all still feeling sick, since the doctor didn't get to finish taking care of us."

The collie glanced dartingly at each of the chickens on the bridge and grinned nervously. "Well, uh, Son, the doctor had to be—"

"I know, Dad," the captain interrupted. "But she had some medicine designed for us. It's in the computer banks under the name Libby-Alpha. If you could just...synthesize it with the teleporters, then we wouldn't—" The kitten glared at the chicken who'd brought him to the bridge. "—have seizures any more. *I know you don't want me to have any seizures.*"

If Sphynx kittens had laser eyes, the chicken alien would have been a well-cooked turkey by the time the captain stopped glaring at it. Why, they wouldn't have needed tricks, teleporters, or telomeric transform waves at all!

"Let's take a look at the file," Cmdr. Wilker woofed, ignoring the impatient chickens.

Back in the schoolroom, Lt. Unari paced, black tail twitching. She was also impatient.

Leslie Keller kept pace behind the kitten, whispering questions to her whenever she caught up. "*How will we know if the captain's succeeded? How long will it take? What do we do once the chickens are little? Even a fledgling chicken could do a lot of damage with those talons and sharp beak...*"

The black kitten whirled around and stared at the Irish Setter puppy with fierce green eyes. It was probably a good thing that kittens, in general, didn't have laser eyes. "*All we can do right now is keep the children here safe.*"

Leslie Keller nodded and reached a red-furred paw out to take hold of one of Lt. Unari's black paws. "Come on," she woofed, leading the black kitten toward the circle of children still watching the GCT. "The best way to do that is to pretend to be one of them."

Lt. Unari skewed an ear and stifled an amused smile at the puppy's implication that she wasn't one of the children. Someday, this puppy was going to make an excellent officer.

In the middle of the room, the GCT had taken the form of a giant amorphous blob and was reciting poetry when the chicken guard suddenly took an interest in it.

"Do you have my species on record, bock?"

"Of course!" the GCT answered, transforming into a chicken alien with yellow and white feathers fluffed out. "The Pollengi are a primitive race of avians who bargain for technology from more advanced species rather than inventing it themselves." As the GCT bocked, the actual chicken seethed. "The Tri-Galactic Navy has minimal contact with the Pollengi due to its desire to refrain from influencing a less evolved culture. Would you like me to sing a Pollengi love song?"

A choir of "yes, please!" rose from the kittens and puppies, but the chicken alien drew its blaster. This time, the blaster's red energy bolts zipped across the room into the lumo-projector rather than the projection itself. The projector burst with a rain of white sparks, melted in the middle, and crumpled over.

The GCT disappeared into nothing: mere photons dissipating into the ambient light of the room.

Kittens cried and puppies bayed.

The chicken alien aimed its blaster at the nearest puppy, a St. Bernard with the presence of mind to look terrified. "This is what you mammals think of my people, bock?! I'll show you less evolved!"

A blur of yellow fur streaked across the room, and Lt. Vonn knocked the blaster from the chicken's wing. She might be small now, but she still had years of training in five varieties of martial arts.

The yellow lab puppy growled, keeping the chicken's attention away from any actual children. The chicken squawked and aimed its sharp beak at her. Lt. Vonn dodged like a puppy playing dodgeball, but the chicken pecked vigorously. The security chief couldn't keep out of its reach for long.

Suddenly, the chicken sparkled with quantum energy. "Bock!" it squawked, flapping and shrinking and sparkling. Its wings flapped so hard, downy white feathers flew off into the air. Then, long yellow pinions floated into the fray of feathers. The angry chicken disappeared in a cloud of feathers and a puff of sparkles.

When the sparkles winked out and the feathers settled, all that was left was a porcelain-white ovoid.

An egg.

"A ball!" the St. Bernard puppy woofed. "Let's play ball!" She aimed a giant puppy paw at the egg, and Lt. Vonn was only barely able to tackle her down before she could kick it.

"No!" Lt. Unari meowed jumping in front of the egg. "None of you touch this egg! We will be judged on how we treat our prisoners of war!"

"Huh?" The St. Bernard rubbed her floppy ear where it had been pinched by Lt. Vonn's tackle.

Leslie Keller edged up to Lt. Unari and whispered to the black kitten, "*Let me translate for you.*" Then, to the crowd of puppies and kittens, the Irish Setter woofed, "This egg is valuable and delicate, and if anyone breaks it, the teacher will be furious with them when he gets back."

Puppies grumbled, and kittens skewed their ears. But none of them messed with the egg.

All over the *Initiative*, chickens reverted to eggs. This was a case where the answer to the age-old question was clear: the chickens had come before the eggs.

Once Cmdr. Wilker and the kitten captain had re-taken the ship, they set to work rescuing the crew—a simple matter of teleporting chickens on the planet's surface back into eggs and teleporting cats and dogs back aboard.

They left a clutch of Pollengi eggs on the planet along with a distress signal calling for the golden Pollengi vessel to return and rescue them before they hatched.

Then, Cmdr. Wilker set a course out of the system.

The kitten captain awaited word from the doctor. No longer stuck in the schoolroom with all the children, he'd returned to his own quarters to sulk and count the years he'd have to live through as a kitten, waiting to become a captain again, if Doctor Keller couldn't reverse the effects of the teleporter accident.

A chime at the door let him know he had a visitor.

The captain meowed, "Come in," and the door slid open, revealing a black kitten and yellow lab puppy.

"We thought we'd wait with you," Lt. Unari meowed.

"I brought scratch-colors," Lt. Vonn woofed, holding up a set of coloring books designed to be drawn in by claws capped with tiny crayons.

"I haven't done scratch-colors," the captain meowed with amusement, "since I was..." He trailed off, ears skewing.

"A kitten," Lt. Unari offered. "Me either." Her ears skewed too, and her tail tip twitched.

The puppy and two kittens settled down to color. Lt. Vonn scuffed her paws over one page after another, filling them with disorganized riots of color. Lt. Unari carefully sketched pictures of each of the plant samples she'd taken from the forest moon, giving special care to her rendition of the purple bell-flowers that had caused so much trouble.

The captain's paw hovered over the page, crayon-tips not quite touching the paper. He couldn't decide what to draw. He didn't want to accept this fate.

He didn't want to be a kitten.

"I don't want this," he meowed.

"It won't last," Lt. Vonn woofed. "Doctor Keller's never let

113

anyone down who depended on her. Not ever. So, you might as well enjoy it while you can."

Captain Jacques smiled. That was true. He would trust his fate in the paws of any officer on his ship, but especially Doctor Keller. She was probably in the medical bay curing the problem of aging right now. He'd have to tell her how admirably her puppy had performed while she was gone.

But for now, the captain put his paw to the paper and colored.

"Can we duplicate it?" the captain asked in a rush.

DAZZLE JOINS THE SCREENWRITERS GUILD

SCOTT BRADFIELD

Scott Bradfield's recent books include Dazzle Resplendent: Adventures of a Misanthropic Dog *(Red Rabbit Books, January 2017), and* Why I Hate Toni Morrison's BELOVED: Several Decades of Reading Unwisely *(Red Rabbit Books, July 2013). He lives in London and San Luis Obispo.*

Dazzle found his first script conference a lot less painful than he expected.

"I see a dog with severe personality disorders," envisioned Syd Fleishman of Sony Tristar, seated in his overstuffed leather arm-chair with a plastic liter of Evian propped between his knees. "I see a dog with closeness issues, and issues about his dad. I see a dog with lots to say about the terrible problems facing mankind—such as the destruction of the ozone layer and the rainforests, and the tragedy of Native Americans and all that. But I also see a dog that, well…If he spots a human being in trouble? That dog comes running. An all-faithful sort of dog, but an all-faithful sort of dog with *attitude*. You gotta *earn* the respect of a dog like that. But once you earn that respect, he's your buddy for life."

Syd was flanked by the Head of Creative Development and the Vice-Head of Corporate Production. Dazzle couldn't remember the names of either of these high-flying, barely-post-graduate executives, but throughout the entire 45-minute conference nobody let him forget for one second that the CEO's name was Syd.

"It's a bold new animal movie for a bold new millennium, *Syd*," piped-up the Head of Creative Development.

"It's got heart, *Syd*. It's got action. And what's more," interjected

116

the Vice Head of Corporate Production, "it's got abstract topicality. Abstract topicality, see, is this term I kind of invented."

Dazzle was leafing through a telephone-book-sized legal contract. The redacted passages alone were terrifying in their opaqueness.

"Kind of like Capra or Spielberg," continued the Vice Head, even though everybody had already stopped listening. "You know, like stuff that *seems* to be about current affairs? But once you look closely, it's not about anything at all."

This particular lull wasn't on the morning agenda.

"Any questions?" Syd asked, getting to his feet. It was the only appointment that Syd was never late for: lunch.

Dazzle took this opportunity to gesture at the as-yet unsigned contract with a flaky forepaw.

"Look, Syd. I've been reading through this rancid sack of worms, and if you don't mind my asking, I'm still hazy on a couple details."

Syd, frozen in an attitude of benign departure, smiled stiffly.

"What a cute little doggy," whispered the Head of Creative Development. She looked about nineteen years old. "He wants to discuss his contract. He wants to be part of the legal process, too."

Three sets of executive eyes, Dazzle thought. And once they start exchanging ironic, bemused glances, it's impossible to tell them apart.

"As I understand," Dazzle went on, "you guys aren't trying to produce a major motion picture based on my life. Rather you're buying the rights, and I quote, 'to develop a long-running, multi-format entertainment entity based on the [possibly fictive] events and characters inspired by the legally-recognized intellectual-commodity-unit known as Dazzle.' Which leaves me wondering, guys—why so much trouble and expense? Why not just make up your own character and call him, oh, like Harry the dog, or Bozo the cat or something? Then, you could 'develop' any damn thing you pleased, and you wouldn't have to pay me anything, or negotiate so many clause-belaboring details with my annoying agent. I may be a dog, guys, but that doesn't make me stupid. All I'm asking is what could I possibly possess that you guys can't invent for yourselves? Give it to me straight, *Syd*. I really want to know."

Syd was smiling at the memory of something he had once said, or a person he used to be. It was a self-enclosed, inviolate sort of smile. He didn't have to share it with anybody.

"That's simple, Daz. You got the only thing money can't buy in this town."

Dazzle waited. So did everybody else.

"Authenticity," Syd said.

And left the building.

According to *The Who's Who Hollywood Guide to Selling Your First Screenplay*, Fred Prescott had won an Oscar during the Eisenhower administration for his collaborative work on some long-forgotten skirt-and-sandal bio-pic, and his consequent A-list status had carried him through lean years and fat. But his work habits were rudimentary; he lacked even the crudest of social graces; and most mornings, his biggest achievement seemed to be dragging his sorry butt out of bed for black coffee and a cinnamon bagel.

"You can't make a whore of Lady Inspiration," Fred often said. "You can only leave the front door open and hope she stops by for a while. Never sweat art, Daz-baby. That's rule *numero uno* at the House of Fred."

Dazzle, who had never stared into the eyes of a looming contract deadline before, couldn't quite adopt Fred's free and easy manner. He knew it made him sound pro-establishment; he just couldn't help himself.

"I'm not saying we should make a whore of Lady Inspiration, Fred," Dazzle explained in his most laid-back, diplomatic manner. "I'm just saying it's been three weeks, and we don't have a title, or even a two-sentence plot summary. Just that rather vague opening scene in the garbage dump with two topless teenagers, which you say is modeled on Italian what?"

"Post-war existential *nouvelle-vague*," Fred said sharply, giving Dazzle a slow once-over, like a school guard scanning for concealed weaponry. "Are you saying you've never heard of Antonioni, pooch? What sort of writing partner did they saddle me with, anyway?"

The funniest thing about movie people, Dazzle thought, was that no matter how laid-back they pretended to be, their fuses were always incredibly short. It was as if Dazzle had to apologize constantly for all the things they thought he said.

"I'm not saying I don't like the garbage dump scene, Fred. In fact, I probably like the garbage dump scene a lot. I just don't think it's enough material to deliver to Sony after six weeks' work. It might need, you know…a little embellishment."

It was like prodding an open wound.

"So you want to embellish our natural-birth baby, is that it? Like wrap it up in pretty bows and whatnot and shoot fireworks out its ass? Why don't you, a first-timer who struck it lucky, explain the business to me, the Oscar-winning sole-credited story-designer of *Solon the Magnificent*, *War Bond Baby*, and the recently rediscovered 'AMC forgotten comedy-classic,' *I Can't Stop Dancing!* Maybe *I* need an introductory scriptwriting lesson from a dickless wonder like yourself."

By this point, the remains of Fred's cinnamon bagel were starting to look pretty tempting, causing Dazzle's tail to thump impatiently at the polished hardwood floor. But then, so did the long blue beach extending beyond the smudgy picture window, and the endless California summer filled with leathery-skinned, once-attractive people playing volleyball and frisbee golf.

In his long and shaggy life, Dazzle had never actually explored Zuma.

But maybe it was high time he did.

Dazzle was usually returning from his second or third walk of the morning when it came time to pay that morning's piper.

"Hi, Daz. Got Syd, Steve, and Becky on the line. Put 'em through?"

Dazzle wished he had never learned how to work the speaker phone in Fred's cluttered office. He could feel his heart sinking when he replied, "Sure, I guess." Then counted to three, four.

"Daz honey!"

"Dazzy-sweetheart!"

"How's it hanging, hot stuff! You got our through-line yet? You ready to pitch this mother to the assholes upstairs?"

It was always more enthusiasm—and coming at him from more directions—than Dazzle could handle. Especially since Dazzle had never been what you might call an optimistic or forward-yearning sort of dog.

"It's, well, yeah," Dazzle said slowly, as if he were trying to lick a burr from his coat. "We're, you know. Really making progress and all that."

At which point, Dazzle permitted himself a hasty glance out the buggy window at Fred, who was sleeping off his third breakfast Margarita in the patio hammock.

"We're working out a few kinks, and developing the, what-do-you-call-it, the plot or something. And of course the central character—that is, *me*—he's getting more interesting by the minute. Hell, even *I'm* beginning to like him."

A long corporate hush emerged from the telephone receiver like a voice from beyond the grave.

"Wow," it breathed.

"Cool."

"Bitchin'–I mean, that is, if you don't mind me using the word 'bitchin'"? Is that okay with you, Dazzle-babe?"

There was so little you had to do to please these people, Dazzle thought.

"Absolutely fine," Dazzle said. "In fact, under these circumstances? Bitchin' is like the most perfect word there is."

"The only freedom you ever really enjoy in this business," Fred liked to remind Dazzle, "is during the always-blissful period when nobody knows what you're doing. And the longer they don't know, the more freedom you've got. So here's how I interpret this contractual 'delivery calendar' you're so worked up about, Daz, and it goes like this. Sign the contract, get the bucks, and enjoy freedom freedom freedom, birdies singing, tra-la-la-la, la-la-la-*laaah*. Then, deliver the pages, receive your delivery check, and it goes like this–hassle hassle hassle, mega-hassle mega-hassle, mini-hassles ad infinitum, talk talk talk, hassle hassle hassle. From the moment you give them what they say they want– which is the goddamn script they don't know what to do with–they'll be climbing up and down it like they've found themselves a new asshole. They'll turn it upside down and every which way. They'll schedule conference calls and studio meets, and before you know it, you'll have execs calling you from fucking Afghanistan and Tamaleland and places you never even knew existed, and they'll all be telling you what to do and how to do it. So stop worrying, my obedient little doggy. Chill out, enjoy the sea-breeze, and share some of these canned martinis. They're better than they look."

It was very annoying of Fred, Dazzle thought, to act as if he were some sort of "obedient" little doggy, when all he wanted to do was get the studio execs off his back. It was especially irksome that Fred did it with such eloquence and conviction.

"I'm not trying to sound like Mr. Obedient," Dazzle countered wearily. "I'm just trying to do the right thing. These jokers paid us a bundle, Fred. And we did agree to start delivering pages by, well, last month or something. I know they're jokers, and *you* know they're jokers, and believe me, I'm hip to the whole 'stop and smell the roses' philosophy. But you're not the guy who answers the phone around here. In case you forgot, these people are incredibly persistent. And to be fair, shouldn't we at least have a title by now? Or some minimal idea of the whaddayoucallit? The narrative arc?"

But of course Fred had already passed out in the hammock, a warm dented can of Make-U-Mix Chilled Martinis cradled against his chest like a begging cup.

It was so Fred, Dazzle thought. You couldn't help but like him.

Dazzle loved the beach. He loved the salty sand between his toe-pads, and the distant tease and crash of rubber-clad, seal-like surfers frolicking in the waves. He especially loved the air that felt both clean and astringent, as if the sea weren't simply providing an alternative to city soot, but was actually scrubbing away its residue, like swarms of hungry, eco-conscious animalculae. It was the perfect place for people without jobs, Dazzle thought.

"Like hey there, doggy-dude! How's the creativity-thing going? You should find a wet suit with four little doggy legs and I'll teach you to surf."

Diggy Bop was scrubbing his chapped, freckly face with waxy sun-screen and sucking diet soda from a can. At various times in their conversations, he had claimed to hale from the midwest, the east coast, the Gulf of Mexico, and the former Republic of Sudan, but most of the local surfers knew him as a native Whittier boy, born and bred. It was one of the few qualities Dazzle had learned to respect in these otherwise-unpalatable human biped types—the capacity to dissemble. The alternative seemed to be human beings who were perfectly happy with who they already were.

Yuck, Dazzle thought.

Dazzle sat down to rest beside Diggy Bop's stash of sandy boards and crumpled wet suits. "I'm afraid it's not going well at all," Dazzle conceded. "And to be perfectly frank, I don't think my so-called writing partner's giving it his best shot. All we seem to do is lie around the house watching TV."

Diggy Bop was looking at the vast Pacific. He had just finished his soda.

"Sometimes a guy's gotta wait for weeks to know what he's waiting *for*," Diggy said softly. "A girl, a wave, an inspiration. You can't go looking for it. It can only come looking for you."

At which point Diggy scooped up his board and sprinted towards a whitecap forming in the blue distance. Diggy wasn't much of a talker, Dazzle conceded. He was more of a doer.

And thank God for that, Dazzle thought.

By the time late afternoon came around, Dazzle had usually given up on receiving any help from Oscar-winning screenwriter and former Writer's Guild Assistant Secretary Fred Prescott, so he ventured alone into Fred's messy office and stared at the antique, dusty Selectra for a while. It was a peculiar, dense little machine with a revolving print-ball that Dazzle found infinitely amusing. What he didn't find amusing, however, was the alert thrum and snap the machine emitted whenever he activated the black power button, as if it had been waiting all morning for Dazzle to show up.

And now it was time for Dazzle to deliver the goods.

ACT I, Dazzle would type clumsily with his stubby, inarticulate fore-paw. SCENE 1. DAZZLE ENTERS. DAZZLE SPEAKS.

It was as far as Dazzle's imagination ever took him. Perhaps because the subject that least interested Dazzle was himself.

Dog meets bitch, Dazzle thought, recalling a notorious Faulknerian parable. Dog loses bitch. Dog finds bitch again.

Coming soon to a theater near you.

But sometimes, things don't tie up in a pretty little bow with appropriate theme music, Dazzle thought. Life just unravels until there's nothing left.

So then, Dazzle deployed all of his worst narrative instincts. He thought about stupid movies he'd seen featuring big name stars grimacing in tight close-ups on multi-media-formattable movie posters. Like a grizzly, Bruce Willis sort of dog, with a flamethrower strapped to its back. Or a telegenic dog who plays basketball. He toyed with ideas of a precognitive dog, a flying dog, and a dog who saved children from imminent catastrophes. But try as he might, Dazzle couldn't get his creative juices flowing. And no matter how long he sat there trying to appease the hungry Selectric, he never once progressed beyond the same unhappy phrases:

DAZZLE ENTERS. DAZZLE SPEAKS.

Dazzle wished, Dazzle thought.

"Speak!" he told the Selectric. "Open your stupid maw and let it out!"

But, of course, machines don't talk. And dogs don't talk. Only human beings talk.

And that, in terms of Hollywood-style creative development, was the rub.

122

The only time Dazzle actually liked to hear the phone ring was when he sat down to do the work he couldn't do. Which was why he was always so quick to activate the desktop speaker—and utter the only word he could usually muster:

"Woof."

It didn't sound right even to Dazzle.

"Wow, Dad. You just fall out of the hammock or something? It's me, Benny. Your kid. Remember?"

It was the sort of voice Dazzle was accustomed to having directed his way. Short, curt sentences without modifiers. Simple animal expressions of calm and appeasement.

"Woof," Dazzle replied. "Woof woof."

"Gotcha, Dad. Know you're busy, just wanted to make sure you hadn't killed yourself with those damn TV dinners you're always stuffing down. Too bad I don't have any Hollywood connections. Maybe then I'd be worth your while for lunch or coffee or something. Or maybe even some minimally polite inter-personal conversation."

Click.

It was a lot of unlived life to live with, Dazzle thought, gazing out the window at somnolent Fred in his hammock, hearing the dial tone recommence like an endless, audible ellipses. Three divorces, four angrily neglected kids, seven undelivered scripts, a pending mega-deal at Paramount, and an irate Columbian lover with her own dry-cleaning service in Sepulveda. No wonder Fred got up so early each morning. It took a lot of time to get your head around doing so little.

You can't outlive bad karma like this guy's got, Dazzle thought.

You could only arrange to fall fast asleep before it came knocking.

Unlike pages, the weeks were mounting up. And whenever Dazzle felt especially panicky about his contractual responsibilities, he called his agent.

"You got five minutes," Bunny said, her voice a deep echoing mine of patience with itself. "You speak, and I'll listen. Shoot."

Bunny started off every conversation as if it were a race between Dazzle and her preconceptions about him. A race, of course, that Dazzle was always destined to lose.

"Oh, well," Dazzle muttered slowly. "Nothing new, really. I'm just getting nervous. We don't seem to be making any progress. And I don't mean to sound judgmental, but it's all Fred's fault. I was never born to write, Bunny. I'm just a goddamn dog. But Fred hasn't lifted a finger, and I think he may be burned out or something. So this is what I was thinking. Maybe we could just, you know, give them their money back, and I could go home to Big Sur. I'd even be willing to surrender all my rights to, you know, my life and identity. Really, I don't mind. Money's never mattered to me; basically, I'm happy with a few berries and wild mushrooms and a splash of clear spring water when I need it. I want my old life back, even if I don't own the rights to it anymore. So what do you say, Bunny? We tear up the contract, Sony brings in another, as they like to call it, 'creative team.' And we all go our separate ways."

Bunny's silence was potent enough to frost glass.

"Look, Daz-baby. We got you paid, right?"

"Well, yeah," Dazzle conceded. "But–"

"And now you're working with one of the most venerable and widely respected scriptwriters in the profession, right?"

"Sure, if you want to call Fred *venerable*, Bunny. It's just that–"

"So let me say one last thing, and listen to me good. I'd tear off my left tit before I gave Sony back a dime. I'd even tear off your balls, if you had any. So get back to work, and call me when you're ready to deliver. Otherwise, I'll turn you in to the dog pound so fast it'll make your head spin. No offense, Darling. But I'm making you a Hollywood success story or my name ain't Bunny Fairchild."

It was like living with plutonium, Dazzle thought. The unwritten script emitted black radiance through every room in the house.

"I don't think you appreciate who you're working with," Diggy often told him, as they exchanged lukewarm cans of Coors over a sputtering, illegal campfire. "That's Fred Prescott on your team. He's like a filmic genius or something. He's like the only soulful person in the entire Hollywood community. Why, a list of all the great movies he *could* have made would astound Michelangelo–at least that's how Fred tells it. Like his totally disrespected seven-hundred-page film treatment for *Finnegans Wake* starring Nick Nolte–*that* got totally dissed by the powers-that-be. Or what about Fred's genre-bending concept about a boxing-promoter on Mars? That got totally crummed on, too. Whenever the suits want to pretend they're artists, they hire Fred Prescott for a draft or two, and pat themselves on the back all over Rodeo Drive. Then they turn every script he delivers into a vehicle of mush for Hugh Grant and Drew Barrymore. But Fred endures the toil and struggle, Daz. He marches to the beat of his own drum. Give the

124

guy a chance, and before this job's done? He's gonna teach you bozos what art is all about."

Dazzle wanted to believe Diggy–and in Diggy's vision of Fred. But the only way to believe in Fred was to disregard the daily pageant of shame and desuetude that constituted his 'routine.'

Art is never easy, Dazzle conceded. Maybe, just maybe, Fred knew what he was doing.

"Hey there, Daz baby. Stu Sanderson at Sony. Would you pick up the phone, Daz? We know you're in there. And we're totally sympathetic to your creative needs as an artist. But we really *gotta* touch base with you on one or two important concept points before we forget them. Isn't that what writing's about, Daz-baby? Writing down every little detail and pawing over it endlessly in high-power executive lunchrooms? Sally, have you got the concept points we discussed at yesterday's meeting? I need to read them to Daz here… Okay, point one–we need humor. Got that? It has to have *some* humor, Daz, but not *too much* humor, because comedy's not our department, but a *little* humor's okay, and actually pretty necessary, especially when it comes to talking dogs. Get me? Point two–and this is a little something Syd and I developed in our meeting with Roger last week–Daz is a dog, but he acts more like a cat. How do you like that one? Syd and I came up with that by ourselves. He's sort of a cat-like dog, with all these feline needs and desires and so forth, the audience will really eat it up. Like he digs catnip or something, or peeing in kitty litter–I'll leave the gory details to you creative types. We did this survey, or somebody heard about this survey, we're pretty sure a survey was done anyway, that says people are either cat people or dog people, and doing a dog movie alienates the cat-viewership and vice versa. So this way, we appeal to every possible demographic. We could sign any A-list director with a concept point like this one, Daz. You and Fred need to incorporate it into your treatment right away."

As Dazzle grew less concerned about their long-broken contract deadlines, Fred slowly awakened from his stupor like a bewitched maiden in a castle. Some days, he even ventured out of his hammock before noon, and could be found browsing yesterday's sun-stained *Los Angeles Times* on the deck, or shoveling through a plate of Maria's huevos rancheros while tapping a pencil against a tablet of yellow fine-lined legal stationary. When he felt unusually perky, he cranked up his old LP-player and treated the beach-side sun-worshipers to a mega-decibel-blast of Stan Getz being mellow, or Paul Desmond pouring cool Hi-Fi martinis. It was like watching a space-captain emerge from suspended animation, Dazzle thought. He was still groggy and blood-sore. He couldn't quite work his lips.

"Hey, Fred," Dazzle would say as he padded to the kitchen, where Maria would stop brushing cobwebs off the ceiling with a damp mop, waddle to the stove, and happily scoop Dazzle's favorite lunch from a simmering pot: soft-shelled chicken tortillas with extra hot salsa and sour cream.

"*Mucho buenos, Señor Perocito,*" Maria liked to say, scratching between his ears, just the way Dazzle liked it. "*Escritor con Señor Fred es muy difícile, no?*"

Meanwhile, Fred examined the tip of his yellow Ticonderoga pencil with a piercing, level-headed gaze.

"The first thing you've got to do is walk away from what the world keeps telling you," Fred announced softly. "Like a penny saved is a penny earned, that sort of crap. Or how better mousetraps are always the rage, and the world will beat a path to your door. You don't need to be human to recognize human turds when you smell them, right, pooch? You just gotta clear your mind of all distractions and think for yourself.

"We're not trying to 'hound' you, Daz-honey. Get it? We're not trying to *hound* you?"

"We're just worried about the, you know, legal implications of all these delays and binding contractual clauses and modifying clauses which, you know, we can't just keep modifying. Unless there's an act of God or something."

"Nobody'd *hound* you, Daz baby. If it was an act of God–"

"But we need words, sweetheart. We need some–I know you hate this word–but we need some *pages*. Syd isn't the most patient chief executive in town, but he's not the least patient, either. He's just doing his job, Daz. And whether you like it or not, we're just doing ours."

"We've got families to support."

"We've got wives, ex-wives, ex-semi-permanent live-in love-mates, and so forth. We're as human as the next guy. Which isn't to cast any aspersions on you, Daz baby. It's just an expression."

"Can we at least drive out and have a little meet at Cross Creek or something? We can watch Goldy play with her kids. You could show us some rough thoughts on a napkin and talk us through. You don't even have to tell Fred. It'll be our little secret."

"We could buy you a nice big bowl of naturally carbonated spring water. Or maybe a beer."

"And you could tell us, right, Daz-baby? You could finally tell us what this movie we're making is all about."

Dazzle knew his days of Hollywood fame were numbered, so he tried to close the door securely on his way out. He instructed his accountant to dump his earnings into a series of 501ks and offshore investments. He set up a trust-fund for his ever-widening (and increasingly errant) canine family back in Big Sur, and arranged a lump sum guaranteed-annuity with a Hartford insurance firm. He gave himself a flea bath, had his nails clipped at the canine beauticians, and even endured what he hoped would be his last-ever full-body upper and lower GI polyp-palpating exam at the local vet, who turned out to be a well-groomed man in his mid-fifties named Dr. Leroy Ferguson.

"I guess I moved here in the late sixties and never looked back," Dr. Ferguson confessed, as he gently posed and reposed Dazzle through a panoply of the usual indignities. "Where I came from, back in Ohio? We had nothing more interesting to do all day than go to the laundromat or visit the bank. Farmers would sit in Bob's Big Boy complaining about their cattle, or some leaky roof. And on your first (and often only) date, you drove to the woods in your third-hand car, screwed, got your girlfriend pregnant, and unhappily married, and not necessarily in that order. Personally, my only viable career choice was to become either a mortgage broker or a vet, and being a vet meant nothing but performing livestock viral exams and animal husbandry. You wouldn't see a decent doggy or kitty for weeks at a time. You were too busy driving across Farmer's Brown's scrub-strewn land in a truck. But then I got crazy and came to California, where everything was different. Suddenly, I was living with movie stars. I was spaying and neutering full-blooded Manxes and Siameses and even, I swear to god, an actual declawed leopard from Borneo once. And now my life is like a beautiful movie. I walk on the beach every morning, my kids go to great schools and marry entertainment lawyers and software executives, and my third wife, Patty, wow. She's got tits out to here, and they're almost all hers. I have never felt more fulfilled as a veterinary surgeon and animal health-care-worker in my life, and my golf swing, Jesus. I'm knocking seagulls out of the air with my seven iron. I've gotten that good."

Even the doctor's hands, while they probed Dazzle's weary orifices, exuded confidence. It was like visiting one of those Shiatsu places at the mall. And when it was over, and Dazzle was gently lifted down from the paper-shielded metal table by a pair of bountiful young starlet-like nurses, he felt like a million bucks.

"I've just never met so many happy people in my life," Dazzle told Diggy over chocolatey cappuccinos at one of the Cross Creek picnic tables. "It's not like I originally pictured at all. I expected some sunny den of despair, where everybody's constantly enraged by the bastards who screwed them over on the last project that fell through. But when you look at Malibu for what it is, everybody has so much free time. Their nannies are taking care of the kids, their administrative assistants are answering the phones, and most of the time, all these people do is wander around clothing outlets, drive back and forth to Blockbuster, and eat lunch. In fact, now that I think of it, I hardly see any signs of depravity whatsoever, even from the sixty year old guys with twenty-something wives. They seem just as boring as everybody else. Except, of course, that they have a lot more money to be boring *with*."

But as Dazzle had learned from a lifetime of pissing on the lampposts of polite society, he always spoke way too soon. And the moment Diggy dropped him off at Fred's, he encountered a fleet of chickens coming home to roost simultaneously. These particular chickens were driving Arnold Schwarzenegger-style 'energy-efficient' re-tooled Humvees, decked-out PT Cruisers, and four-wheel drive off-road vehicles thumping with Wagner, Patti Smith, and mid-seventies progressive rock.

"We know you're in there, Pop!" shouted a twenty-something version of Fred in a linen sport coat and Levis. His features were so well-tended that they seemed shellacked. "You shut down, passive-aggressive, family-abandoning old hack! The worst part about hating guys like you, Dad, is that you never even show your face, or give us a chance to make fun of that hypocritical sixties get-up you wear! And then to hear you spouting all that outdated bullshit about marching to your own drum and beautifying the muse, Jesus! It makes me want to puke! You practically ruined my life, Dad! And if Mom hadn't met that property developer in Pasadena, you'd have ruined her life, too!"

The fleet of well-mobilized chickens represented the depth and breadth of middle-aged, middle-income California rage. Some of it, like Fred Junior's, had been fanned into a hot flame by years of assertiveness training and self-actualization therapy. But some of it had been twisted into bizarrely serene, flowery zen-like shapes by inner tranquility regimens and TM.

(To Dazzle's way of thinking, this second type of rage was the most frightening type of rage in the world.)

"We just stopped by to see how you're doing," Syd Fleishman said gently, flanked by various heads of development. "We're not like these other people. We're here to help. Maybe you'd be so kind as to let us in, Fred, and we could share some of our disillusioning experiences with the corporate entertainment industry. And then, you know, if you felt like it. Maybe you could show us some of the, ahem, you know. Some of the—"

"*Chingo tu madre!*" shouted the hot little Columbian woman in a low-slung white cotton blouse and tight-fitting lime-green toreador pants. She was shaking a large loose pallet of ironed white shirts on a set of clattering wire coat hangers. "Take your dry cleaning and shove it straight up your butt, Fred Prescott! Screw you and your creative thought process—you miserable queer without balls!"

It was terrible, Dazzle thought, how bad karma could come revving into your driveway like this. It always seemed to know where you lived.

"You owe us for five months of gardening, Señor Piss-artist!"

"You stole my action concept at a Sizzler restaurant in Tustin, you lazy old ponce!"

"I bore you three children, listened to your endless pronouncements about art and liberty and beauty, and when it came to the settlement, you screwed me so bad I could hardly afford new sprinklers for the yard!"

"We only want to share the burden of creative development, Fred! We're not like all those other men in suits! We're here to help you make the most of your dreams and ambitions!"

Jesus Christ on a crutch, Dazzle thought. If life was a choice between these awful people and that filthy hammock, I'd probably be swinging my flea-bitten haunch in that hammock right now.

Then, as if a tiny displacement had occurred in the atmosphere, the entire crowd of belligerent shouters went totally quiet. And everybody blinked simultaneously at Fred's snail-tracked blue front door.

And watched the door open slightly—and a pale hand extrude, depositing a yellow foolscap legal pad on the thick brown horsehair doormat.

The door closed again. And like one thinking feeling organism, everybody looked directly at Dazzle.

It took Dazzle a moment to catch up with all the attention. Then, once he caught his breath, he spoke the only word he had in him.

"Woof." Dazzle shrugged sheepishly. "Like what did you expect me to say?"

As if they were drawing a line with a laser, the crowd's attention moved slowly from Dazzle to the sheet of yellow foolscap paper on the doormat. And when they spoke, they spoke through one individual at a time.

"Who's the dog?"

"*El perro es muy* exacerbating."

"I told you I smelled something special about that mutt. I don't know what it is exactly, but I'm pretty sure I like it."

"I didn't even know Dad had a dog. All my life, as a kid, I'm begging for a dog. But he never gets one until I'm already grown up."

Feeling self-conscious, Dazzle trotted across the brown lawn, picked up the legal pad with his teeth (he hated when dogs did stuff like this), trotted over with apparent dutifulness to Syd Fleishman of Sony Pictures Tristar, Inc, and laid it down at his feet.

"I think," Dazzle said humbly, "that this is what you came for."

The suits separated from the crowd like the yolk from an egg.

"What's it say?"

"It's definitely Fred's handwriting. But it's hard to read."

"That's a tee and that's an aitch and that there—"

"Through-line. It says through-line. And right after that. It's a date."

Then, Syd came forward—pushing everyone out of his way.

"I pay you guys to think, and you can't even read." He held up the yellow legal pad like Moses carrying tablets down from the mountain. And then he told everybody what it said.

Cool dog. Cool guy. Buddy pic. Big shots get thrown out of buildings, set on fire, the works. Politically conscious, eco-wary, funny with a heart. Explosive finale, two week pre-opening ad campaign on VH-1, Family Network and Animal Planet. 60 mill opening—secure.

It was as if the entire crowd of gang-haters gasped at once. Everybody waited for somebody to say something. Finally, somebody did.

130

"You're the fucking *man*," Syd whispered under his breath, holding the sheet of yellow foolscap in the air like an Olympic torch.

And slowly, like a chant, the entire crowd began whispering it, too.

"It's like I always said," Dazzle explained to Diggy, on the day he was dropped off at the Burbank Greyhound station. "I'm not cut out for the writerly life. I don't have creative genes or something. The worrisome part is that I don't even recognize a decent writer when I meet one. Seriously, I had Fred pegged as a tiresome old hack with delusions of grandeur, but what do I know? Now, without any help from me (his supposed inspiration) he's taken our script to 'the next level', as Stu put it. They're bringing in six-figure rewrite teams. They're coordinating tri-agency talent deals to develop, cross-market and cast. And the concept's so hot it's being passed around at pool parties and Bar Mitzvahs, and all I ever did was answer the phone, lie to people I don't know, and walk on the beach."

Diggy's car was littered with fast food wrappers, expired bottles of sun screen, and yellowing dead-winged pages of the *Los Angeles Times* and *Coast Mall Shopper*. You could perform a fairly accurate sociological survey in this screwy Toyota, Dazzle thought. The ratio of fast-food franchises to miles driven by the average surfer, or something totally useless like that.

"I told you, Daz. Fred doesn't compromise, dig? He remains totally faithful to his beautiful muse."

It was the smoggiest day Dazzle could remember, and the funny thing was? It had never looked more beautiful or benign. Pink and orange and purplish clouds rimmed the horizon, like one of those multi-layer liquor-cocktails served as lady-drinks in phony, overpriced west-side bars.

"Yeah, well, maybe you're right, Diggy," Dazzle concluded wistfully. "And I'll definitely never remember good old Fred without smiling. What a life. What a profession. I guess somebody's got to do it. I'm just glad it's not me."

"Looks like your bus, Dude. You come visit soon, and I'll teach you to boogie board. It'll be awesome."

It was the best part about any animal, Dazzle thought. The part that got enthusiastic about things. (Even boogie boards.)

"I'll do that, Diggy," Dazzle said sincerely, as he climbed out of the car. "And if you ever make it to Big Sur? I'll teach you the only thing I know anything about. And that, of course, would be taking really long and meaningful naps."

"Do what you do best, dude. Or don't do nothing at all."

And of course Diggy, as always, was right.

NOTE: "Dazzle Joins the Screenwriter's Guild" originally appeared in Fantasy & Science Fiction, *October/November 2008. It got an Honorable Mention in* The Year's Best Science Fiction: Twenty-Sixth Annual Collection, *ed. by Gardner Dozois (St. Martin's Griffin, July 2009); and it was read by Ace Antonio Hall on* Clonepod *("Voices of Tomorrow Podcasting Today's Science Fiction and Fantasy"), Episode 26, January 10, 2009. It is reprinted here from* Dazzle Resplendent: Adventures of a Misanthropic Dog *(Red Rabbit Books, January 2017), a collection of eight Dazzle stories written between 1988 and 2011. Dazzle is introduced as "a dog with bushy red hair, fleas and an extraordinary attention span – especially for a dog." He was particularly fond of pastry, philosophies of language and Third World political theory.*

A LATE LUNCH

BANWYNN OAKSHADOW

BanWynn Oakshadow aka Suta Sunmanitu (Tough Coyote) is a hermit, hippie, experimental beat poet, speculative fiction writer, nature photographer, cultural historian, social activist, pipe carrier, husband, father, adult survivor of child abuse, mentally ill, aphasic, dyslexic, gay, pagan, disabled veteran, and a Cancer with a criminal record. He uses every bit of that in his writing. This Jack-of-All-Trades/Master-of-None has no degrees in eight interesting majors. He loves to create but hates the job of finding good homes for his work and is attempting to train his Border Collie to become his agent. BanWynn lives on a small, 400-year-old farm in southern Sweden in the middle of a remote forest grown over a Viking village gone a thousand years.

The dragon spat repeatedly, his eyes scanning the landscape below for a likely place to unload his burden. Finally, he spied a remote crevasse and banked toward it. His claws unclenched when he was close and, with a sigh of relief, he circled to follow his load's trajectory. He enjoyed the crunching, wet splat as the princess became part of the mountainous, granite landscape; it was almost as funny as the day that idiot au pair lost her grip on her umbrella.

The splats were the only part of his job that he actually enjoyed. How many times had he applied for a different position? But, no! The Union just kept assuring him that he was perfect for the job. That he was doing an absolutely marvelous job—that the villagers could not be happier with his work. The villagers? Who cared about smelly, dirty, uneducated peasants? What about his happiness? Didn't he pay his Union dues twice a month? Wasn't he entitled to some job satisfaction? What kind of moron placed a gay dragon as a village's evil monster anyways? And if he had to do this damn job, why couldn't the villagers sacrifice princes to him instead?

He had even brought it up at the last meeting of the Union of

Mythical, Magical, and Fantastical Creatures (Local 438.)

"It's just not the way things are done, old chap," they said.

"It would just confuse them, Dragon," they protested, "They like things just the way they are."

Hah! Well, they could keep sacrificing those gold-haired, wailing harpies all they wanted. He would go ahead and bite their heads off, spread some blood around for the villagers to "Ooh!" and "Ahh!" and "Ugh!" about, but he would be damned if he was going to eat the revolting things. Screw what the village charter said.

Dumping princesses was a pain in the ass, though—well, pain in the wings to be precise. He wasn't used to carrying that much weight for very long, and his wings burned from the effort.

To make matters worse, his right wing was aching miserably from a bite he had received in a bit of a scuffle the night before. He had been playing bridge with Cerberus at the gentlemen's club, partnered with the Hound of Hell's center head against the paired left and right heads. They had been doing very well until the left head of the beast had accused him of cheating. In the ensuing struggle, the dragon had barely managed to swallow the cards that the hound had seen him palm, and had taken a bite on the shoulder for his efforts. That bite and a torn ear, when Cerberus' center head attacked the right, had been the only injuries inflicted before others arrived and broke up the fight.

Still trying to remove the taste of maiden's blood from his toothy maw, his leathery wings began carrying him to someplace where he could gargle away the leftovers from today's job and, maybe, find something worth eating. It wasn't difficult to find fresh, clean water to drink. A glacial lake did that job nicely as well as providing welcomed relief from the pain of the bite. Finding a decent meal proved to be more difficult. Deer, bears, cows, and peasants were plentiful, but the former wouldn't satisfy his particular appetite, and eating too many of the latter was a sure way to find a herd of those pesky knights in their tin-can suits strutting outside his door. Not that he had anything against knights, mind you; it was just that roasting them was about the only way to make them stop waving their swords about...and eating roasted food was no fun at all.

He made sure to swing round the hill with the old tree to add another dragon turd to the already huge pile under which Rip Van Winkle was sleeping—well, probably not merely sleeping anymore, considering the size of the dung heap. He spied three goats engaging in a 'one-up' boasting contest in a meadow, and considered grabbing one of the Gruff boys for a moment. But he decided that they were too close to the bridge with that damn troll and his fucking rocks to bother with. He saw a large hare napping against a stump and was about to swoop down, dinner selection made, when his sharp eyes caught sight of a large tortoise lumbering down the path a couple miles away. He'd heard about this race; and the chance to have some truly twisted fun overruled the grumbling in his belly. He changed course, and large talons plucked the unsuspecting tortoise from the ground. Rather than turning him into lunch, the dragon dropped him and watched the shell roll to within a few yards of the "Finish Line" banner that hung across the trail.

He was about to give up on lunch and return to his cave when sharp, draconian eyes caught a metallic flash from a copse of trees about a mile away. Wings tucked, he plummeted toward the woods to investigate. With a snap, his wings caught the air a moment before scimitar claws sank into the ground. His head snaked forward to part the branches and peer within. He growled a happy growl of delight at what he saw.

A large, white rabbit was struggling in a mass of blackberry vines. Their tiny thorns kept catching in his fur and plaid waistcoat, holding him tight.

"Damn Br'er Rabbit's idiot cousin!" said the rabbit, "Damn him! 'Oh no. Take this shortcut instead,' he says. 'Save you half an hour,' he says. Didn't bother to mention miles of brambles to catch me like a spider in a web, did he? And now, as if I wasn't late enough already, I am going to be very late. Very late indeed. Ouch!"

The dragon watched the trapped rabbit for a bit, feeling an excited clenching in his stomach and a tightening in his groin. He saw the metallic flash again as the rabbit managed to free a large, round watch from his vest pocket and click it open.

"Oh no! Oh, so very late indeed. If I can just free this foot...Ah there...Damn! Now, my arm is caught again. Oh, I hope they don't pour tea until I get there. Ow! Now my foot is caught again! If only Honeypup hadn't had that silly doctor's appointment today, I wouldn't be in this fix. Damn all the Br'ers! Damn them, I say!"

The dragon was enjoying the show and almost hated to end it, but his belly was starting to growl, and his wings were still burning from having to carry that cow of a princess. The rabbit seemed to be a fancy-pants posh sort, but the dragon figured that he could pull off posh if he

136

tried. With a concerned huff, he pushed his head further into the brush and made his presence known.

"Oh my! You seem to be in quite a fix there, sir. Do you require any assistance?"

The rabbit froze with a tiny 'eek' and appeared to have a major coronary when a cart-sized, green head full of very long, very white, very sharp teeth appeared out of nowhere. In fact, the rabbit was sure that he was in full cardiac arrest until he realized that it was because his heartbeat had sped up to a flutter rather than its usually reliable 'thump-de-thump'. When he determined that the giant, red maw was not about to pluck him from the brambles like a ripe berry, he remembered his manners.

"Oh, pardon me. You startled me," he said, doing his best to straighten his waistcoat with only one paw, "Uhm...yes, I do seem to be in a bit of a fix, don't I? Although I believe that I could free myself eventually, a spot of help would not be unwelcome. I am late, you see. Late for a very important date."

The dragon smiled brightly; a potential problem had just been solved. One of the greatest dangers of carrying dinner back to his cave was that the dinner might be seen. The Union frowned on members eating other members. If he flew too low, then the sneaky eyes of nosy neighbors might spy his burden. If he flew too high (far over the flight paths of fairies, griffons and broom-straddling witches), his dinner was likely to arrive either frozen or asphyxiated. A willing passenger was the perfect solution; but, almost impossible to arrange.

"Well then. We cannot have that, can we?" said the helpful dragon, "Let me see what I can do to extricate you from that rude mass of brambles. After that, I would be most honored if you would permit me to offer you transport to your appointment. Then, you would not be late."

"Oh! That would be most wonderful, I'm sure!" said the rabbit.

Then, "Eek!" said the rabbit, as the huge mouth opened and lowered toward him. The "Eek!" became an "Oh my!" when the mouth closed daintily on the neck of his vest and lifted him carefully, while the dragon's sword-like claws made short work of the brambles.

It took but a moment before the large, white bunny was freed, and he found himself being lifted up through the canopy and deposited safely on the dragon's back.

"There you go, good sir. Right as rain! And now, where is your destination, that I may carry you there in the shortest time?"

Things were happening a bit fast for the rabbit, and it was a tad hard to gather his startled wits, but he pulled himself together and managed to answer his rescuer.

"Right as rain indeed. I thank you, sir. I was on my way to the home of my dear friend, the Mad Hatter. We were to have a tea party and, as you can see, it is very nearly time for tea just now. I have a hole not too far from here that will take me right to his place."

The rabbit attempted to settle himself comfortably on the dragon, sliding slightly in front of the wings and wedging his ample posterior between two of the spiny projections running down the dragon's back. As he did so, he noticed the dragon untying what, at first, appeared to be a scarf from around his neck; he realized that it was actually some type of cloak when his rescuer handed it back to him.

"It would be my pleasure to convey you there. If you would be so kind as to slip this cloak on and drop those long ends down either side of my neck, we can make sure that you are both safe and comfortable during the ride. It gets quite chilly up there, you know. And I am afraid that I am not all that used to carrying passengers. The cloak will both keep you warm and also allow me to hold you safely on my back during take-off and landing."

The rabbit did as he was asked, donning the large, flowing cloak and raising its hood to better keep his ears warm (and, not coincidentally, became virtually invisible from above in so doing.) He saw that dangling from the forward corners of the cloak were two long, tether-like contraptions. As he passed one down either side of the dragon, he saw that the garment was of almost the same color as the kind gentleman's reptilian skin. Personally, he thought that a soft blue, or perhaps teal, would have looked nicer.

He felt the dragon take the two tethers and pull him down more securely in his seat, and he began to actually look forward to being in the sky. Quite an adventure when he stopped to think about it. Yes, quite an adventure indeed! He would have a story to tell at the tea party. One that would make even the Dormouse sit up and take notice.

A dinner-plate eye looked back over the dragon's shoulder to make sure that he was all set, and the eager passenger gave what he hoped was a jaunty thumbs-up while checking his watch once again.

"Hmmm...Maybe not so late after all. I might even arrive before the Dormouse steals all the raisins on the scones again. And arrive with a jolly good story to boot!" he said.

With a mighty bunching of muscles and an even mightier flapping of huge wings, the dragon was airborne while the rabbit watched the ground falling away…and his stomach with it. Gulping desperately, he began to think that this was not such a marvelous idea after all. Even a rousing good story was not worth the side-to-side and up-and-down-and-up-and-down and…*gulp!* But then, the dragon achieved his desired altitude, and the flight suddenly became very smooth. The dragon seemed more to glide than to fly, and soon the rabbit was admiring the view.

"My!" exclaimed the rabbit, "What an absolutely wonderful view one has from up here. Why, I quite imagine that I can see the whole of the world!"

"Kind of you to say so, I'm sure," replied the dragon, "I'm so glad that you enjoy the view. Some folks do not have the stomach for it, but it appears that you hares are made of sterner stuff."

"You are too kind, good dragon," said the rabbit, choosing to ignore being called a hare.

"Not at all! Now, you mentioned a hole that would take you to your destination. Can you tell me how I may find it so that we can get you to your tea in the shortest time possible?" said the dragon as he pondered how to get his meal home without it suspecting anything.

"Quite right, old chap! I'm glad that one of us is keeping his head about him," said the rabbit as he tried to get his bearings. "Let me see… Ah yes, do you see that wood over there off your right wingtip? Starboard I believe you aeronautical types call that, don't you? Right, yes. Uhm, in that wood is a certain witch's house. Quite unique it is, made of gingerbread of all things. Do you know it?"

"Oh, I should say so!" said the dragon, "That icing-covered roof is a true and reliable landmark to all of us who use the higher roads."

"Wonderful! Well eastward of that house lies a meadow, and my hole is at the edge of that meadow nearest the mountains."

The dragon smiled as the rabbit indicated the forest at the foot of the very peak in which he made his home. He would be able to fly right over the meadow in question and have the hare safely in his cave before his dinner even realized that anything was amiss. Assuming, that is, he could keep the rabbit quiet and avoid the other nosy users of the aerial byways. Since taking off, he had been keeping his eyes peeled for anyone who might spy his dinner and spoil it before it even began. He would have to skip his habit of flying over the Emerald City and taking his daily wizz on the Wiz, but sometimes sacrifices just had to be made. Damn. He really loved the green tinged rainbows that his spray made.

139

Far below he could see an old man walking from tree to tree and tacking something up on the trunk of each. It was probably old Geppetto putting up more "missing child" posters. Ground traffic seemed to be otherwise scarce, and so he turned his attention to the skies.

He didn't think that he would have to worry about Tinker Bell. Ever since Peter Pan had been arrested and his "Lost Boys" kiddie porn site taken down by the Feds, she'd been spending most of her time selling Pixie Dust to kids at playgrounds and trying to avoid the cops. Mother Goose had already flown south for the winter, and Mercury had pulled a tendon at the Mt. Olympus mixer last week. There might be some risk of running into that nosy, old bitch of a witch who had become a troublesome busybody since being disqualified from the Competitive Transformation Circuit for cheating. Now she was constantly approaching anyone who didn't flee at the mere sight of her to try to get them to sign her petition for readmission to the competition. This, along with her involvement in the Prince Charming trial, made her rather unpopular. In the meantime, she was stuck with temp agency jobs using her broom to skywrite ads for toothpaste, catching lost dogs, and such.

Even as he thought this, he saw her broom launch itself from the Three Bears' house. In her wake, Papa Bear roared at her and pointed to the new "No Trespassing" signs tacked to the picket fence all around his house.

The damn hag spied him and was headed his way while waving a sheaf of papers wildly. The dragon glanced back at his passenger, to make sure that the rabbit was looking the other way, then snaked his neck toward the old bat and belched forth a ball of flame.

"Damn! Missed!" he griped as the screeching bag dodged and took off in another direction with a stream of curses that seared the air almost as thoroughly as his fires.

The rabbit was busy cooing excitedly and giving a running commentary on virtually everything he saw. "Marvelous! What a view...and there, the Yellow Brick Road. I didn't know that it had a branch out this way. How I wish my Honeypup were here to see this. He would love flying, I am sure. Oh! I say. What was that sound?" inquired the rabbit.

"I beg your pardon. Something I ate must have disagreed with me," the dragon lied.

"How unfortunate," said the rabbit. Being a proper gentleman, he had nothing more to say on that subject and struggled to find a suitable topic of conversation, "I had an aunt who was mad, you know. Very sad. One day, she took to thinking that she was a harpy. She decided to fly to the Enchanted Forest on holiday, and that was the last we ever saw of her. "

Before the dragon could respond, the rabbit squeaked and bounced in his seat.

"Look there! That's the gingerbread house, is it not?" said the bunny.

"Quite right you are, good sir. Hold on tight as we turn here." So saying, the dragon banked into a steeper than necessary turn that forced the rabbit to tuck himself tighter against the dragon's neck. This, consequently, made him even less noticeable on the dragon's back. They were nearing the mountains now, where there was more likelihood of aerial traffic, as locals made their way to and from their cliff-side homes. This close to his destination, the dragon was taking no chances on being spotted.

Soon they were over the meadow that the rabbit had mentioned and, soon after that, a white-furred paw was pointing to a dark opening in the ground a short distance from where a young girl in a blue dress and white apron was napping under a tree.

"There it is. My shortcut. And in such good time, too. Far from being late, I may even end up being unfashionably early. I say!"

The dragon smiled a twisted, draconic smile and began his descent. He waited until the ground was rushing up to meet them and then intentionally snapped his left wing back, sending them into a roll that very nearly unseated the rabbit.

"A cramp! A cramp! Ow! My wing," the dragon cried out in a pitiful voice.

The rabbit was, at that particular moment, too busy trying to hold onto the dragon's neck while attempting to separate earth from sky, as they appeared to tumble one over the other, to ask questions. He was quite relieved when the horizon steadied itself with the ground in its accustomed position under the sky, and he still in his position on the dragon's back.

"Are you alright, Sir Rabbit?"

"*Gulp!* Uhmm... Yes, I appear to be altogether in one piece. Are you alright, Sir Dragon?"

"I fear that I am not at my peak at this moment. I am unaccustomed to carrying passengers, even ones as light and pleasant to travel with as you. My left wing has cramped, and I do not believe that I can land safely until the pain subsides," he moaned, "We shall have to circle a bit until the spasms ease."

In fact, the dragon was not altogether pretending. The aborted landing, intended to terrify his passenger, had also caused a very real stab of pain in his shoulder radiating from the tooth marks left by the Hound of Hell.

"Oh me! I feel quite horrible to have your generosity on my behalf bring you to this state." The rabbit patted his companion's neck in what he hoped was a comforting manner. "I feel quite responsible and insist that you not apologize. Take whatever steps are necessary to ease your distress, good sir, and I shall not object even if it makes me late to the party, after all."

"You are too kind, sir. Are you sure that you don't mind?"

"By my word, good dragon! What kind of gentleman would I be to ask you to injure yourself simply that I might get first pick of the tea cakes? I declare! And after you went out of your way to assist me in the first place. Not only do I not mind, I insist!"

"Well, if you are sure..."

"I am!"

"Because, you see, my cave is... No. Forget I mentioned it. I am sure that I can get us down safely and can get my medicine after." The dragon allowed himself to slip from the thermal that he had slowly been spiraling up, causing them to drop a good twenty feet in a single hair-raising heartbeat.

The rabbit, who was now starting to view the dragon's supposed injury in light of basic survival instead of merely good manners, did his best to urge his heart to cease its attempts to leap from his throat and resume its accustomed place in his chest.

He finally managed to gasp, "Medicine? Cave? Please, do illuminate."

"Well, it is just that I have a certain liniment in my cave just up a bit from here that I normally use in such circumstances. The cave is easy to land at, being a 'straight in and land' matter rather than a 'drop down and pull up' affair. But I cannot ask it. It would surely make you late for your engagement, and then the rescue will have been for naught."

The rabbit did not take long in weighing the disappointment of being late for tea with his friends against the disadvantage of becoming a permanent addition to the meadow itself.

"You are injured, good sir," he quickly replied, "And while I admire your bravery in being willing to make the attempt, I cannot in good conscience allow you to risk further injury to yourself on my behalf. I insist that you seek first the ministrations of your medicine. No matter if I miss the party altogether, since the Hatter has these affairs on a regular basis."

"Well, if you insist."

"I do."

Having forestalled the possibility of alarmed cries for help that might alert his neighbors, the dragon hid his victorious smirk as he spiraled a bit higher, and then darted toward the granite cliff to disappear inside the entrance to his cave.

Settling himself daintily on the lip of his lair, the dragon assisted his soon-to-be lunch in dismounting and ushered him inside.

"Welcome to my humble home, sir. Please make yourself at ease while I tend to my shoulder. Feel free to look around."

The dragon followed his charge inside and smiled at the shocked and somewhat disappointed expression on the rabbit's face. While the rabbit was preoccupied, he took the opportunity to silently close and bar the door behind him.

Almost everyone expected a dragon's cave to be a huge, dismal affair furnished only by the glimmering pile of gold and gems serving as draconian bed. This cave was full of gold all right, but it was gold lamé cloth draped over a delicate settee and gold tassels rimming the edges of floor lamps that made his abode glimmer. Drapes rich with gold velvet and purple silk hung on the walls on either side of framed posters of Judy Garland and Madonna. Bright, tiffany lamps shed their light on a small statue of an aroused David standing next to a book of Tom of Finland's more 'forceful' works.

Most folks cringed at the explicit drawings of overly endowed men portrayed in the latter, but the rabbit's eyes brightened in delight.

"Oh, I say! That one is one of my Honeypup's favorites. He would love this place, you know. He has such an eye for decorating. But don't tell anyone that, I beg you. He would be mortified if anyone knew that he was more than the rough and tumble brute he shows the rest of the world."

"Your Honeypup?" inquired the dragon, not really caring.

"Oh, I am sorry. My pet name for him, the dear. If you have ever found yourself at "The Manhole" on a Friday night you may have met him. His name is Cerberus, a large, muscled hound with three heads."

"Indeed," said the dragon, suddenly caring quite a bit, "I do know of whom you speak. Wears lots of leather? Has quite the nose for cards as well, I understand."

"Yes, that's him! You know him. How marvelous! We have been together for a couple years now."

"I am quite happy for both of you, I am sure," the dragon smiled with delight as the rabbit supplied an unexpected dessert to the forthcoming meal. Not only a wriggly repast, but also revenge on the muscle-bound hound that had bitten him. It was altogether too perfect!

"Feel free to wander around while I find the liniment. In fact, you might be quite interested by what is in the alcove behind that tapestry to your left."

Watching the rabbit with undisguised glee, he made no move for the nonexistent ointment but instead kept his gaze locked on his guest's face as the bunny pulled the tasseled, gold rope near the wall hanging.

The delicate tapestry drew back to expose a small room, bare but for several wooden plaques mounted on the walls and some pedestals in the center of the floor. Each was adorned with what appeared to be random objects, the significance of which took a moment to sink in. The rabbit's gaze slowly traveled from item to item as he took in what he now realized were pieces of morbid memorabilia.

He saw a curly pig's tail and mason's trowel on one. Next to it was a plaque holding a large omelet pan, to which several huge pieces of eggshell had been glued. A large 'H' was engraved at the bottom. A wreath of blackberry brambles encircled a fox tail and pair of rabbit ears on another. Three balls of fluff that took a moment to identify as rabbit tails bore the names "Flopsy", "Mopsy", and "Cottontail". A very long longbow leaned in the corner with a jaunty huntsman's cap perched atop it. The leather bag with 'Tax $$$' written on it sitting on the floor beside the bow was empty.

These were not the only pieces of the private museum. Several pedestals were positioned around the area, each topped with its own collection of memorabilia.

He saw a handful of beans spilled out of a bag next to a large bowl of goose feathers, a harp with no strings, and a single golden egg. The pedestal beside it held a small miner's cap, a long lock of black hair, and the wrinkled remains of a partially eaten apple.

The rabbit pointed to the apple and accused, "That...that's the missing evidence from the Snow White date-rape trial!"

The dragon just snickered, "A shame really. Prince Charming may have avoided the headsman's ax if anyone had believed his poison apple defense. Doubtful, though, considering that the Red Queen was presiding as judge."

The rabbit jerked as if he had just been punched. Wide-eyed and trembling, he backed away from his host. Even then, he could not keep from looking at what was on the remaining displays.

A small, silver sword propped against a pair of thigh-high, leather boots that smelled strongly of cat piss crowned the third pedestal. The final one held what, at first, looked to be a pair of broken sticks with wooden shoes pushed onto the ends, and a few dangles of black string.

With growing horror, he turned back to the dragon who was now smiling at him with something less than his former friendliness. His rescuer's huge, golden eyes now spun with a hunger that went far beyond food. Thick, gelatinous strands of saliva now dripped from his grinning maw.

"He kept telling me that he was a real boy," said the dragon, "A real boy! Do you have any idea how painful it is to spend a week picking splinters out of your ass?"

The rabbit suddenly understood the piss smell on the boots as his bladder released, and he felt the warm flow of urine soak the fur of his legs.

The dragon merely smiled wider, showing even more sharp teeth and inhaled deeply with obvious pleasure, eyes closing to mere slits, "I do love it when my dinner is self-marinating."

"D...d...d...dinner?" came the squeaked reply.

"Of course, dinner. It is too late for lunch," drooled the dragon.

"B...b...but you can't! The rules! The union! You can't do this!"

"Oh, but I can," hissed the dragon over the rumbling of his belly, "Don't you think that each of your predecessors carried a union card just as you and I do? It didn't make any difference then, and it won't now."

"The law! The law will catch you! You don't want to spend the rest of your life in prison, do you?" The rabbit's eyes took in the closed and barred entrance as he backed away from the dragon, knocking a wooden leg to the floor.

"The law? Hah! Who saw you come here? When have I ever even met you before? Anyone looking for you will first question the Mad Hatter and your other tea party companions. When the authorities give up there, it will be your adored Honeypup's crap they sift for your remains, not mine.

"I can see the papers now," he taunted, "Those fundamentalists with their Predator/Prey separationist propaganda will have a field day. 'An unfortunate lover's spat turns to murder, and the poor, little bunny is feared eaten by his horrific lover.' I won't have to do a thing to get even with that rabid bastard. You will do it for me"

The rabbit suddenly took note of the bite mark on the dragon's shoulder and exclaimed, "You are the card cheat! You mean to kill me simply because my lover caught you cheating at cards?"

"I didn't cheat! And no, I am not going to kill you because of him. I am going to eat you because it is going to feel so exquisite to have you squirming and kicking your way down my gullet. Revenge on your flea-ridden bedmate is merely an added bonus."

The rabbit had backed himself all the way into a corner of the trophy room by this point, and had begun shaking so badly that speech became impossible. With a squeal of purest terror, he bunched his legs under himself and launched at the closed door, too terrified to even wonder how he was going to lift the heavy bar.

Huge, curved claws pinched the collar of his vest and held him swinging back and forth as he was slowly raised to eye level with the reptilian face.

"Oh dear, how rude! First you accept my assistance when you are in trouble; you use me as your own personal taxi; you accept the hospitality of my home; and now you rush to leave without even a 'Thank you'. You, my rude little friend, are not going anywhere."

The dragon relished the way the bunny kicked and struggled in his claws. He watched with delight as his prey's expression flashed from terror to desperation to anger to hopelessness and back again. He was in no hurry to eat his well-earned repast, though. No matter what mothers told their children, playing with your food was half the fun.

When the rabbit had exhausted its struggles and hung limp in his claws, the dragon darted out a long, forked tongue to flutter about its furry face, tasting its fear. This made the poor creature begin its kicking and screaming all over again. How delightful!

Lifting his other paw, the dragon slowly dragged a single claw up the back of the squirming victim's plaid waistcoat and felt the cloth fall away until it ripped altogether, spilling the naked coney to the floor. With surprising dexterity, he reached into the vest pocket and pulled out the large, silver watch he had seen earlier.

"Yes, the plaid of the vest will make a nice backdrop to the watch when I add them to my collection on the wall. Don't look so revolted.

It is no different than keeping a book of matches from the restaurant where you had a particularly fine meal."

The rabbit began a frantic scrabbling around the room, clawing at curtained walls seeking a door or tunnel...anything that would allow him to escape his insane captor. The dragon watched his desperate captive with glee, until the rabbit's frenzied racing sent the small David statue crashing to the floor. Even as the shattered pieces were still coming to rest on the hand-woven rug, the dragon's head snaked out to catch the fear-maddened rabbit between his teeth and drew him back out of harm's reach.

Spitting his catch out into a scaled palm, he closed his clawed fist about the rabbit and began to squeeze, "How dare you! Those are my things that you are destroying. My possessions! My treasures!" his voice slowly climbed in volume until his roars made the smaller items on tables and shelves dance. Rage made his eyes blaze in swirls of purple and red. All dragons were insanely protective of their hoards, no matter what form they took. It was only with great effort that he was able to calm himself and slowly open his hand before the rabbit was crushed to jelly in his grip.

At first, he was afraid that he had killed his dinner, but soon determined that the small creature was merely catatonic with fear. Well, it was not his first time facing that particular problem. He reached into a nearby cupboard to bring forth a small vial. Opening the rabbit's jaws with the tip of one claw he poured the contents down its throat. He didn't worry about drowning the bunny. A potion of healing couldn't harm anyone whether it was poured on a wound, swallowed, or even inhaled.

He wasn't even bothered by the loss of a very expensive potion. He'd planned on using it on the rabbit anyways. He always did; a healing potion helped his meals wriggle and kick so much longer than they ever could otherwise.

"You are going to pay for that, you son of a bitch," he said as the rabbit came round, "You are going to pay very dearly indeed."

Loss of his chance to escape also seemed to have taken away any hope, and, with it, fear.

"What could you possibly do to me that is worse than you already plan to do?" asked the rabbit boldly, "Go on. Bite my head off and get it over with, you monster!"

"What could I do that would be worse?" the dragon teased. "Probably not much. But it seems that I need to clear up a small

147

misapprehension that you appear to be laboring under."

"I have never planned to 'bite your head off' as you so eloquently put it. Oh no. That would be no fun at all. If I bite your head off, how will you struggle as you feel yourself slowly sliding down my throat? I will merely tilt my head back, thus. Then open my jaws very wide, like this. And then I will hold you a moment, just here so that you can look down past my teeth and see the moist, pink lining of my throat as it opens in anticipation of your imminent arrival. And then I will close my mouth around you and let go. And then...Well then, you will be a late rabbit indeed."

So saying, the dragon lowered his fingers a bit and allowed his jaws to close around them and the rabbit suspended there. He allowed his tongue to play over the body of his prey, tasting it, and laving it with the saliva flooding his mouth. He enjoyed the kicking and scraping of feet against the roof of his mouth, and delighted in the cries muffled behind his scaly lips. After several long seconds, he let go. The rabbit went down with a gulp.

A few hours later, the dragon was picking his teeth with the splintered end of a wooden leg. He belched contentedly as he placed the torn waistcoat and watch onto a freshly varnished plaque. It was true what they said: the day after, nothing beats the hare of the dog that bit you.

"Feel free to wander around while I find the liniment. In fact, you might be quite interested by what is in the alcove behind that tapestry to your left."

RIDDLES IN THE ROAD

SEARSKA GREYRAVEN

Searska GreyRaven makes her lair in sunny South Florida and has been telling stories for as long as she can remember. When she isn't tapping away at her keyboard, she might be found tending her bees, devouring her weight in sushi, or cavorting about the internet. Her work has been previously published in several anthologies, the most recent of which are ROAR 8 *and* Dogs of War.

Once upon a time, there was a fox. It's always a fox, isn't it? But this isn't just any old fox, no ma'am. This is the King of Trickery, Lord of Thieves and Thief of Hearts, Reynard T. Vulpes. You've probably heard of him. He prances through a lot of tales these days.

Now, Reynard was a wandering fox, and he liked to roam far and wide. No mountain was too high, no cave was too deep for his trouble-seeking ways, as anyone well-acquainted with him is quick to lament. Once, he even made it as far as Yggdrasil, tricked and fought a dragon there. But he grew weary of the cold North, and, after fleeing from a scandal he no doubt caused, Reynard made his way to the balmy coast of the Aegean sea. His feet had barely settled into their first footprints upon the sandy shore when Reynard began plotting his first theft: breakfast.

Our foxy friend was just getting his grubby little paws on some lagana flatbread to go with the dish of saganaki he'd pilfered, when he saw something moving at a distant crossroads. It was barely more than a hint of movement, a flicker of interest, but it caught the wily fox's eye and drew the trickster like a moth to tallow flame. He snatched the lagana quick as you please and tucked it into his vest for later, then made his way toward the crossroads.

The short grass along the road brushed Reynard's black-furred ankles, and the blue sky yawned above as he munched on his stolen saganaki. He tore a chunk from the lagana. Divine! *They know how to eat here,* he thought, licking his lips. *No more lutefisk for me! I've had enough of that to suit three lifetimes.* He trotted along, visions of bread and honey dancing through his mind, and still the thing by the crossroads remained. It seemed to flit from one corner to the next, never staying in one spot but never leaving the crossroads completely. Reynard was intrigued. *Could it be a fey of some kind? Perhaps a nymph?* He'd heard of nymphs. Lovely, immortal, capricious; as likely to love you as curse you. Just Reynard's sort! His pace quickened, slowed again. *Or perhaps it's a maenad.* Reynard recalled the story of one King Pentheus' encounter with such creatures, and he had no interest in having his head parted from his body. He needed his head right where it was, thank you very much, and was dearly attached to it. He approached more cautiously, ears flicking, tail twitching, and his pawsteps as silent as a cat's upon the sandy road. The canny fox would not be caught unawares! Finally, he could see clearly what manner of creature haunted the crossroads.

It had ceased its restless flitting and at last sat stock still, gazing up at Reynard. Sitting primly in the center of the crossroads, one front paw crossed primly over the other, was a sphinx.

She was a lovely creature, with tawny fur that shone gold in the bright sun and a long, black mane that fell like a waterfall across her feline paws. Great dark wings were folded neatly across her back, every bronze-colored feather in perfect order. She gazed at Reynard through slitted eyes and flicked her serpent's head tail. Reynard frowned. *No mere serpent,* he thought. *A sand viper.* Dark diamond markings traced across the snake's back and disappeared behind the sphinx's muscled haunch.

"Well, well, well. What have we here?" she purred, tracing a swirl in the sand with one golden claw.

"Greetings, m'lady," Reynard said, bowing low. He was a thief and a scoundrel, but he knew his courtly manners. Besides, it was unwise to be rude to any creature in a strange land, and downright stupid to be inconsiderate to someone with such wicked-looking claws.

The sphinx regarded Reynard and tilted her head to one side. A pair of leonine ears perked up through her dark mane and pointed his way. "What business does a fox have here?" she asked.

"No business, really. Just passing through. Lovely country you have here. Best food I've had in ages!" Reynard exclaimed, rubbing his ivory belly.

The sphinx smiled faintly and nodded. "It's even better when not stolen," she rumbled. A grin split her face, revealing very, very sharp teeth.

Reynard went still. "Stolen? This? No, I found it. Fell off the back of a cart."

"Plate and all, still warm?" The sphinx snorted. Her tail lashed, the serpent's head hissing softly. "I think not. You should return it, Reynard."

"I'll do no such—wait, what did you call me?"

The sphinx's smile widened. "Reynard, you're known even here. Rumor of you flew on Hermes' heels to my ears, and I waited for you to arrive."

"Waited…for me?" Reynard swallowed, his mouth suddenly dry.

The sphinx nodded, just once. Wine-dark eyes gazed at him, steady as sunlight, and it made the rogue fox squirm.

He recovered quickly, as rogues do. Reynard barked a laugh and hopped back a step. "If I'd known, I would have made better haste! I hate to keep a lady waiting. What could I—a mere vulpine veteran—do for you?" He wagged his tail, doglike and charming.

"You're not a veteran; you're a villainous vexation. And you can start by returning what you stole," the sphinx retorted.

Reynard didn't reply. He merely shoved another bite of stolen flatbread into his maw, licking his muzzle from corner to corner. He smirked, shameless, and groomed his fine whiskers.

The sphinx hissed. Her serpent tail arched over her back, and she bared her fangs, her hackles raised high. "Have a care, fox. It's been a long time since I've had a proper meal. You come to my home and blaspheme, blatantly violating one of our most sacred customs. Do not think you will walk away unpunished."

"What, the middle of the road is your home? No wonder you're hungry."

"Greece, rocks-for-brains," the sphinx said. "You break xenia with your thieving."

"I broke what?" Reynard asked, wiggling one finger in his ear.

"Xenia, you illiterate swine! Hospitality! Gods above and below, how have you not come to a messy end already?"

"Because I'm clever and cute," Reynard replied with a wink.

"Ugh," the sphinx replied. "Waste of breath. I should have simply devoured you from the start." The sphinx crouched, her powerful hind legs bunching to spring. "Pity, really, that my first meal in a hundred years is something so scrawny and mangy. But it will have to do, I suppose."

Reynard backed up and held his paws out before him. "Hold a moment! My deepest and humblest apologies, madam. I sincerely did not set out to offend. Please, allow me to make amends."

The sphinx growled and sat up once more. Her tail lashed, venom dripping from the viper's long fangs, and Reynard readied himself to flee. But the sphinx nodded and ceased the restless motion of her tail.

"I will forgive your trespass and make amends to the shops you have pilfered, on one condition: you entertain me with a riddle contest until the end of the day."

Reynard blinked. "That's all?"

"If you fail to amuse me, I'll devour you and rid the world of yet another yapping fox."

"And if I don't agree to this contest?"

The sphinx grinned very, very wide. Much wider than Reynard thought was strictly necessary or anatomically possible. He shuddered.

"Then, I get to find out if you taste as funny as you look," the sphinx growled.

Reynard nodded emphatically. He had no desire to see if the sphinx's teeth were as sharp as they appeared. "I agree," he said. "May I finish my meal first? I'm starving."

"Of course. It is only proper," the sphinx replied.

Reynard finished his lagana and saganaki, and after he'd licked the dish clean, settled down on the side of the road. "Would you like to begin? It is your home, after all."

The sphinx shrugged and began, "What walks on—"

"A man," Reynard interrupted, smirking.

"Gorgon's blood, but you're an ass," the sphinx replied.

"No, I'm a fox," Reynard replied with a grin. "Use a less tired riddle, and I'll behave."

"That's funny, you look like Midas' brother. 'Twas the ears that fooled me."

Reynard covered his ears with his hands. "Low blow, sphinx. Low blow," he whimpered melodramatically.

"Bah, like you've never hit below the belt before."

"It might be a more pleasant use of my time than sorry riddles from a droop-winged sphinx!"

The sphinx laughed. "Very well, Knave of Thieves. Answer me this: There is a building. One enters it blind, and comes out seeing. What is it?"

Reynard rested his elbow on his knee, and then his chin upon his closed fist, and pondered. "That's more like it," he said.

The sphinx smiled and groomed the length of one golden paw. Reynard lost his train of thought when the sphinx flexed, flashing her wicked claws. She sheathed them again quickly, though, and waited patiently for Reynard to answer. If not for the occasional flick of her ear or tail, Reynard could have sworn she'd turned to sunset-colored stone.

He thought and thought again.

"A school," he said at length.

The Sphinx beamed and nodded.

The corners of Reynard's lips curled upward. "My turn, then. I've watched many a maiden take to this thing. They store it in nooks and watch as it swells, pushing upon its covering. And when it has reached its peak, many a maiden takes this boneless hunk between her hands, and with her apron covers the tumescent thing!"

"Lewd!" The sphinx cried.

"That you took it in such a way says more about you than me!" Reynard chuckled.

The sphinx sighed and pinched the bridge of her nose with one velvet paw. "Bread, you insufferable cad. The answer to your riddle is bread rising."

Reynard tapped his nose and gifted the sphinx with a canine grin. He scratched vigorously behind one ear, causing the sphinx to wrinkle her nose.

"Fleas," she muttered grimly.

"What's a few fleas between friends?"

The sphinx didn't reply. She merely looked at Reynard, who shrugged and sheepishly ceased his scratching.

"Very well, my turn again. What we caught, we threw away. What we didn't catch, we kept. What did we keep?"

Reynard backed his ears and huffed. "Why would you not keep a thing you caught?"

"Well, if you can't answer it…" drawled the sphinx.

Reynard growled and curled his lip. He hmmed and hawwed, and the shadows grew shorter, then vanished altogether. Bright, noonday sun beamed down upon his russet back, and still, Reynard had no answer.

"Seems I'll be having a fox for dinner!" the sphinx said, and licked her lips.

154

Reynard whined and scratched behind his ear again, wondering where he'd picked up such annoying pests, and suddenly, "Ah-ha! Fleas! The answer is fleas!"

The sphinx settled back down and pouted. "That one vexed even clever Homer. Clearly, they make foxes of different stuff in the North."

Reynard preened and puffed out his chest with pride. "I *am* the cleverest of all foxes," he said. "I've stolen gold from a box without hinges, key, or lid!"

"You stole an egg and no doubt ate it too! And I'm counting that as your riddle." The sphinx rustled her wings uncomfortably.

Reynard opened his mouth to protest, but the sphinx interrupted him. "Riddling is such hungry work. Perhaps a snack to tide me over? Oh, something red and ripe would do just fine!"

"They say that hunger is the finest spice," Reynard said. "The day is young, yet. Perhaps we let this red and ripe meal stew a bit longer?"

The sphinx snorted, then said, "Oh, very well. Here is my next riddle: Out of the eater came something to eat, and out of the strong came something sweet."

Reynard blanched. "I've heard this one. One moment, what was the answer, ahhh…"

The sphinx settled back and yawned. She stretched, catlike, and spread her wings to catch the failing light. Black shadows reached across the road, kissing stone, and sand, and grass. The ocean glimmered, diamonds upon sapphire, as the sun dipped below the horizon.

"Ah, yes! You've a morbid mind, Lady Sphinx. What is sweeter than honey, and stronger than a lion? I believe the answer is bees, making honeycomb within the body of a lion. That's a bit of a cheat, don't you think? If Samson's wife hadn't been sweet on me, I'd never have known the answer."

The sphinx threw back her head and laughed. "Oh, you *are* fun. Tell me another one, please."

Reynard bowed—a tricky feat for a sitting fox, but he managed—and said, "Here is a thing that, when you name it, you have destroyed it. What is it?"

The sphinx thought for a moment, and watched the sun sink lower and lower into the azure sea. "Silence," she said at last. "You've entertained me all day, and that is no small thing. Solve this last, and I'll consider your deal fulfilled: There are two sisters, one gives birth to the other and she, in turn, gives birth to the first. Who are they?"

The sun set, turning the sea wine-dark, before Reynard finally answered in perfect ancient Greek, "The sisters are night and day," he said. "Night and day being feminine in the old tongue." The moon rose and cast silver light upon the road where the pair sat, side by side.

The sphinx smiled and nodded. "And here I thought you were simply ignorant of our ways."

"Merely careless," Reynard replied. "I am truly sorry to have caused offense."

"All is forgiven. But here, I'd ask for one last riddle from you, for the road, shared from one friend to another."

Reynard looked up at the sky, and the last riddle came to him. He picked up the dish that he'd pilfered, that once held the stolen saganaki. It gleamed in the moonlight.

"A silver dish is set upon a black velvet cloak. All around, diamonds twinkle, and I can trace the paths between them with story after story. What am I?"

The sphinx rose and stretched, and flexed her wings. "You speak of the night sky, Reynard Riddle-Master. You've entertained me all day and into the night, and for that, you have my forgiveness and my thanks."

The sphinx took the dish from Reynard, and sprang into the sky. The night swallowed her up, and Reynard was left alone. The only trace at all of his encounter was the place beside him, where the crushed grass still lay flat.

"Riddling is hungry work," he muttered. He turned around and regarded the city behind him, light from torches flickering to life. The scent of incense drifted past his nose, laced with the aroma of burnt offerings to the gods. Reynard grinned. "I wonder if that baker still has any bread left."

"Greetings, m'lady," Reynard said, bowing low. He was a thief and a scoundrel, but he knew his courtly manners.

THE LOST UNICORN

SHAWN FRAZIER

Shawn Frazier's career as a writer has been a learning journey to say the least. After completing his MFA, which he found to be useless, he learned the craft of writing after graduating with a massive financial loan. He returned to taking writing workshops at the Taos Writers' Toolbox (Nancy Kress and Walter Jon Williams), and Callaloo*'s two-week craft workshop and critique held at Brown University. In Kansas, but sadly without Dorothy, he spent two summers at the James Gunn Center for Speculative Fiction (with Kij Johnson and Christopher McKitterick). Then, things started to roll. His first published story, "The Hoodoo Nigger," was published by* Quail Bell*. "Jacob and The Owl" won the Mary Shelley Contest and was published in* Rosebud #57*. He received honorable mention in a short fiction contest in* Ragazine*. His short story "Nne" is featured in the special edition of* SQ*. Flapper House Press published "How Emma Jean Crossed the River" in their #8 Winter issue. His most recent publication is "The Shadow's Insomnia", published in* Flapper House #12 (Winter 2017)*.*

A Unicorn quietly trotted into the Gardener's wilted garden. The Gardener sat knee-deep in the dirt and didn't notice the animal approaching him. His eardrums were plugged with music. He hummed a song and yanked the weeds growing in the dry soil. Three weeks ago, he had planted seeds. Nothing grew. He wished for a miracle to save his crop. For days, a cold wind had lingered through the town of Darlington. The carrots, cabbage, tomatoes, and other vegetables refused to blossom in the frigid weather.

The Gardener felt a warm breath on his neck. The shadow of the mythical animal blanketed him. He jumped up and grabbed his pick-shovel to defend himself.

"Michelle, come on out here and look at this!" In a pink bathrobe and bunny slippers, she peeked out the back door. She went out to join her husband. The two looked like Rodin statues in their backyard.

"What in the…Who lost their horse?" the Gardener said, standing beside Michelle. She lifted her bathrobe and circled the animal.

"That isn't a horse. That's a Unicorn. See that horn? Gold!"

"A what? I see it, but I can't believe it!" The Gardener began panting. "What circus did it run from? They're going to charge us with stealing this thing," the Gardener bellowed.

"Darling, no circus or zoo has a Unicorn like that." The Unicorn stepped up to the Gardener. With its short, thick head and long ears, it lowered its body for the Gardener to mount. "It wants to give you a ride, baby. I wonder where to."

"To its owner, that's who. Why else would this broomstick want me to ride on its back."

"Owner? Who owns a Unicorn in South Carolina? I bet that thing belongs to a…a Fairy."

"A Fairy? What the shit are you saying?" He laughed. No…he hollered at what she just said. "Do you know how you sound? There is no such thing. Next, you'll say it was running away from the big bad wolf in the woods."

Michelle walked up and tapped her knuckles gently on the Unicorn's golden horn. "That's gold, alright. Solid. Didn't make a tinge. I bet a fairy or a virgin maiden is trying to find it. Lost it while riding. I read all about stuff like that. Poor thing. Let me get it something to eat." Michelle went back into the house and came back with two granny apples and a worn leather book.

"This Unicorn has got to be worth something. Maybe we'll get a reward for returning it to its owner. Who let a beauty like this run free?" The Gardener gently opened the unicorn's mouth to peer at its teeth.

"This reminds me of something I read before," Michelle was flipping through the pages of the book. "Remember this book that got delivered to the house?"

"Yeah. The one that the new mailman delivered by mistake. When is he going to get that our last names aren't Doyle? How can you confuse Durham with Doyle?"

"Oh, stop it! Jimmy is young. You should be happy he ain't in the streets selling dope and hustling." A white flickering light brightened behind a brick wall. Michelle came beside her husband, tugging him by his arm to go back inside the house. The Unicorn began to move toward the light, sneezing rainbows out its nostrils. The soil became moist, ending months of drought.

"Why ain't you returned that book yet?"

"I did. Three times. Went to the post office, stood in line, and gave it to the clerk. But the book keeps being sent back. So, I read it. It's a tale of a soldier returning home in a storm. As he walked across a long bridge, it collapsed. A Unicorn trotted to his rescue. Just like this one. At first, the Unicorn was all sweet and cute. The soldier didn't know where it came from and who it belonged to. He needed the animal's help, or he would have perished from cold and hunger." The Unicorn ate the apples out of Michelle's palm. The Gardener rubbed the thickly coated creature and lifted his fingers to his wife to smell.

"Lilacs. I know that smell from a tree on Stone Street."

"If something as beautiful as this can walk in here, it can't be all that bad from where it came from. Nope."

"You fool? Is that what you think? Listen. This soldier mounted on top of the beast, and it carried him over the water to a place that was far from his home."

"Why didn't the fool Unicorn take him home?"

"The soldier steered it off its path. He'd heard of material riches in this far, far away place. I never got to the end."

The Gardener shook his head.

"We are miles from any river. Second, Michelle, just look at that Unicorn's face. Polished teeth, cleaned and brushed mane, braids falling down its back. It ain't wild at all."

"No?"

"No! What if it ran away because someone tried to take its horn?" Tears welled up in Michelle's eyes hearing her husband say those words. She went back to the house, trying not to step on the soil the Gardener had tilled. She tip-toed around the edges, the soles and ears of her bunny slippers getting covered in damp dirt. When she reached the back door, she took her shoes off and banged the heels against the steps. "I am going to make a call to the police!" The back door shut behind Michelle.

The Gardener shouted, "And you're gonna tell them there's a Unicorn in the garden? Why, they'll lock you up for being crazy. Those folks don't have time for nonsense, Michelle. I will take care of this." *Besides, they might steal the Unicorn for themselves,* he thought. The Gardener stepped back from the animal, eyeing the Unicorn as if he was buying a brand-new Cadillac. "Hey, we could get a reward for returning this broomstick."

"To pay off months of mortgage? You read the letter, huh? They

160

stapled it on the door yesterday," she shouted from inside the house.

"Yeah…I read it," the Gardener replied in a hushed voice. The fear of losing his land returned to him. As they waited for the police, the afternoon turned into night. The Unicorn's white coat illuminated the dark. Inside the house, the Gardener's wife watched from a second-story window as her husband mounted the Unicorn and began trotting away. She emerged from the house, screaming for him to stop.

Michelle rushed to the back of the yard. She saw nothing but its hoofprints ending at the back-brick wall. Michelle knew nothing could go through it. *I wished I went to church this Sunday. The Lord would have told me what to do now.* In the air, rain fell. She dodged through the garden to return to the house, protecting her new hair perm with the cloth of her pink bathrobe. Michelle waited for her husband to come back and the police to answer her phone calls.

The Gardener and the Unicorn came to a virgin place where not a person, bird, building, house, store, statue, or street appeared. Only a tree-studded field that stretched endlessly. Clusters of sparkling blue vines covered trees that were sky-high. In the grass, carnations blossomed from out of the ground. The Gardener wondered where he was. "Help…Anyone here?" he yelled. All that answered was the echo of his raspy voice. Frigid winds made the Gardener wish he wore a jacket.

The Gardener gave the Unicorn a mean look. "Where did you take me?" the Gardener said. The Unicorn trotted to where a rainbow shined on an old-style two-story mansion made of stucco brick exterior with cast-iron porch railings. He opened the cast-iron gate, leaving behind his ride. The Unicorn stayed on the spot. Octagonal posts supported a pair of arches. "Is this where your owner lives?" the Gardener asked the Unicorn.

The Gardener walked up to the front door and knocked on the brass iron knocker. The door was opened by a dark-skinned woman like he was, but dressed in Antebellum clothing. He wondered if he had come to a costume party and wished he had dressed differently. She wore a headscarf and an apron covered in grease. Was this Hattie McDaniel? What kind of party did he come to?

"Why didn't you come around the back? And look at what you are wearing!" The Gardener looked around her, at a high-ceilinged room with velvet cushioned chairs and a carpeted floor.

"Who does this Unicorn belong to? I found it in my backyard.

Would you know where I can locate the owner?"

"I hope she didn't cause you no problems." The woman stepped out and waved at the Unicorn. "We were about to go looking for you. Go in the barn, Sally, and wait. And get yourself washed up. And I bet you're hungry, too. Shame on you for scaring folks." The Unicorn trotted away leaving the Gardener. He was instructed to go around to the back of the kitchen. He waited at the door there for thirty minutes before the maid led him to a small closet. A double-breasted frock coat hung on a coat hanger. She held two full cloth bags that looked as old as the house.

"After you finish changing, I'll tell you where you can get your reward."

He came out of the closet dressed like an officer in a Civil War film. "Now follow this here map in the bag, and take this deed for your reward of forty acres and a mule. Wait." She paused. "I better tell you how to get there myself. Just go and follow the North Star and..."

"—I can read."

"Oh...I heard about those who do. You from the North?" The Gardener blinked his eyes and shook his head. "No"

"Hmm. Now just take this here bag I packed for you." He peeked inside and saw a wrapped sandwich, bottled water, and an Adams Revolver, which the Gardener had never held or fired in his life.

"Any questions before you go?"

"Why do I need this to claim my reward?"

"There might be soldiers who think you shouldn't have it. Tell them that you earned your forty acres and a mule, if they have any questions. Sit down in the kitchen and read it a bit if you can. You said you can, right?"

"Yes." The maid's cartoonish eyes popped wide open.

On foot, the Gardener traveled until he came to a spot on the map that read, *Cemetery of the Forgotten*. A dirty mule running loose kicked a headstone with its horseshoes. It pissed, then moved to another plot and peed again. It went to another and this time shitted. "Get out of here," the Gardener screamed. The headstones showed the names of Sojourner Truth and Harriet Tubman. "Don't you know who these people are? They're not forgotten." He lassoed the mule with some rope he found in the sack and led the beast from the Land of the Forgotten.

"You damn fool. What is the matter with you?" the Gardener said.

The mule eyes teared up. It reminded him of his sweet Michelle back home. As the sun was setting, the Gardener traveled to a plot of land that had bright Bee Balm and Helen flowers. He tiptoed through the garden. "It's here. I knew it would be. Oh, Michelle. I can't wait for you to see all this." He shook himself, closed his eyes, and reopened them. He patted and rubbed the mule gently to be sure this was all real. The Gardener thought of what he could do. Plans that he had for his backyard could be used here, to raise a whole botanical garden of fresh flowers.

He was too lost in Mother Nature's gifts to hear a troop of soldiers approaching. Dust billowed from the soft stomping of men's feet on the ground. The sky became covered by a dark cloud over the garden. The Gardener was shaken out of his momentary celebration. Confederate soldiers marched and crashed through his reverie. Men wearing caps and bullet-hole-worn attire stepped up and began to sing:

> *I hate the Yankee nation and everything they do.*
> *I hate their Declaration of Independence, too.*
> *I hate their glorious union, dripping with our blood.*
> *I hate their stripéd banner, and fit it all I could.*

Heads wrapped and bandaged, the mangled army of soldiers wobbled on the saddles of their horses. If a wind blew, they'd be scattered to pieces. Foam filled the mouths of the water-drained animals. Withered, hungry faces stared at the mule. Stomachs somersaulted at the sight of the beast. Images of the animal turning on a roaster filled each one of the soldier's heads. The men licked their lips.

"This is my land. See." The document was shown in the torchlight. Night had already fallen. The bright flowers glowed in the dark. Before a soldier snatched away the paper from the Gardener's hand, a wind landed on their commanding officer's hard-ridden boots. His toes from his left boot showed.

"Boy, you damn silly coon." The soldier bent down and picked up the paper. He lit it with a torch he held.

"It says that I am the owner."

The soldiers huffed and puffed.

"This ain't real."

"How's it not?" The soldiers began to lick their lips and rub their stomachs with thin pencil fingers. A musket clicked. The Gardener turned his head to the barrel and heard another click. Click.

"Oh, shit. I ran out of bullets. Who has any left?" asked the armed soldier. All the soldiers nodded their heads, no. They had all ran out. While the men searched to see who had a rope to use, the Gardener slipped away unnoticed with his mule. When they were a fair distance away, he began to see the light that he entered through with the Unicorn. A river ran between where the greenkeeper stood and his home. After going through so much, he returned with nothing to show for anything. The waters bubbled and foamed from the lake. He stepped away from the water, remembering the story his wife told him. The mule went to the edge, submerged its head, and drank. The Gardener watched the animal in the full-lifted moon. He tried to cross without using the ass as a boat. His stomach made a soft cry. A branch in a plain tree above him lowered an apple. The Gardener plucked and bit it, thinking of how he was crossing the river. Slowly, he felt a surge of energy. A revived spirit reverberated in him. He took another bite of the apple and ate it.

"You took me to my forty acres, and now it is up to me to claim it. No one will take away from me what I am promised."

"Hee-Haw, Hee-Haw," the mule replied, raising its front legs, its face drenched from drinking the water. It rubbed its head on the Gardener's leg. "There, there now. Just don't go into that graveyard, you hear? You hear me?" The mule nodded to show it understood him.

"Now, go and get. I got business to handle."

Michelle heard the clicking of hooves echoing down the street and poked her head out the second-floor window. A fog covered the road. She rushed outside, trying to see through the thick mist if her husband and the Unicorn had returned. Michelle opened the front door. Rather than seeing the sparkling blue eyes and white fur coat of the Unicorn, a mule in black waited at her doorstep with a bouquet of flowers sticking out of its mouth. When it dropped the flowers on the welcome doormat, white doves flew from out the chimney of the house. She bent down and patted the mule. The bitter and stale aroma of death clung to her fingers.

The animal's tail hung stiff as a rope as it trotted off in search of a new owner to claim his forty acres. The mule's ears turned slightly backward as it clicked its heels and vanished into the thickening fog. Michelle picked up the flowers. She knew now that the Unicorn and her husband were forever in another place and time.

"This is my land. See." The document was shown in the torchlight. Night had already fallen. The bright flowers glowed in the dark.

BOOMSDAY

JENNY BRASS

Jennie Brass is a New England soul stranded in corn fields of the Upper Midwest. Growing up in the rich folklore of the coast gave her a fondness for taking a bit of history and turning it on its head into dark fantasies. The vast majority of her casts include anthropomorphs or tales told from an animal or monster's point of view. Many of the characters that inhabit her worlds originate from her artwork, stepping out from the portrait and into the written word. Her work has been published by Time Alone Press, Gold Fever Press, Bards and Sages Quarterly, Dragon Roosts Press, and Horrified Press. Follow her writing on www.facebook.com/BrassQuill/

Enfuego the chihuahua pressed her thumb against the game remote's joystick. She shoved the control all the way to the left. In the middle of the field, the mouse twitched and veered left. Stitches along the side of his head held an incision together.

"Ninety-nine bottles of tequila on the wall," Enfuego belted off-key. She rammed the control to the right.

The mouse jerked, spun on his heel to the right, then shuffled off in the new direction.

"Ninety-nine bottles of tequila. Take one down, drink it on down." In a quick series, she mashed the buttons.

The diminutive mouse pirouetted with dull eyes locked open in a vacant stare. In his torn jeans and bloodstained t-shirt, he looked like a zombie rodent.

"Ninety-nine bottles of the tequila on the wall." She shifted the cigarette lodged between her teeth and hit a few more buttons at random. "Ninety-nine bottles of—"

One moment, the mouse was there.

Boom!

The next, he was gone in the flash of a small crater.

Her eyes glimmered for a moment. Her tail wagged in a furious blur of long fur. Then, it dawned on her. She stared at the remote and wailed.

Alsadair slid the barn door open. The pine marten folded her arms across her chest over her lab coat. "Did I just hear *another* explosion?"

Enfuego nodded her head and pointed out at the field. "My toy broked."

"What did you think would happen to it in the mine field? Don't you remember where you buried your booby traps around our compound?"

Enfuego opened her mouth to reply.

Alsadair raised a silencing paw. "That was rhetorical. You have to think in the first place, which I know is beyond your mono-neurocellular capabilities."

"You made more of the mousies, right?"

Alsadair smirked and reached into her lab coat pocket. She dangled another diminutive mouse by its tail. "The neuro-implant surgery for each of these takes me several hours. You have to stop treating them like they are disposable. There are not many mice left that are foolish enough to come to our compound after all their friends never coming back."

Enfuego grabbed for the mouse just as it was pulled out of her reach. "Pfft! There's plenty mouser volunteers in the dives. I gots 'em hooked; they do anything for a fix. Now gimme. I'm just gettin' good at driving the lil' buggers."

She put the mouse back in her pocket. "You have another task. Go to your ammunition shed and get the bombs prepared. I want to raid that warehouse at nightfall for my shopping list."

Enfuego stuffed the remote into the pocket of her leather duster and kicked up her heels. "*Dañoso!*"

She dashed to the shed around the side of the old barn. The barrel of the super death ray stuck out of the loft window like a planetarium's telescope. The device was just a few dozen feet too large to fit inside. With a giggle, she unlocked the padlock and slid the chain free from the shed door. It seemed so silly that Alsadair didn't trust her to store her explosives in the barn.

What could possibly happen?

She tossed the spent cigarette aside and pulled a fresh one out of her jeans pocket. Her lighter flame caught the end as she puffed on the cigarette.

Ah, sweet smokes. Not as good as tequila, but then not much is. Mmm mmm!

The door swung open on well-oiled hinges.

Daylight poured inside the empty shed.

Enfuego's ears shot up. She shut the door. Rubbed her eyes. Then opened it again.

It remained empty.

"No!" She collapsed to the center of the empty shed. Her claws clattered against the floorboards. "All my lovely TNT! My dynamite! My C-4! Even my rocket launcher!" She tugged the red bandanna from her head and sobbed into it.

By the time she looked up, Alsadair's shadow fell across the floor. The pine marten raised an eyebrow.

"Someone stole mis *amigos*!" Her paws flailed in the air. "When I catch the *gilipollas* who did this, they gonna pay!"

"That was at least several tons of explosives." She gave Enfuego a wry glare. "Unless you have been moonlighting, again."

"No benders since the last time. What? I swears it!" She shook her head and held a paw to her grimy shirt. "I ain't raided any bars for tequila in at least three days."

Alsadair sighed and lowered her face into her palms. "In that case, who knows how long then, seeing as how that's as high as you can count. So, you haven't been in here for a few days?"

Enfuego shrugged and patted her jacket pocket. "I still gots a bottle of tequila. I still good. But someone stole my stuff!" Her fist rammed against a floorboard. The wood shot up and clattered, leaving a hole behind. She reached down into a tunnel. "What the—" Tearing free a few more boards and casting them aside exposed the smooth contours of the dirt shaft.

Alsadair switched on a flashlight and watched the curve of the tunnel devour the beam. "Well now, a covert underground operation. This explains why we didn't notice any strange activity."

The stale air carried a musky tang to it. Enfuego stuck her head through and perked her ears. Nothing. "Whoever they are, they not here no more." She dropped down and landed with a soft *oof* in the loose dirt.

A moment later, Alsadair joined her. The flashlight illuminated the long tunnel before fading into the distance.

Enfuego took a deep gulp from her tequila bottle. "Ahhhh. Ok, now we can go bust this thief's chops."

"Yes." Alsadair scowled. "We wouldn't want you to do anything sober."

"Heh, I be sober when I be dead." She tucked the bottle back into the inside pocket.

"Can you tell what animal is our subversive?" Alsadair asked as they padded through the musty shaft.

Enfuego sniffed at the dirt. "Smells a bit like you when you're not doused in that smelly stuff."

The pine marten narrowed her eyes. "That is a very special concoction designed to mask my natural musk. I'll have you know, I spent many years finding the perfect ratio of vinegar and lavender."

The chihuahua blew out a ring of cigarette smoke and grinned. "You still stink."

"How long ago did our thief pass through here?"

"Oh, he here no more than an hour or so. See the soggy track?" She pointed to the water-filled depressions. Marks from webbed feet sprawled in the loose soil.

Alsadair peered down the beam of the flashlight. The illumination revealed a wall in the distance with a large hole in it. She clamped her paw around the chihuahua's muzzle.

Enfuego narrowed her eyes. The moment her muzzle was free, she plucked out the crushed cigarette and glared at it. She flicked it into the puddle where it hissed. "Not going in without a light, *amigo*."

The pine marten tapped her footpaw on the ground as Enfuego pulled out her lighter and a fresh cigarette from her pocket. She took a few puffs before even noticing the glare of her associate. Alsadair held out a paw and grumbled, "May we proceed, Enfuego?"

"Sure. I ready now." She slunk up and peered into the hole. Her large ears, flared out like satellite dishes, picked up the whine of a metal grinder. The room beyond held crates and boxes bursting at the seams with ordnance. Three times more than her shed could hold. Enfuego's eyes shot wide open, her heart practically burst from her chest. "I died, right? This be my heaven."

Enfuego's eyes gleamed, her tail spun like a plane's propeller until Alsadair grabbed it. She kept her voice low, "If you think a twisted little psychopath like you goes to heaven when they die, you're more delusional than I—"

A voice cut Alsadair off. Muttering came from somewhere in the center of the room near a dark looming shape draped in tarps. "There we are, Lotus my love."

Ignoring the voice, Enfuego squealed and pointed at a box overflowing with yellow sticks of TNT. "Look! Me *amigos*!" She dragged Alsadair into the room.

Alsadair grabbed her muzzle and hissed, "We're not alone, you ignoramus!"

From atop the draped platform, a sinewy figure appeared. He immediately discarded the grinder to pick up a rocket launcher. "Shh, Lotus. Don'tcha worry now. Ol' Skveek will protect you."

"Oh good," Alsadair tugged on her comrade's ear, "he appears to be as deaf as you are dim-witted."

Enfuego freed herself from the hold and cocked her head at the figure. "Is that a mask or your face, *asno?*"

Burying her face in a paw, Alsadair muttered between clenched teeth, "That wasn't a request for a demonstration, Enfuego."

"Eh? Visitors?" Skveek the otter cackled and pushed back the welder's mask. Over his shoulder, the rocket launcher tipped precariously. From his perch, he glared down at the pair. "You should never have come here. Now that you have seen my stash, you must die."

Alsadair plucked up a grenade from the box, turned it over in her paws, then set it back with a sigh. *Oh great, Enfuego's intellectual twin. This should be stellar.* "Hit the trigger on that, and we'll all be incinerated, genius."

He blew through his whiskers. "Hogwash. The power of the Great Oyster will protect me." He reached beneath the welding apron and produced an oyster carcass on a string.

"Phew! That stinky thing?" Enfuego snorted. "Eh, Whiskers, you know that thing's deader than a spent ignitor, right?"

"No!" He clamped a paw over it. "The Great Oyster has promised me a smorgasbord of fishes for my service. All I have to do is fulfill the plan."

Alsadair rubbed her forehead. "Oh wonderful, another crackpot with delusions of grand dining. Here we go again." She folded her arms and smirked. "So lay it on us: what did the little mollusk tell you was the path to salvation?"

Skveek's grip on the rocket launcher loosened as he gazed at the piles of ammunition. "The way must be made clear for the bivalves. A path must be cut for them from the reservoir where they suffocate to the ocean's clean waters."

"Clean?" Alsadair's ears tilted up. "I'd love to know what standard you are using to measure that. The last I looked the coastlines still glow in the dark. That's not bio-illumination, either. Nothing lives in that

170

muck."

"Nonbeliever! The bivalves will save us. They are the key. Nothing will stop them."

"They told you that, didn't they?"

His obsession gleamed in the fog of his cataract-laden eyes. "You will see. You will all see."

She held up a paw. "Let me guess. Villain plan 101. You're going to blow up the reservoir dam and flood the valley."

"Oh oh." Enfuego rummaged through her pockets and pulled out the lighter. "Can I help?"

Skveek stared. "I don't need a rat's help."

At that, Enfuego froze. The guard hairs on the back of her neck flared up, pushing against the collar of her duster. Her lip curled into a snarl. "What did you call me? I no' no rat, Whiskers!"

Alsadair reached into her pocket and pulled out the mouse. She set it on the floor and tapped its head just above the incision. "Primed."

Enfuego discarded the lighter into her jacket pocket and grabbed a roll of duct tape.

Skveek barked a laugh. "A mouse? You're going to send a mouse? That's nothing compared to Lotus!"

He stomped his foot, and the platform moved. The tarps fell away to expose a twenty-foot-long snapping turtle. On her back, the otter had mounted a Gatling gun. She opened her striped eyes and hissed. One clawed foot struck and cracked the floor.

Alsadair grinned and inclined her muzzle. "One mouse and one deranged chihuahua are all I need. Besides, you stole Enfuego's stash. Nobody takes her toys and remains in one piece to tell about it."

Enfuego finished duct taping a C-4 bomb to the mouse. She set the timer without glancing at it. The moment she had the remote in her paws, the mouse toddled forward toward the turtle.

Lotus didn't pay the mouse any attention. She stretched her neck, eager to take a bite out of the intruders. That was until the mouse scampered up her leg and into her shell. Her motions now became an odd dance, shifting back and forth in a drunken jig.

Enfuego blindly drove the mouse deeper into the shell.

Lotus panicked and pulled into herself. Her head and all four legs retracted, dumping the shell to the ground in a tremendous thump.

Bawoom!

Smoke belched from all five holes.

Skveek gaped wide-eyed over the edge. "Lotus? Lotus, my love?

171

Speak to me!"

Enfuego licked her lips and ribbed Alsadair. "Didn't you say I never cook? Look, I made turtle soup. One easy step!"

The pine marten sighed and buried her face in her padded palm.

Skveek dropped the rocket launcher and swung the Gatling gun's muzzle at them. "You killed my love! Now, you're both going to die!"

Alsadair reached into the pocket of her lab coat and pulled out a purple-capped test tube. "Enfuego, eat your cookie."

She wrinkled her nose. "But they taste icky with all the dotes in them."

"The word is antidote, not dote. Do you want to die twisted by poison?"

"Umm. No." She wagged her tail furiously. "You know I wanna go out in an explosion heard round the world." She spotted the tube and immediately fetched a cookie from her pocket. "Ohh, got it."

Alsadair flashed her teeth.

Skveek hadn't noticed. He set out a string of curses as he struggled to get the gun's safety to disengage.

She opened her fingers and let the tube fall, remarking dryly, "Oops."

It smashed on the floor and dispersed a fine mist into the air.

She pulled out a notebook and started to write. "Purple cap. Subject: male otter. Age: adult."

"Ahh! There we are. Now you're gonn... ack!" Skveek stiffened. He clawed at his throat. "No." He rasped, "No ... the bivalves ... must ..." He clutched the oyster in his paws. "Must ... bring ... their dawn ... ack." He slid off the top of the turtle onto the floor.

"Time of death in proximity to exposure," she glanced at her watch, "exactly fifteen seconds. This is a potent strain. It was a little melodramatic, though. It's so hard to manufacture a good death on such a short time span."

"We get a Gatling gun! We get a Gatling gun!"

She sighed, still making notes. "Yes. You may take the Gatling gun if you must. It may prove useful." After a short time, she realized things were quiet. Too quiet. "Enfuego, what are you doing?"

She glanced back over her shoulder to find Enfuego reaching one paw into the turtle's shell. "Dinner. What? You expect me to move all this gear back on an empty stomach?"

"Well, hurry up. I still want to hit that warehouse, if we're going to be on time to blow up the dam. Mollusk migration? What an

172

unambitious plan. Once the valley is flooded I can begin to build my army of remote control northern pike. That's when the real fun will begin."

The tarps fell away to expose a twenty-foot-long snapping turtle. On her back, the otter had mounted a Gatling gun.

OH! WHAT A NIGHT!

TYSON WEST

Tyson West was born on the south side of Boston a long time ago. He has worked a wide array jobs in his life, including farmer, contractor, property manager, bartender, and teacher. He moved to Eastern Washington many years ago where he is at home with the coyotes, magpies, bears, and deer in the Ponderosa pine or sagebrush of the Columbia Plateau. A veritable seagull of a writer, he has published poetry of various types, including haiku and related minimalist poems, fibs, rhyming verse, and free verse. He has also published fiction in a variety of genres, including steampunk, suspense, erotica, pulp detective, sci-fi, horror, and western.

He communicates with his totem animals, a Canadian lynx and a rock hyrax, who give him inspiration and ideas for his writing. As a pagan, he believes that although divinity is everywhere or in everything, art creates meaning against the chaos of the indifferent universe.

When John H. Truehart first strolled into the dockside bar at the Coeur d'Alene Resort overlooking the marina with its rows of yachts, houseboats, and huge sail boats bobbing at the docks at the edge of the large inland lake, he smiled at the incongruity of big, expensive boats so far from the ocean, against the backdrop of the Rocky Mountains with their tall fir and pine trees.

Coeur d'Alene Lake is a deep, cold lake, and the resort on its north shore had been a popular destination for wealthy Californians seeking anonymity and the company of their own kind. It counted many movie stars and sports figures among its guests, as well as other celebrities and billionaires. John, at first, appeared to be one of those handsome fox movie stars. With his graying temples against his red fur and bush tail, he dressed in a dapper manner in expensive but discrete casual clothes. These were, however, the foundation of his appearance that he capped off with a bit of bling. He wore several large gold rings, including one with a five-carat diamond, and a heavy gold chain around his neck

175

against his furry chest. With his excellent manners and upper class accent, he appeared to be a fox of substance with a hint of the rebel.

He made no attempt to draw attention to himself, but sat in a corner after ordering an expensive scotch whiskey. The waiter, Jimmy Strong, noticed John right away. Jimmy was a hardworking skunk who waited tables in both the formal restaurant and the more casual grilles at the resort. He was covering a shift in the bar for Luella, a hare who'd fallen sick unexpectedly. Jimmy, suffering the slurs and jibes of less redolent species, was alert to each animal around him, moreso than the wealthy patrons who strutted in expecting to be waited on paw and hoof and who paid heed only to their own. John, careful to order expensive scotch, paid for his drink with a C note from his massive wallet bursting with cash.

As he tossed the hundred-dollar bill to pay for the twenty-dollar drink, John displayed to Jimmy the bills in his fat wallet which all seemed to be hundred dollar bills. Jimmy immediately took note of John, but he also noticed John was watching him with more care than the average wealthy patron.

John smiled, "I've been here for about an hour looking at the beautiful mountains and the boats, observing the help and patrons. You seem to be a skunk who's on the ball."

Jimmy nodded. "Thank you, sir. I do my best to make sure every one of our guests has a pleasant stay."

"I'm up here doing some business. I just sold a high tech startup company, and I'm looking for investors. As a waiter, young skunk, you, I'm sure, have a better idea of folks that might make sense to make my acquaintance."

Jimmy, in his late thirties, hardly considered himself young. Warily, he put on his best submissive smile. "Sir, I do my best to try to understand who our guests are, and how best to attend to their needs."

"I'd like to talk to you in private, if I can. I realize you're busy."

"Thank you, sir, for your understanding. I will be on my break in about twenty minutes, and I can meet you over by the smoking area. We can go a little ways and talk in private if you wish, sir."

"I certainly would like to do so."

Jimmy noticed that John was not a heavy drinker. The fox had ordered a water as well, and was discretely watering his drink to look like he was drinking more.

He nodded to Priscilla, the raccoon who was tending the bar. "I'm going to be heading out on break here pretty soon. Do you think you've got everything covered for now?"

"Just do one quick round of the tables, honey, and let me know if everybody's got what they need."

"Glad to do that for ya."

Jimmy walked out onto the outdoor portion of the bar. He asked a rather stately looking grizzly bear if she'd like to have her wine cooler refreshed. Next to her, her niece, a slender mink who was wearing shorts and a tank top that showed off a lot of her smooth twenty-two-year-old fur, was drinking a non-alcoholic lemonade.

"I just want to check with you ladies to see if there is anything else I can get you."

"Yes," Brunhilda the bear mentioned casually. "I noticed that rather dapper looking fox in the corner. I wonder if he's attached."

"I'll be glad to find out, ma'am."

"Yes, you can bring me another wine cooler, but I think Honey is fine with her lemonade."

Honey grinned. She had a beautiful smile. They had arrived just yesterday, and Jimmy still didn't know what to make of them. They both dressed very well, and appeared to be at the resort simply relaxing. He figured that Honey was the niece of the older lady, and Brunhilda mentioned something about vacation and getting Honey away from a boyfriend the older woman didn't care for.

Jimmy brought her the cooler. She paid and gave him a dollar tip.

He brought the funds back to the bar, and handed the tip to Priscilla to go in the tip jar and the payment for the drink to go into the till.

"For a grizzly as wealthy as she claims," Priscilla grinned, "she sure is not a very big tipper."

Jimmy laughed. "She tips like a lot of rich ladies. You got to take them as they come. I'll be back in about fifteen," Jimmy muttered as he turned to leave for his break.

Jimmy walked to the smoking area. Sure enough, John lingered near the boats, making it seem as if he weren't waiting at all.

Jimmy said, "How can I help you, sir?"

"Let's go down to the dock and talk where we won't be disturbed."

They went beside a doorway, and John held out his hand. "Pleased to meet you, Jimmy. I am John H. Trueheart. I'm here for a week or so, and I'm trying to relax after selling my latest business for a billion dollars."

Jimmy showed absolutely no sign of any emotion on his face.

John thought, "This guy would be a hell of a poker player."

Jimmy spoke deliberately, 'That's wonderful to hear, sir. Congratulations."

John reached into his pocket and pulled out his massive wallet. He peeled off five hundred-dollar bills and handed them to Jimmy. "I need somebody to be my eyes and ears while I'm here and to help me with things from time to time. I was wondering if you might be my special helper."

As the bills touched his paw Jimmy responded, "So long as no criminal charges come my direction, I'm perfectly glad to make your stay as pleasant as I can."

"Good, good. And if everything works out well," John smiled, "there'll be another tip for you when I leave."

Jimmy bowed his head slightly, "I will do my best to see that all your needs are met."

"First thing I need, is to satisfy my curiosity. I'm looking for new investors for my newest venture. Do you know of any folks here that have mentioned that they may be interested in investing some money, or talk of it at all, and have the wealth you think to make the investments?"

Jimmy looked down at John's shoes. John was wearing two-thousand-dollar Italian loafers. Jimmy thought, *Whether he's the real thing or not, he sure knows how to play the part.*

"I was speaking with a charming lady from La Jolla, California who's here with her very charming niece."

"That would be the grizzly bear sitting on the deck with the young mink."

"Yes," Jimmy said. "She was talking with a friend about what poor returns they're getting on their investments. Her niece appears to be a little bored, but she wants to spend time with the pups her own age. She seems very restless. And by the way, Brunhilda did ask me to make inquiries as to whether or not you are attached."

"Ah? Of course, of course. I am very much unattached and very much non-committed."

"With your permission, sir, I will relay that information to her."

Jimmy very quickly and discretely pocketed the five hundred dollars, then gave John the lowdown on the various guests and their standings and stations.

John spent the next couple of days working carefully to ingratiate himself with the guests. John took boat trips and played golf. With his genial personality, John made acquaintances of just about any guest who had any resources who were staying at the resort.

Soon after he probed the denizens of the marina, bar, and golf course, John decided to invite Brunhilda to go sailing. Not being much of a sailor himself and without a boat, he talked to Jimmy about how to handle the situation.

"We got lots of sailboats for hire, but you need a good man who knows how to keep his mouth shut and give you your privacy and knows how not to run aground. I recommend Will Johnson, a quick young marmot who can handle a boat and knows how to stay silent."

"Sounds good to me," John asserted. He was disappointed so far. He thought by now he would be able to find someone he could get close to and pry some funds from. Brunhilda looked like his best chance.

The other guests turned out to be pretty savvy business animals. They asked John telling questions, but kept him at arm's length when he mentioned business. However, they enjoyed drinking with him as well as playing golf and boating, especially when John bought the drinks.

That evening, John sat observing Brunhilda and Honey from afar. He was waving at some of his newfound friends, and joking with them as they passed his table.

He strolled slowly to the big window overlooking the marina. As he walked past Brunhilda's table, Honey was busy texting. She was wearing a short skirt and short sleeved top that showed off the sleek, glistening fur of her legs and her arms.

John grinned as he thought to himself, *W. C. Fields once said, 'Women are like elephants. They're fun to look at but I wouldn't want to own one'.*

He enjoyed watching Honey as she was frantically texting someone. Suddenly, as he walked by, the phone slipped out of her hands and fell onto the floor in front of him.

John reached down automatically and picked up the phone. He handed it to Honey with his best elegant smile.

"Oh, thank you, sir," she smiled, leaning forward showing her cleavage.

My, what a cute girl, he thought.

"Oh, sir," Honey asked, "please, will you come sit with us?

"Thank you."

"Are you from California?"

John wondered why she was asking him such a question so warmly.

179

He wondered where this was leading.

"Why, yes. I'm from San Jose. I'm in the high tech business."

"My goodness," Honey smiled. "You must have a lot of money."

"Well, I've done all right," John demurred.

"Please sir, maybe you can help us," Brunhilda turned to him. "Would you care to have dinner with us?"

"I could ask the waiter to move everything over here as well."

"We'd really appreciate your company."

"*Enchanté*," John replied with a slight bow.

He crooked his finger toward Jimmy, who was waiting tables, and asked him about his moving to their table.

Jimmy with an absolute straight face, nodded. "I'll be glad to get your things moved."

John sat down next to Brunhilda, and she reached over and put her paw on his arm.

"You don't know how glad I am to find somebody here like you. I just don't know how to get a better return on my money. My husband died leaving me millions of dollars, but when you're down to your last hundred million dollars, you kind of wonder if you could do better."

John nodded wisely. "Of course, you can do better, ma'am. I did that well when I sold my special app 'Claw and Talon' to Furbook."

"Why, yes, Honey uses that app all the time. But I thought that Preston Badger was behind that app."

"He had a few silent partners, and I was one of them. Please, however, don't spread that around. I only share it with my closest friends."

"Of course," Brunhilda smiled, "you must be a very clever fox."

"I've taken my chances, and I've had my share of success."

John focused on Brunhilda.

However, as he focused on Brunhilda, he noticed Honey was not going back to her texting but hanging on his every word. It made him uneasy, that such a young attractive mink would pay attention to him. He didn't want her to notice as he was working. Suddenly, the idea that she may be interested in him worried him. He preferred not to have a tangle of such feelings pop up. She was so beautiful.

They shared a delightful dinner, which John paid for out of his fat wallet.

"It's been such a wonderful time with you two ladies. Would you like to go sailing with me tomorrow? I miss my yacht down in San Jose so much that I had hired a sailboat for tomorrow to explore this beautiful lake. You're welcome to join me?" he asked, looking suggestively into Brunhilda's hard eyes.

She radiated a lovely smile, "Why, of course. Perhaps, we can talk more of investments. I really would appreciate your help."

John turned to Honey, who had been watching him, as she replied, "I'd love to come along."

John was a little disappointed that Honey would be along, but perhaps she would be focused more on the water, or the young marmot who was their guide, than on his coaxing her aunt to trust him with some of her funds.

The next morning, John was impeccably dressed in his yachting outfit, including worn boating shoes he had bought at a thrift store. New shoes would have looked too fake. It was a beautiful day, and he was glad to see Will, a muscular young marmot, who looked good with his shirt off. Perhaps he would distract Honey, while John poured his attention on Brunhilda.

To his surprise, Honey strutted up to the dock wearing daisy dukes and a soft cotton halter top covering her minimal string bikini.

John smiled. He would certainly enjoy watching Honey, but hoped that Will would absorb her attention. As she climbed over from the dock, Honey stretched her long legs onto the sailboat. John noticed Will held out his hand and was attentively helping her onboard.

Good, John thought, *I can get her out of my fur.*

John in turn helped pull Brunhilda's bulk aboard, then escorted her safely to the cockpit of the boat.

"You've got to be careful," John shepherded, "to keep your head down. If the wind shifts, the sails may shift. Sailing has always been a passion of mine. This boat is a little smaller than my sixty-footer, but the principles are the same."

"What happens if the wind doesn't blow?" Brunhilda asked innocently.

"That's why we have an auxiliary motor."

"I'm not so familiar with this lake, so I'm glad we're having Will come along."

"I hope we can sail the entire length of the lake."

John pulled out a chilled bottle of sauterne and glasses for the two of them as well as snacks, then went to work.

"Such an attractive widow as you, I wonder why some man hasn't come and swept you off your feet."

Brunhilda giggled, "Maybe it's just that I haven't met the right man that I feel comfortable with."

They caught a light breeze that moved them slowly southward. Will was expertly tacking the boat, and Honey had gone to the front deck where she had taken off her cutoffs and tank top, and lay sunning herself in the slightly cool breeze. John noticed her nipples popped up pleasantly. The resort faded away smaller and smaller astern.

John felt a warmth as he sipped the glass of wine. He had Brunhilda right where he wanted her—alone and comfortable and asking him about investments.

"No, no. I would not think of letting you invest in anything that I do. I feel that they are risky investments, and although the rewards, as I've shown, can be very great, it's not the kind of investment we would want to encourage widows and orphans to involve themselves in."

"Still," Brunhilda persisted, "I've got to do something to get something better. Don't you have something you could help me with?" she asked, reaching out her paw to hold his.

"Well, perhaps there is something," John said hesitantly.

Suddenly, walking along and holding on carefully, Honey appeared from the front deck, and sat right beside John. Although John enjoyed looking at her grace, she couldn't have picked a worse time.

"Do you think I could have a glass of wine," Honey asked as she meekly batted her eyelids.

John turned his eyes toward Brunhilda. "Why of course, Honey. You're old enough to drink. You've had wine before."

John gallantly poured a glass of sauterne and handed it to her. He caught her musky scent. She might be in season.

"Thank you," she said, as she took the glass from John's paw, touching his paw with hers for a few seconds longer than John thought appropriate.

"Isn't it beautiful out here," she whispered.

"Yes. Maybe you could help Will with the sailing. Have you ever been sailing before?"

"No. I was hoping you could teach me as a seasoned old salt."

"I'd love to, but I want to make sure your aunt is comfortable."

Brunhilda puffed up. "Why thank you, John. After you finish your wine, dear, why don't you go to Will and see what you can learn."

Honey took a sip from her glass, with her big, dark eyes open innocently, admiring John, "I'll be glad to help how I can. I just was hoping I could talk to John some more. I appreciate his wise advice."

Brunhilda puffed, "And so do I, but Honey, sometimes we have to

182

be alone."

Brunhilda and John huddled the rest of the afternoon, and concluded with her expressing an intent to invest five million dollars in his latest venture.

John nodded his head, tentatively, very tentatively, to give his reluctant consent. Inside, he excitedly thought this could be the score of his lifetime.

"Which room are you staying in?" Brunhilda asked innocently.

"Why the Admiral Suite upstairs. And which room are you staying in?" he asked Brunhilda.

"Why, we're on the fourth floor in the Ensign Suite."

"Oh," he said, "perhaps we can get together and visit." He smiled at Brunhilda as he helped her and Honey disembark.

"Perhaps," she said. "I do need to talk to my banker."

"Certainly," John delivered his lines. "And you can wire the funds to my account. We're taking investments right now, and I'd hate for the window to close if you are willing to take this chance. I am not encouraging you, but I feel an obligation to help."

Honey, with her cutoffs and tank top on again, and a big sun hat, with her tiny, delicate hind paws in flip flops, smiled. "I don't know what you're doing, Auntie, but I'm sure John wouldn't lead us astray."

John smiled confidently and strode calmly across the dock, as he said goodbye to the two ladies. His first thought was to find Jimmy as quickly as possible.

Jimmy was waiting tables at the dockside bar. John signaled, "Can I see you at your first break?"

"Why certainly," Jimmy nodded. "Meet me at the usual place."

John had been staying in a sleazy motel several blocks away from the resort, and he was afraid Brunhilda would discover his incorrect representations of his quarters. "I have a problem. I need to borrow the Admiral Suite for a few hours."

"You're lucky," Jimmy smiled. "It's five thousand dollars a night. Why don't I make arrangements for you? I know it's vacant. They keep us help apprised, and there ain't nobody there tonight."

"Do you think you can get me in for a few hours tonight?"

"You mean sneak you in? I might be able to do that. But it may require an extra tip for the desk clerk. And you better damn well not make any mess, and you better damn well not stay there all night."

"That's fine," he said, "I just want to be there for after hours later this evening. I might be having an elderly bear visit me for a night cap.

183

And I will, by the way, fold the bed back and leave everything as if nobody was there."

"As long as you don't get us in trouble, we're quite happy to accommodate you."

John pulled out his enormous wallet and handed to Jimmy a couple of C notes. "Here's a tip for you for the extra help. And here's one for your friend."

"He'll meet you there in about an hour out in front of the suite."

John met a bouncy, eager chipmunk who used his master pass card to get into the room. "Here's a card, when you're done give it back to Jimmy. I didn't have nothing to do with this. We also arranged to have the cameras in the hall turned off while you get in there. Once you're in, stay in. I understand a lady may be coming by to see you later. Please text me at this number, and we'll shut the cameras off for a few minutes while she shows up."

"You got it," John sighed. "Thanks for the help."

John immediately entered the suite, carrying his suitcase. He hung some expensive suits in the closet and put some of his expensive shirts in the drawers. He had brought in a bottle of cheaper wine which he poured into an empty bottle of expensive wine and a couple of glasses so that it looked as if room service had been there.

He turned on the light discreetly, and went to the balcony where he sat. A text came in from Brunhilda's phone.

"I'll be up to see you in a few minutes."

John was relieved. It looked like the money he had been shelling out would be paying off. He just hoped the portly bear would not try to get physical.

He texted the chipmunk to have the cameras shut off in the next few minutes. He heard a soft knock at the door.

Wearing a smoking jacket, John was prepared to do what he needed to do to seal the deal and persuade Brunhilda to part with her funds. This could be his biggest payday yet.

John was shocked. In a soft silk dress that came just above her knees, stood Honey, looking soft, frail, and vulnerable.

"Hi," she whispered suggestively; "can I come in?"

To his credit and as a testament to his self-control, John kept a polite, smiling, and welcoming look on his face, in spite of his great disappointment. "Why of course, young mustalid, I always enjoy visiting with a charming mink such as yourself."

She sauntered in very softly, flaunting her dress and form. After he shut the door, she held his paw, then came over, and put her arms around him. John was completely shocked as he inhaled her arousing scent. She flicked his big bushy tail with her sleek delicate one.

Such a young beautiful mink like this coming on to him was totally baffling. He had enough sense not to reject her outright. He put his arms around her and hugged back in a fatherly way.

"It's always lovely to be greeting a young lady with a hug."

Just an inch shorter than he, she brought her lips up against his muzzle, and she kissed him passionately, though not thrusting her tongue between his lips. After she finished, he was quite overwhelmed but still grasping firmly at his self-control.

"I'm flattered, of course, that you would be paying such attention to such an old man as I. I'm wondering if you are aware of how old I am."

"I'm a lot wiser than I look, and I know what I want. Can I have a glass of wine?"

"Why, of course."

He poured her a glass of white wine from the expensive-looking bottle, and poured himself a glass. When she wasn't looking, he watered his. They sat down together at the sofa. She moved her left leg to touch the side of his right one.

"Let's go out on the balcony," he suggested, "and drink our wine there looking at the lake and the marina."

"Sure," she whispered running her tongue along her lips.

"I thought your aunt was going to be coming to see me," John spoke. "I am pleasantly surprised to see you."

"My aunt takes everything away from me, and she doesn't think I know what I'm doing. I've always had this thing for older men, and especially ones like you, that are wise with the world. She turned in early after our boat trip. She is tired. I borrowed her phone to text you."

John was worried. Honey was definitely wiser than he thought. Living on his wits all of his life, and on the confidence of strangers, he'd done well. He had also avoided the traps set by female wiles.

Suddenly, much to his surprise, he felt an overwhelming feeling of care for this mink. He wanted to shelter her. He wanted to protect her. His plans for a big score started to fade. Honey was younger, but he was not old yet. With his charming manners and wits, he was sure he could make it as a legitimate businessman. He was at least as ethical as a used car dealer. There'd be other Brunhildas in the future, but this was something he needed to do. He would take care of this fragile child. Who knows how long it may last or where it would lead?

"Just a second," she smiled, "I need to go to the lady's room and freshen up."

He picked up his wine and hers.

She went to the bathroom and met him on the dark balcony a few minutes later. She sat down and reached over to pick her glass of wine. She put it next to his. She reached over to hold John's paw and pulled her chair next to his. Her scent started to arouse him.

"Look," she said, "what's that light there down the lake?"

John looked down, and it appeared there was a speedboat moving up the lake.

"Why, just a speedboat," he said and reached over and picked up his glass of wine.

"I don't know if you know how long I've felt this way," she said.

"I'd really like to get a chance to know you a lot better."

"Me too, Johnny. How long have you been in business?"

"Years," he said. "Some of the businesses I've worked in have worked out, and some haven't."

She talked about her life and feelings and relationship with Brunhilda and Brunhilda's great wealth. John felt excited, but as the moon rose over the lake, he tried to reconcile how he could handle making love to the niece and keep Brunhilda from exploding with anger.

Maybe this mink would be the one for him. So much of his life was living on chance. Chance perhaps was bringing him to love.

No, he realized as he looked over the lake. He was a con fox. He could offer her nothing but moving from place to place. Yet still, could he have a night that he'd never forget? Would he destroy her trust if he made love to her and they parted forever? He had never before in his life of risk and calculation weathered such a storm of emotion.

"Let's go inside," she spoke in a lowered suggestive voice, "and get comfortable. I've finished my wine; why don't you finish yours and let's go inside to see where this magical evening leads us?"

John tossed down the rest of his wine. They walked in together holding paws. She squeezed his paw lightly in hers and led him to the sofa in the suite.

He wondered what it would feel like as he watched and helped her take off that beautiful dress and see her long thin body. Seeing her in the bikini had already been a taste of what he hoped he could experience. Tonight would be an evening he would never forget. Oh! What a night!

Jimmy was shaking him.

"What …What …?" John muttered over and over. John was having trouble waking up. He was groggy and had a headache.

As John shook his head hoping to shake out the cobwebs, Jimmy in a low worried voice whispered, "We gotta get you the hell out of here. It's two in the morning. You said you would be out of here by midnight?"

"What…what…" John shook his head.

"Somebody slipped you a mickey," Jimmy stated matter-of-factly. "I've got your stuff packed up. Let's get you gone. Where can I take you?"

"Over to the Paul Bunyan Motel, Room 25, here's the key."

"You got the card for this room?"

"Here it is," he said and reached down to his wallet pocket. The room card was there but his wallet was gone. He looked at his fingers. His rings were gone from his fingers and the big gold necklace was gone as well.

Groggy though he was, he recognized immediately what had happened. "The little mink rolled me. Where's Brunhilda Burns?"

"They left this evening. Got in a car and left saying they were going to Spokane for an early morning flight to California"

"Jimmy, I appreciate everything you've done."

"Well, I sure hope you appreciate it enough that you don't forget to tip me when you leave."

"I'd love to do that, but my wallet's missing. Let me get my stash in my money belt." John took off his belt and unzipped it on the inside. His eyes opened wide with admiration.

"She is really good. She found my money belt and pulled out all of the stash I keep here. I am afraid, my good man, that this is a bad day for you, too."

"Not as bad as it could be. I wondered why Honey tipped me $100 when she left. Let me drive you to your motel room so we can get the hall cameras on again."

When they arrived at John's room, John got into his secret stash in the false wall in his suitcase, and handed Jimmy five hundred-dollar bills.

"It looks like you made more on this caper than I did. We don't need to say nothing about any of this to anyone, do we?"

"No, sir," Jimmy smiled. "It's been a pleasure knowing you."

John grinned. "A pleasure knowing you. I consider you my best skunk."

After he and Jimmy shook paws, John was grateful to be alone. He needed to sort out his feelings. He filled a water glass with ice and pulled out his bottle of Old Overholt rye whiskey that he kept for serious occasions.

He took a sip, and his calculating mind took a careful inventory of his feelings. He was not angry or hurt. He felt nothing but the deepest admiration for the sleek mink. She completely bamboozled him and had done, in John's professional opinion, an elegant job.

She hadn't gotten much. He had won most of the bling in poker games. His fat wallet was mostly counterfeit money that he never passed. He had a few thousand dollars of real bengies on either side of his huge wad of counterfeit C-notes. He was worried poor Honey might get into some serious federal trouble if she tried to pass the bogus bills. He'd met female grifters before, and he'd never been fooled. None was as slick as Honey. What she took from him in money and bling was nothing he couldn't replace in an all-night poker game if the cards fell right.

He took a long sip of rye, and let it trickle around his tongue. Then he laid back and looked at the ceiling.

So, it found him at last...the predator that had been stalking him since he was a pup...the predator he managed to elude by his speed and wits.

He stood up and carefully stepped to the bathroom mirror to look at his tired and rumpled fur and graying ears. He was trapped. He grinned. He was not going to give up on Honey. He would hunt her down to see how she felt. If she gave him a chance, he could court her. If she said no, he had nothing to lose but a little time. Oh! What a night! For the first time in his shucking and jiving life, love had caught up to John.

John, careful to order expensive scotch, paid for his drink with a C note from his massive wallet bursting with cash.

MORAL FOR DOGS

MAGGIE VENESS

Maggie Veness realized a while back that fiction was easier to live with than fact. People do drugs, lie, die, go bonkers, and make mistakes. Look no further than your own family. All that craziness and angst needs an escape-route. Her stories get to the mad heart of things, which isn't always comfortable. From flash to novella length—the **vast majority print-published—***Maggie's* **work has appeared in several countries in a range of eclectic literary journals and anthologies. She lives in a gorgeous seaside town in New South Wales, Australia.**

Dog spots Fish when out sniffing along local wharf. Fish has most attractive scales Dog has ever seen. Dog tries to attract Fish's attention by moon-walking on back legs and barking melody of "Yellow Submarine," but showing off only rubs Fish's scales wrong way. Fish swims off.

Dog is inconsolable. Wanders streets for two weeks, howling, chewing grass, and hurling. As last resort, checks into Lost Dog's Shelter. One night, Snake slithers into Dog's cage and sheds skin. Ooo-la-lahh!

Dog and Snake shack up. Snake soon delivers eight long, thin snuppies with perfect carpet-patterned hair. Everyone loves cute snuppies. When snuppies reach six weeks old Dog places adorable photo in newspaper hoping each will go to wonderful home.

Fish sees ad. Wants cute snuppy. Goes to address.

Snake is out shopping for juicy rats when Fish knocks on door. Dog can't believe eyes. Licks Fish up right way this time. Fish gets excited and lays roe. When Snake arrives home early Fish must jump into toilet and swim under city all way back to ocean. Dog gobbles roe to hide evidence.

Dog's fish-breath makes Snake suspicious. Many fights result.

After last snuppy goes to good home, Dog leaves Snake and moves to beach suburb. Night after night, week after week, month after month, Dog sits on wharf staring out to sea howling theme song from *Titanic*.

Mob of crazed beach suburb residents stalk and kill Celine Dion.

Moral of story: If you leave toilet seat up, you may never see girlfriend again.

If you leave toilet seat up, you may never see girlfriend again.

BROADSTRIPE, VIRGINIA SMELLS LIKE SKUNK

SKUNKBOMB

Skunkbomb lives in McLean, Virginia with his family. When he isn't working an office job in D.C., reading, or writing, he enjoys going to the movies, watching Game Grumps and Smosh, and playing Mario Kart. *He wishes to go skiing or to an amusement park soon. Writing humor is difficult, and Skunkbomb appreciates and respects those who do it well. He will write more stories set in Broadstripe, Virginia, and aims to add a touch of humor into most, if not all, of his stories, no matter what genre. Other anthologies with his writing include* ROAR 7, FANG 7, *and* FANG 8. *He can be found on Furaffinity as Skunkbomb123 and on Twitter and @Skunkbomb123. Skunkbomb would like to thank his writing group for all the feedback he received on this story.*

Skunks had taken over Broadstripe, Virginia. When I woke up each morning, I would take a deep whiff of country air and smell their stink. You'd have to be blind not to catch sight of those white-striped critters in town. When I ordered a meal at the diner, I would sometimes get a stray black or white strand of fur on my plate. God had bestowed unto me, the noble bloodhound, a nose that could sniff out anything, including the truth. Skunks ruled the town, and dagnabbit, I was going to prove it.

Hubert, my grand-nephew, walked in the door sometime past eleven smelling of some raccoon he had bedded the night before. He may not hold my same views on what the skunks are doing to this town, but I was doing my best to pass down my knowledge.

"Come see what I've done read," I said, holding the book up.

Hubert glanced at it. "Why do you have a book on building outhouses?"

I chucked it and grabbed the other one. "Go on, have a look." I opened it on the kitchen table. "This here town was founded by an upstanding hound dog by the name of Uriah Grady after the Civil War. Before he ran for mayor, some lowlife named Paul Underhill—P.U., you see; there's your warning flag—asked to join the town, and he brought all his skunk neighbors with him. Look at this picture. It's nothing but them black and white scallywags."

Hubert took a look. "Grand Uncle Vernon, the book's in black and white, and that there's a badger."

I squinted at the picture. "That's open to interpretation. So thanks to the skunk invasion, Underhill beat Grady in the election for mayor and won the right to name the town. I never done see a hound dog win an election for mayor, but there's always a skunk on the ballot. They have to be planning this out. I see them gather together in their homes or their stores. Well, I'm putting a stop to it!"

Hubert picked up his banjo and plopped on the chair in the living room. "In that case, pick up some tomato juice at the general store before you go bothering those skunks."

"That's like folding before the poker game begins, and I've got a hand of all red cards." I grabbed my cane. "But I will be heading to the store anyways. We're out of bread."

It was a beauty of a walk into town. My hip wasn't giving me too much trouble, and there were sheep-like clouds in the sky. It was the calm before the storm.

If I was going to find out about this next meeting of the skunks, I had to go where the skunks were. In the past, I tried visiting their homes, but they were all so rude. It was all, "What are you doing here?" or "It's 10:30 at night" or "Mama says you're an ignoramus." Skunks were always in town, though. All I had to do was follow my old sniffer and keep an ear out for gossip.

I lifted my nose to the wind and sniffed. Skunk. No surprise there, but there was something else. Tomatoes. Wagon wheels in need of some oil pricked at my earholes as I approached the outskirts of town.

The youngest skunk of the Mire family, Theodore—"The odor," you see, bad news written all over him—was pulling a red wagon stocked with crates of tomatoes and cans of tomato juice. Is it not a crime that the Mire family farm, a farm owned by skunks, was the biggest supplier of tomatoes and tomato juice in town? Skunks go around spraying the bejeezus out of honest hound dogs and get richer

194

when we hand over our money so we can deskunk ourselves. If anyone would know about a secret meeting of skunks, it would be the Mire family.

I hustled up and around the skunk and his wagon. "Well, good morning, Theodore."

The skunk stopped. He only had the courtesy to meet my eye for a moment before staring at his feet. "Good morning, sir."

"My, you're getting pretty big," I said, luring him into a sense of security so he could spill his secrets like beans. "How old are you now? 14? 15?"

"11, sir." Theodore grabbed his tail and brushed it with his hand. It was a clever diversionary tactic, that bashfulness of his. How was I supposed to know if he was about to turn around and spray me if he wouldn't let his tail go up?

"11? Well, you're almost old enough for the adult table," I said. Flattery works wonders. Trust me. It works on me every day that ends in a y. "Now, if you were joining your parents for, I don't know, a secret meeting of some sort, where would that be?"

The skunk shrugged. "Gee, if it were a secret, I guess I wouldn't know either, sir."

"But let's say they done told you."

"If they told me, I couldn't tell you, because it's still a secret, and if I tell you a secret Ma and Pa told me, I'd get in trouble."

I crossed my heart. "But you can tell me. Then, it'd be a secret between us and only us."

Theodore scratched his head. "But if you knew I blabbed about one secret, wouldn't that mean I could blab about another secret? I don't think that's a good idea, sir."

"Oh, come on now!" I barked. "Stop running me around the bush and tell me already."

"Leave the boy alone, Vern."

The skunk behind me was broad-shouldered and chomped on a corncob pipe. He glared at me behind a set of glasses, but I wasn't fooled. The skunk had the aim of a sniper. You could say Obadiah Mortimer Mefford was my greatest enemy in town. Well, Obie and I played cards sometimes, and we talk about football, and he gave me a good deal on the nails I needed to fix up my shed, but he was a crafty old skunk. Any time I had the upper hand, he would fight dirty. Dirty and smelly.

Obie knelt by Theodore. "Could you stock those tomatoes on your own today?"

"Yes, sir." Theodore grabbed his wagon and scurried inside the general store.

"I was just on my way in to buy some bread," I said, walking toward the front of the store.

Obie stepped in front of me, and leaned in so I could really smell him. "For Christ sake, Vern. When are you going to leave us skunks alone? We ain't dogs, but dammit, we belong here just as much as you do."

"Well, hey now, I didn't mean you skunks can't live here," I said, backing up and wrinkling my nose.

"It's bad enough you howl about your dumb conspiracies," Obie said, heading back toward his store, "but Theodore's a child."

My tail brushed the inside of my leg. The old stinker was right. "Hey now, we both got ourselves in a tizzy. Look, I'm sorry. How about we make up with a game of checkers?"

The skunk's tail flicked. "If you'll shut your yap about skunks for five minutes."

I was wagging like someone half my age. Kids don't know squat, but Obie may know something about secret skunk meetings.

Obie brought out two stools and the box of checkers, and we set up the board on a stump next to his store. I was a champion checkers player. While I dazzled the skunk with my expert jumping and king-ing, I'd get him to tell me where his secret meeting was.

I moved one of my black pieces. "Beauty of a Saturday, ain't it?"

Obie shrugged and moved one of his red pieces. "I'm not complaining."

I slipped another black piece forward. Quick and decisive was the way to do it so your opponent couldn't think where to go next. "Slow day for you at the shop. Thinking of closing early?"

"Rather not if I can avoid it."

"Ain't you got better things to do on a day like this?" I asked. "Places to be? People to see?" My tail was wagging something fierce. All Obie had to do was make whatever move he had in mind, and then I could jump—

The skunk jumped over two of my pieces.

"Son of a biscuit! How'd you do that?"

Obie chuckled. "You're not watching the board, Vern."

"I am too!" I moved my piece into position to jump him.

"That's one of my red pieces."

I huffed. "My finger slipped, so sue me!"

In all the 63 years of my life, I had not seen such blatant cheating. I wanted to call the sheriff to report a robbery, a theft of any decency the game of checkers had. No matter what strategy I strategized, Obie captured my poor little black pieces with the ruthlessness only the devil would admire.

I yanked at my ears and gnawed my lip. "Sleight of hand? Witchcraft? Divine intervention? Which was it, Obie?"

"You spent more time chatting and belly-aching than looking at the board," Obie said, adjusting his glasses. "How about you take a walk to cool off?"

"Afternoon, Obie!" another skunk said as he walked toward the store. "Hope to see you at the old town barn tonight. 7 o'clock, okay?"

Obie sighed. "Yeah, I'll be there."

After the other skunk went into the shop, I grabbed one of my pieces and slapped it down on Obie's side of the board. "That, my friend, is checkmate."

Obie pinched the bridge of his nose. "Vern, I know you've got some crazy idea cooking in that dinged-up oven you call a head, but I'm asking you politely. Please don't come. You're not invited."

I got up and walked away, swinging my cane. "Oh, don't you worry, my striped friend. You won't be seeing me tonight."

"Vern, you stay away, you hear? And can you at least help me put the pieces back in the box?"

I chuckled on my way out of town. Picking up the pieces was for the loser, and as far as I could see, I came out the victor that time.

I was halfway home before I remembered I forgot to buy bread.

The old town barn was, well, an old barn. Whoever built it never used it, so the town snatched it up and used it for town meetings, parties, and, as I was about to witness with my very two eyes, secret skunk gatherings. I approached the barn from the back, because who can be stealthy going through the front? What was I, an idiot?

The back doors were open just as wide as the front ones, but no one was watching that entrance. I crept—that might be a generous description with my knees—into one of the stalls. If I laid flat on the ground, I could peek under the gap of the stall door.

I didn't need my eyes to tell me who were on the other side of the stall door. There must have been two-dozen skunks in that barn. I wrinkled my nose. They weren't wearing any sort of robes I imagined a secret society would wear, but they had pointed hats. One of them lit a handful of candles at the center of a table. Then, they gathered in a circle and chanted. I wiggled my finger in my ear and flicked away the wax. I couldn't make out a word they were saying. When the chanting ended, the skunk in the middle of the circle blew out the candles, and the lot of striped ninnies clapped. It was obviously an initiation ceremony of some sort.

The newly initiated skunk wandered over to the stalls clutching a box. I held my breath, and not because of the skunk smell. I let out a sigh of relief when the skunk entered the stall next to me, but I kept perfectly still. Even in the dark part of the barn, the bars between the stalls weren't thick. The skunk might not see me if I didn't move. I squinted at the darkness. If the lighting wasn't playing tricks on me, I was sure that was Ethel Wilcox.

Ethel was easy on the eyes, for a skunk. Her fur still looked soft and full, even with the gray coming in. Her stripes weren't stained with the yellowing of old age. Either that, or she washed religiously.

Now, skunks aren't known for their statuesque figures. They're shaped like pears. Ethel though, she had gams. She lifted her leg up onto one of the rungs of the stall dividers and brushed a bit of old hay from her foot. She reached back, groping for the zipper behind her dress.

My tail wagged. "Need some help with that?"

Ethel screamed and bolted out of the stall before I could clap my hands over my big mouth.

Everything would be fine if I could just explain to Ethel that peeking in on her while she was changing was a complete accident. All I had to do was lie that I was here to be inducted into their society. I walked out of the stall.

As hard as it may be to believe, I've been sprayed by a skunk before. It's the closest a hound can get to Hell while still living. I'd smell the stink on me for months afterward.

I had no less than a dozen skunks bent over, dresses hiked up or pants pulled down, all aiming at me.

I cleared my throat. "Hey now wait just a sec—"

The skunks fired.

I buried my clothes in the backyard, got in the tub, and poured the cold tomato juice over my face and down my body. The dried juice was going to be a pain in the neck to pick out of my fur. I held my nose the

198

whole time, partially to try to keep from smelling myself and partially to block out the stinging in my nose.

Hubert, a clothespin clamped on his nose, plucked at his banjo a good fifty feet away on the porch. "Good thing Obie let me buy tomato juice from him at this hour."

I slumped lower into the tub. "Hubert, I done those skunks wrong tonight."

"I think the whole town can smell that," Hubert said. "So, you finally learned your lesson?"

"The Mire family could pay for Theodore to go to college with the money we spend on tomato juice?"

Hubert shook his head. "Maybe, but that ain't the lesson."

I dunked the old scrubbing brush in the tub and washed under my chin. "Ethel's got nice gams?"

"Does she now?" Hubert said, a little chuckle in his voice. "Wait, no, one more try."

"That I'll need to be more careful snooping around skunks." I bolted up, even if my knees and hip complained. "In the memory of Uriah Grady, I owe it to all the hounds in this here town!"

"Dammit, Vernon!" Hubert said, covering his eyes. "Don't stand up in the tub when you're naked!"

I scratched my head. "What kind of lesson is that?"

"The lesson's that you don't go around pissing off skunks!"

"Well, if they weren't so dadgum sensitive—"

Hubert growled and picked up his banjo. "I'm going out drinking. Sleep in the shed for a few nights, you hear? Maybe if you get it through your thick head that there's no skunk conspiracy, I'll buy you a beer." The screen door slammed behind him.

I crouched back into the tub. After pouring another can of tomato juice on myself, I sniffed. I clamped my hand on my nose and howled. Whether I wanted it or not, the air in Broadstripe, Virginia would always smell like skunk.

I cleared my throat. "Hey now wait just a sec—"

A LEGEND IN HIS OWN TIME

FRED PATTEN

Fred Patten (1940-current) joined the Los Angeles Science Fantasy Society in 1960 while in college and has been an active s-f & fantasy fan ever since. He began writing for and publishing fanzines in 1961 (see zinewiki.com/Salamander), and has written over a thousand reviews of anthropomorphic literature since 1962, irregularly for s-f fanzines in the 1960s, 1970s, and 1980s; for Yarf! *from 1990 to 2003, for* Claw & Quill *in 2004 to 2005, for* Anthro *from 2005 to 2008, for* Renard's Menagerie *in 2008, for* Flayrah *from 2011 to 2014, and for* Dogpatch Press *since 2014. He has written three nonfiction books and edited thirteen anthologies of furry fiction. He founded the Ursa Major Awards and has been on its administrative Anthropomorphic Literature and Arts Association since 2001. He is a member of the Furry Writers' Guild and the Furry Hall of Fame. He co-founded Japanese anime fandom in 1977, and was awarded the Comic-Con's Inkpot Award in 1980 for helping to introduce anime to America. He wrote a weekly column on animation,* Funny Animals and More, *for Jerry Beck's Cartoon Research from 2013 to 2017. A stroke in 2005 has left him hospitalized, from which he carries on his fanac.*

If there was such a thing as an isolated planet, Purity was it. Purity was the only inhabitable world of an out-of-the-way stellar system. It had been settled over a thousand years before (going by the humans' calendar, based upon that of their ancient Earth homeworld) by a faction of humans who didn't believe in mixing socially with other intelligent species, and were willing to undergo real isolation to live their beliefs. Purity was outside the human-settled part of interstellar civilization, in the midst of "alien"-inhabited space. Purity had become more accepting of non-human peoples over the centuries, but it was still satisfied to live mostly isolated and self-sufficient.

Still, it did have some contact with the rest of the galaxy. And the news of how the human-sized, shaggy otteroid *ch'rr'pts'* merchant ship

Victory of Dobleth had helped in the merger of humanity's two greatest space empires a year previously, had won the *Dobleth* a favorable reputation with the Puritan government. The *Dobleth*'s Captain *Brr'ttcheerpt* (Bucky to humans, but don't call him that to his face) didn't especially care for that species, but he didn't dislike them (more than usual), and he was quick to take commercial advantage of the *Dobleth*'s reputation. Thus, the *Victory of Dobleth* had been operating mostly in human space recently, and was now approaching Purity, as one of the rare non-human ships to be granted landing permission there, to deliver a routine cargo for an inflated fee.

The *Victory of Dobleth* touched down at the small spaceport of Virtue, Purity's largest city, and switched off its engines. Captain Bucky was mainly concerned with delivering his cargo, but he did hope to pick up some new cargo to make the return trip profitable. Unfortunately, Purity, being self-sufficient, didn't have much to export. While Captain Bucky searched, he gave the *Dobleth*'s crew shore leave in Virtue. The humans in Virtue were aware from their newscasts that they were being visited by those *ch'rr'pt* who had aided the human space empires to unite, so there were no worries about the Puritans' traditional antipathy to non-humans.

Most of the crew headed for Virtue's drinking establishments, but *Rru'gg*, the *Dobleth*'s most junior crewman and the youngest of Bucky's clan out of puberty, set off alone to explore the city. *Rru'gg*, like many *ch'rr'pt* youths, did like the humans and their customs. One major difference between humans and *ch'rr'pt* was that *ch'rr'pt* had thick fur and humans didn't. As a result, the humans wore colorful clothing, which the *ch'rr'pt* couldn't without overheating and getting their fur mussed. They wore just harnesses to hold pockets, writing implements, and the other small necessities of civilization.

Purity was unusually fascinating because its isolation from the rest of human space had encouraged several unique cultural developments. *Rru'gg* had found numerous examples after several hours of looking around. He was not as much interested in the examples themselves as in what he might be able to sell the more portable of them for back in *ch'rr'pt* space. His long-range goal was to prove himself a canny merchant, and to win Captain Bucky's approval.

By the early afternoon, *Rru'gg* had come to a large central square that was filled with a busy outdoor marketplace. In the middle was an ornate fountain, around which human young of various ages were playing. This looked like someplace where he could find something that was small and portable enough to bring back aboard the *Dobleth*. What to get; what to get? Hmmm. All human clothing looked so exotic to the *ch'rr'pt* that there would be little value in bringing Puritan styles all the way home.

Rru'gg was browsing from stall to stall when he became aware of some commotion on the other side of the square. The people around him stopped to stare. The merchant at the stall he was at frowned and stepped out. She was back in a moment, shaking her head. "Some old lady had a seizure and collapsed. She's being rushed to a hospital," she explained to those around her. *Rru'gg* didn't pay much attention at the time.

Rru'gg went on to the next few stalls. He was currently dubiously looking through an adolescent's comic book; a fantasy-adventure about a ghost-hero in old-fashioned clothes who appeared to help people in danger. It was based upon some long-dead Puritan legendary hero who was probably unknown off-planet. Yes, but again, the comic book looked so similar to those fantasy-hero comics commonly available throughout human space that he doubted that it would be worth the trouble to transport home.

Suddenly, he felt a tugging at the fur of his lower left leg. He looked down and saw a tiny human child beaming up at him.

"Doggy!"

He guessed it was a female from the clothes that it wore. It looked so young—barely old enough to toddle—that he assumed its parent must be nearby. But none of the bustling humans walking past the outdoor stall in their busy marketplace looked like they had misplaced one of their young.

"*Big* doggy!" she repeated, giggling.

Rru'gg wasn't sure what to do. He had a pawheld electronic translator that enabled him to talk with the human adults, but he had no experience speaking to their young. He doubted that one this young would be familiar with talking through an artificial device.

"*MY* doggy!" She wrapped both her arms around his leg.

Rru'gg imagined himself to be a dynamic *ch'rr'pt*, a future leader, full of enterprise. It didn't seem right to just shake off the little human and ignore her. He bent down and spoke to her. "Hello, little one. What are you doing here without your parent?"

She appeared to be fascinated by his voice coming through a pawheld translator. "Hi. I'm Alicia. What's your name?"

He paused. She didn't look like she could pronounce the guttural

Rru'gg, even through a translator. "What are good names for a doggy?"

"Rover! You're Rover!" She giggled again and hugged his leg more tightly.

"All right; Rover will take you to your mother. Where is your mother?"

Alicia shook her head vigorously. "Mommy's not here. Where's Suzie? Grandma brought me and Suzie here. Suzie and me are playing while she's shopping."

That was progress of a sort. "Well, where is Grandma shopping? And where is Suzie? What are you doing here by yourself?"

"Suzie ran away, and I'm all alone. She said to stay in the playground 'til she came back. But she's been gone a long time. Can Rover take me to her?"

Rru'gg stood up. This was something for the humans to handle, not him. He called over the busy shopkeeper of the stall he was at. "Excuse me, but there is a little child here who seems to have become lost from her parent. Can you call the appropriate authority?"

The shopkeeper was engaged in a transaction with another customer. He glanced over at the man-sized otteroid that was loosely holding the arm of a happy human child who was hugging its leg with her other arm. It didn't look like anything worth calling the authorities to his stall about. "The authorities don't like to be bothered except for an emergency. Are you having an emergency?"

Was he? *Rru'gg* didn't know whether the situation was an emergency or not. While he paused, the shopkeeper turned back to his other customers, while simultaneously Alicia began to tug at his leg fur. "Where's Suzie? I want Suzie!"

Rru'gg was at a loss. "Maybe Suzie has come back to where she left you. Can you find that place again?"

Without answering, Alicia began to drag *Rru'gg* through the crowded square. The *ch'rr'pt* were rare enough on Purity that *Rru'gg* drew attention, but the Puritans had been assured by TV newscasts that the *ch'rr'pt* were friendly; and the sight of a skinny, furry otteroid being dragged about by a little human girl reassured them that this was nothing to worry about. Alicia led *Rru'gg* to the square's central fountain, where a playground for young humans was set up.

She looked around. "Where's Suzie? You said Suzie was here."

Rru'gg hadn't made any promises, but Alicia was too young to understand the subtlety. And he could use a break. He sat on a bench for adults. "Maybe she will still come. Let's wait for her."

The large furry *ch'rr'pt* became a magnet for the other human children. They slowly gathered around him. Alicia proudly introduced him as...her pet? "This is Rover! He's MY doggy!" The other parents present saw the friendly otteroid youth who was apparently the guardian of a little girl, and relaxed.

Rru'gg let the little humans stroke his fur. A couple clambered into his lap. Several of the other adults produced photographic devices and took pictures and videos of "Rover" being climbed over by little humans. Alicia continued to claim him as "MY Rover." *Rru'gg* considered that if his translator's data banks were correct, Rover was a pretty good name for him. The *Victory of Dobleth* and its crew did rove throughout the galaxy, never making any new planet their permanent home. He and his shaggy crewmates were all rovers.

He suddenly realized that the large stone statue dominating the fountain was of the same ancient Puritan hero that the comic book had featured, and was more realistic. He walked over and studied it more closely. There was a metal plaque. "Georg Bazalgette, 1 A.L.—71 A.L. 'Guide Georg,' the founder of Virtue. The third human born on Purity, and the leader of the first expeditions from Purity's original landing site to create settlements around the planet. He was always there to bring aid to new towns in distress." The statue was of a short-bearded man wearing an explorer's work garb, looking with an "upward and onward" expression, suitable for legendary heroes.

As the afternoon wore on toward evening, the other children and their parents or nurses began to disappear. *Rru'gg* became annoyed that he was wasting his time, but he was more worried about what might happen to Alicia if he just abandoned her. He hadn't been finding anything worth bringing back to the *Dobleth*, anyway. Alicia grew more fractious, becoming visibly worried. "Where's Suzie? Where's Grandma? I want to go home!" *Rru'gg* decided that they had waited long enough. He stopped one of the last human adults present who was about to leave with a small boy. "Excuse me, but I found this young child wandering alone in the marketplace several hours ago. I brought her to this play area where she said that her Grandma had left her, but there is nobody here for her. She is too young to leave here alone. What should I do?"

The matron frowned. "Well—hmm—this really sounds like a matter for the police. They take care of lost children. Should I call them?"

"Yes, please do. I think that it is time for them to take charge of this little one."

A policeman was called, but it wasn't that simple. Alicia, now crying, refused to let go of "Rover." "No! Where's Grandma and Suzie? Rover, find them for me!"

The officer gave up trying to pry Alicia away from *Rru'gg*. "Sir, would you be willing to come with us to the station? The little girl doesn't want you to leave her." So, *Rru'gg* accompanied them to the police station to keep Alicia calm.

Alicia was examined at the police station, and was found not to carry any identification. The police agreed that if she had been abandoned for this long, and that a presumably equally young Suzie was also missing, something was seriously wrong. A lost-child specialist among the police decided to start out by showing Alicia on the TV early evening news and requesting any relative to contact them. Alicia still did not want to let go of *Rru'gg*, and the TV news team agreed that including the exotic otteroid in the news story would make it more than just another help-us-find-this-lost-child's-parents appeal.

That evening, all Virtue saw the tear-streaked little girl hugging her big furry guardian. *Rru'gg* was briefly correctly identified, but Alicia's name for him as Rover was louder and more frequent. Even the human newscasters were addressing him more often as the more easily pronounced (by humans) Rover than as *Rru'gg*.

Rru'gg visored the *Victory of Dobleth*. He was afraid that he had become embroiled in a situation that would get him into trouble, but that he'd better not put off calling the ship any longer. Fortunately, there didn't seem to be anything to worry about. *Akkk'rrchk*, the *Dobleth*'s first mate who took his call, wasn't happy, but he agreed that *Rru'gg* was doing the best possible in an awkward situation. "I'll tell Captain *Brr'ttcheerpt*. For now, keep doing what the human authorities ask you to do. Don't do anything to get yourself or the *Dobleth* into trouble." And so *Rru'gg* continued to appear on TV with little Alicia in his lap. He was identified as Rover, a friendly visiting otter-like alien who had found a lost child and had interrupted his own affairs to get help for her.

A few hours later, the mystery was solved when a frantic mother contacted the police. The old lady who had collapsed in the square earlier in the day had been Alicia's grandmother. She had brought Alicia and her slightly older sister Suzie with her from a nearby town to Virtue on a shopping trip. Suzie had been left to watch over Alicia in the playground while the grandmother shopped. Suzie had been panic-stricken when Grandma collapsed nearby, rushed to her, and had been taken to the hospital with her. Suzie had been old enough to tell the hospital how to call their home, but by then nobody knew where Alicia had been except "back at the playground in Virtue," where she was no longer. The TV newscast had not been shown in Alicia's town, where her worried parents had called the local police. Fortunately, a family friend in Virtue had seen the newscast and had called Alicia's parents. A happy ending ensued. Virtue's newscasts covered Alicia with her parents gratefully thanking *Rru'gg* and the whole crew of the *Dobleth* (trying to look friendly without smiling and showing their sharp teeth).

The only problem was in getting Alicia to let loose of "my Rover." She reluctantly agreed when her parents promised to get her a dog of her very own, "just like Rover." Just before the *Victory of Dobleth* left Purity, it got a home video of Alicia hugging her new Bearded Collie, nearly large enough for her to ride, that had long hair over its eyes and down almost to the ground. The other *ch'rr'pt* thought this was hilarious. *Rru'gg* didn't consider himself nearly *that* shaggy.

A few weeks later, the *Victory of Dobleth* was back in interstellar space, returning to the more thickly-populated parts of the galaxy. Their publicity, which had spread throughout Purity, had made it easy to assemble a new cargo for the return trip. Captain *Brr'ttcheerpt* was actually pleased with *Rru'gg* instead of just indifferent toward him. *Rru'gg*, relieved, had settled back into being the *Dobleth*'s most junior crewman.

Rru'gg was double-checking the fastenings on their latest cargo when he became aware that *Akkk'rrchk* had quietly come over and was staring at him.

"What?"

"Do you know what you've done?"

Rru'gg immediately tried to think of what he could be in trouble over.

"Apparently Purity's planetary government had been having the latest in a series of political debates on whether to join the rest of civilization, when we visited. Your helping that little human female made the difference. The newscasts didn't die down after the *Dobleth* left. Instead, they spread all over Purity. The humans got some of the other photographs and videos of you at that playground and added them, showing the little human children crawling all over you while you were looking confused but trying to be kindly toward them. Some newscasts even called you a giant otter, that Earth animal we resemble, instead of a *ch'rr'pt*. Purity has just voted to join some human space confederation. And it looks like you are going down in Purity's history as Rover, Purity's equivalent of the "Pied Piper," whoever that is."

Akkk'rrchk reached over to shake the stunned *Rru'gg*'s paw in the human custom. "Congratulations on becoming Rover, the human children's friend who comes from outer space to help them when they're in trouble—their latest legendary hero."

"WHAT? But I—that was just one little girl and me! That was just during one afternoon …"

Akkk'rrchk nodded. "That's how it starts with the humans. I researched some of their legendary heroes, going back to their beginnings. It's really very fascinating. There's an ancient one named Herakles or Hercules. Some of their scholars think that he originated as a real man of greater-than-usual strength during their prehistory, who grew through legends after his death. He's one of their legendary demigods today, the son of an almost-as-old god called Zeus.

"Another ancient human named Gautama, a young prince in an insignificant kingdom in a place called India, even evolved into a major human god worshipped in many kingdoms, their Buddha. About a thousand years later, a Buddhist priest in one of those other kingdoms, China, got worried that the Buddhist teachings in China had become corrupted. He wanted to go to India to get authentic teachings, but the king of China wouldn't allow it; so he sneaked out of China and went alone. His journey took seventeen years, and he returned to China with a whole caravan, riding on one of the first elephants seen in China. The same Chinese king who had forbade him to go was so impressed that he welcomed him as a hero and gave him his own Buddhist monastery. But after another thousand years of legends, that priest, Xuán Zàng, had become a comedy-relief supporting character in his own legends, a hapless nobleman protected from ferocious demons on his journey by his three imaginary magical monkey, pig-demon, and sand-demon bodyguards.

"On the other side of the human world, when their North American continent was being settled from their continent of Europe, there were pioneers named Daniel Boone, David Crockett, John Chapman. They became legendary heroes called Dan'l Boone, Davy Crockett, and Johnny Appleseed. The same thing happened in reverse with the humans' legendary villains. A real ruthless warrior prince called Vlad Drakul became in later centuries the legendary Dracula, an immortal monster who drank blood and could transform into a flying animal called a bat."

Akkk'rrchk grinned in the *ch'rr'pt* manner. "I hope that you like being called Rover better than Captain *Brr'ttcheerpt* likes the name Bucky. You can be sure that he's trying to figure out how to best take advantage of this."

He left to return to his first mate's duties. *Rru'gg* remained stunned. The Captain would probably remain in human space just so the *Dobleth* could promote itself as having the one, the only, Rover among its crew. He had thought that becoming "Rover" was only a momentary incident on an isolated planet, and that it would be unknown off Purity and become quickly forgotten. Instead, it now looked like he could expect to be Rover, the Giant Space Otter, the Living Legend, throughout human space (at least) for the rest of his life.

"…The humans got some of the other photographs and videos of you at that playground and added them, showing the little human children crawling all over you while you were looking confused but trying to be kindly toward them."

THE CAT'S MEOW
(*LE MIAULENT DU CHAT*)

LISA PAIS

Growing up Lisa always wanted a pet; the answer was always no. Not easily deterred however, Lisa sought alternative measures to obtain a furry friend, truly convinced that possession would be the most effective form of persuasion. As luck would have it, and much to her classmate's surprise, one of his mice was male. Lisa brought home her first pet. But a cardboard box with air holes is not a proper dwelling, and, if you ever saw The Brady Bunch, *you know what happened. Next came the snake. Not furry of course, but a pet was a pet. Upon learning that snakes subsisted on a diet of mice and bugs, he was set free, back into the yard where he'd been caught. Over the years, a menagerie of small rodents, cats, and dogs were rescued by her and her sister only to become the beloved pets of other people. It wasn't until adulthood that she finally got her very own dog. Lisa still loves animals and lives in coastal New England with her husband and dog, Buddy. She writes speculative fiction and often provides her heroes and heroines with an animal sidekick. Her current WIP is a YA fantasy about a girl with the ability to communicate with dogs. She has also completed YA fantasy (time travel) for which she is seeking representation. Some of her short stories can be found online at www.BewilderingStories.com and* Nebula Rift *digital magazine.*

Kitty Pierre, a white and orange tabby, rolled over onto his back like some enraptured heroine on the cover of a romance novel. One insouciant paw was strewn across his furry little feline face. He'd been lounging atop the back of the couch staring out the window, but had quickly rearranged himself into a more dramatic pose as soon as Scruffy, the dog, wandered into the room. Kitty Pierre loved an audience. He also fancied himself French and would affect what he considered an authentic Parisian accent. It sounded a lot like Lumière from Disney's *Beauty and the Beast*, though his cattitude was more in line with John Malkovich from *Dangerous Liaisons*.

Kitty Pierre sighed loudly. "Nevair in my entire lives 'ave I *bean* SO bored. Mon dieu! I hav still got another eight to go! 'ow am I to bear eet?"

"What do you mean? There's loads of stuff to do," Scruffy said, pausing momentarily from his present and, in Kitty's opinion, favorite occupation.

"One can only lick oneself for so long," he uttered disdainfully. Though unable to fight a sudden and overwhelming urge to do the same, he quickly lapped a spot on his own backside.

Kitty finished only to find Scruffy eyeing him with amusement. Kitty aimed his most haughty feline glare at the aptly named terrier, and then turned away. Scruffy went back to business. *Peasant,* thought Kitty.

"Why don't you go out and climb something?" Scruffy suggested. Wet snores came from the *other* one.

"Tis too cold."

Torturing small rodents, chasing birds—he'd done it all before. *Kitten stuff.* He eyed the curtains, but even that didn't arouse him. *Are my claws asleep?* He sighed heavily wondering how he might get himself out of this slump.

Scruffy's ears perked up, and Pugs awoke. Scruffy and Pugs ran to the door, tails wagging. Somehow, they always knew of an arrival before Kitty. This vexed him to no end. *Needy beasts.*

The door opened, and in walked the Bipeds, bringing with them a cold wind, a little snow and a flurry of energy and chatter equally matched by the eager greeting of Scruffy and Pugs. The quiet Saturday afternoon was broken. This should have made Kitty happy, but somehow he felt even more annoyed and depressed.

The kitchen buzzed with excitement. The biggest of the hairless Sasquatches carried a large square something. He set it down with a thud and a groan.

"Open the box, daddy," cried the smallest squatchlet.

Box? What is box?

Curious, Kitty Pierre decided it might be time to investigate. The outside of the box, which was plain white, provided no clue as to its contents. He tried sniffing, but it was devoid of any smell that would tell him what might be contained within. Kitty wound himself around the legs of the Bipeds, but he was quickly shooed aside. Not one to give up easily, however, he tried again. This time, he was picked up and dumped unceremoniously into the other room along with Scruffy and Pugs.

"Stay out," the squatchlet commanded. Adding insult to injury, the door was shut in his face. After a while, the outer door was reopened, and the dogs were led outside. Kitty Pierre followed.

Bad move. Ice and dirt collected between the creases of his paw pads, and wet snowflakes caught in his whiskers. But Kitty decided he'd take advantage of the situation to do some reconnaissance. He hopped up onto the window sill to see what all the fuss was about. The Bipeds blocked his view. *Foiled.*

Just then the boys barked, a signal to the hairless ones to open the door and let them in. Kitty ran in ahead but was quickly stopped in his tracks.

"What eez zat?" Kitty Pierre purred. "I 'ave never seen anything so wonderful."

Day two, Kitty spent all morning and afternoon staring into the box the Bipeds called TANK.

It was alluring. "Ooh, it eez a kaleidoscope of color," Kitty squealed in delight. "See how they catch the light? They shimmer like many jewels."

Scruffy looked up at the tank. "I don't get it."

"I am enraptured. Watch as they glide silently through space, dancing to a symphony that only they can hear." Kitty made kissing noises just as Pugs walked into the room.

"Been hittin' the catnip pretty hard, eh Pierre?" Pugs said and grinned at Scruffy.

"*Don'* be reedeeculous!" Kitty's accent matched his indignation.

"I still don't get it," said Scruffy.

"Don't sweat it, we're color blind," Pugs assured him.

The following day, Kitty Pierre and company were finishing breakfast. Kitty dipped a paw into the leftover bowl of cereal that one of the little hairless Bipeds had left for him. He let a big fat creamy droplet of milk fall into his open mouth. He then lapped the "sticky" from his paw, savoring the rare treat with obscene pleasure.

"Nevair has le lait tasted so sweet, so pure."

"Ah jeeze, I'm gonna hurl," Pugs said, eliciting a chuckle from Scruffy.

Pierre sauntered past the boys, flicked his tail and resumed his perch in front of the tank.

"Bonjour, my precious ones." His paw tingled and the claws popped as if spring loaded. "Why hello, *mon ami*," he said, raising his paw for a better look. "Ripper, you are awake."

Pugs had been watching and commented. "You've finally lost it. For good this time."

Kitty hissed. "What do you know about eet?"

"I know that you can't have them things, in there," Pugs said and gestured, "and that it's driving you crazy. It's hilarious."

"Eedeot," Kitty spat. "Now, go away. I wan' to be alone weeth my…What *do* you call these theengs?"

"Dunno," Scruffy said scratching himself.

Later that evening…

"I know what they are," Pugs announced to Kitty who still sat at his perch. "Fish."

"Feesh?"

"No, not *feesh*. Fish."

"Oh, my lovelies. Now, I know what you are. Feesh."

Pugs shook his head and trotted to the other end of the living room. Kitty remained in front of the tank, totally absorbed.

Two days later, and Kitty was still no closer to getting his paws on the fish, something he desperately wanted to do. He was just now beginning to put his plans into action. Unbeknownst to the prickly "petit tigre," however, Scruffy had been observing him under half-closed lids for the past hour. Kitty had fashioned himself a zip line of sorts. It reached from the curtains to a point just over the middle of the tank, using the TV cable and an extension cord.

Scruff yawned and stretched, then padded over to where Kitty was working.

"Whatcha doing there, Pierre?"

"Nevair you mind," Kitty said, not bothering to turn around. He finished tying off the end of the cable wire. "Wait. On second thought, I could use your help." Though Kitty was loath to admit it, there were times when the mutt came in handy, this being one of them. "I want you to retrieve sometheeng."

Scruffy's ears perked up, and his tail began wagging vigorously, an involuntary response to his supreme enthusiasm at the unexpected prospect for a little afternoon fun. Retrieving was one of Scruffy's greatest joys in life, next to eating and sleeping. "At your service!"

Kitty stroked the fur under his chin, his very own beard of evil.

"Your mission, should you choose to accept eet," he began, "involves the recovery of one official Batman utility belt with real fly wire. But we weel need to move fast, before the Bipeds return."

"Ya, ya, ya. Plenty of time," Scruffy said, then bounded up the stairs.

"Wait, you fool!" Kitty smacked his paw against his forehead and shook it in disgust. "Amateur." But Scruffy was long gone, and so Kitty scrambled up after him, finding his canine ally waiting in the hall at the top of the stairs.

"Which one?" Scruff asked.

"Thees one," Kitty indicated with a nod of his head to the second door which was open a crack. Scruffy pushed through nose-first and trotted inside. Kitty's tail twitched anxiously, and he waited a moment, surveying the landscape before stepping gingerly into the bedroom. He kept close to the wall, his spidey senses in overdrive. He had to wend his way around and over the various landmines strewn across the floor. Dirty socks, a scattered assortment of orange and blue Legos, and what appeared to be a Tootsie pop that was now one with the carpet under the foot of the bed. Meanwhile, nose to the ground, Scruffy sniffed the perimeter.

"Say, what does a Batman thingy look like?"

"There," Kitty pointed. Slung over the back of the desk chair was the Batman utility belt with real fly wire. "That ees eet. Fetch."

Scruffy made a beeline straight for it, then stopped. He pulled up short only inches within reach and turned back to Kitty.

"You didn't say the magic word."

"What?"

Scruffy sat down on his haunches, grinding himself stubbornly into position.

"Go get it."

Scruffy ignored him.

"Cookie?"

"Where?" Scruff swiveled around and then realizing his mistake, rolled his eyes. "Come on, Pierre, you know the word."

Kitty huffed but relented, "Please?"

"Winner winner chicken dinner. That's the one."

Scruffy had to get up on his hind legs but was able to grab the belt with his teeth and pull it off the back of the chair. Kitty grabbed the swim goggles on the floor beside the desk.

Back downstairs, they got to work. It wasn't easy, but Kitty, with

Scruffy's assistance, managed to secure the belt around his waist. He was about to attach the fly wire to the cable line, when he paused and turned to Scruffy. "Something ees missing." Scruffy looked left then right.

"Like what?"

"Wait 'ere," Kitty said and dashed over to the laptop computer, booted it up, then typed in the password. SCRUFFY15. It vexed him to no end that it should be Scruffy's name and not Pierre's that allowed him access to the digital world. A quick YouTube search yielded the results he was after, and he bade Scruffy to join him at the keyboard.

"When I geev the signal, just place your paw on top of thees pad, and then give it a quick double tap." Scruffy cocked his head. "Maybe we ought to practeece," Kitty said. It took a few tries, but Scruffy eventually got the hang of it.

Kitty stopped at the tank before getting into position. "Eet won't be long now, my lovelies," he cooed with great longing before pulling himself away. He climbed to the top of the bookshelf and strapped the hook from the belt he wore onto the cable wire which he had attached to the curtain rod.

Just then, Pugs wandered in from the other room. He stopped, mouth falling open at the sight before him.

"What's this?" he asked. He peered up at Kitty Pierre who was now dangling upside down in the makeshift harness.

"He's going to get his lovelies," Scruffy told him. "I'm helping."

Pugs laughed so hard that he farted, which sent him into another fit. He fell to the floor and rolled onto his back. "Wait, wait," he said trying to get it under control. "Hold on, I want a good seat for this."

"You just wait," Kitty said.

"All set there, Pierre?" Scruffy piped up.

"Cue the music," Kitty said, then adjusted his goggles. The theme from *Mission Impossible* filled the living room. Kitty started his descent toward the tank, zipping across the room. He made it all the way to the tank and had begun to drop down a few inches before stopping abruptly. He hung, suspended in mid-air. His arms and legs were outstretched, making him look like a furry mobile. All he needed to complete the look was a cape. He tried pressing the button on the belt, but nothing happened.

"What's wrong?" Scruffy called out to him. Pugs just sat there shaking with laughter.

"Zee wire, it eez stuck." His accent grew thicker along with his frustration.

"Try again."

But no matter how many times Kitty tried pressing the button, the fly wire would not release. The *feesh* remained frustratingly out of reach.

Once again, Pugs and Scruffy were alerted to the unheard approach of the Bipeds. They began their daily ritual of running back and forth to the door and barking. "They're here, they're here," Scruffy shouted, a mixture of panic and excitement balled into one.

"Get me down."

"No time. Just stay put. They won't notice."

Upon the arrival of the squatchlets and the teenage goat-herder (a.k.a: the babysitter), the dogs were let outside to do their business. Scruffy had been right about one thing; the Bipeds zoomed through the living room without so much as a glance in Kitty's direction, while the goat-herder had her eyes glued to the square with the bright light, her fingers flying. That one, KP noted, could navigate any terrain without looking up from her iBox. At least it gave him the chance to climb back up and swing himself, paw over paw, along the wire. He unhooked the harness and jumped down onto the couch. "Ha! Stealthy as a neenja, I am."

When the back door opened, he had once again taken up his position in front of the tank, with none the wiser of what had gone on earlier. This was a setback, for sure. But he had not given up on his goal. There had to be a way to get inside the tank.

"Why don't you just climb on top of it?" Pugs said.

"Why don' you jeest mind your own beezness?"

Just then, the squatch-herder came over to the tank. She stroked Kitty's back, and a purr of pure pleasure escaped him. *You are weak*, he scolded, totally disgusted with himself. He was about to jump down when he noticed that she was now holding the little bottle of flakes in her hand. KP watched as she opened the cover. It was so simple. It had been all along. *Ha! Victory will be mine.* Kitty looked over at the boys then back at the tank. Scruff raised a paw, not quite a thumbs up, but the idea behind the gesture felt the same, and he took it as such. Kitty turned back to the tank. He put first his paws and then his face against the glass. "We shall be united soon, my lovelies."

At this, Pugs headed into the other room.

"I'm not sure how much more of him I can take, Scruff."

"Give it time, Pugs. A month from now, he'll be onto something new."

All of a sudden, a loud splash followed by an even louder screech was heard.

"You know, you may have a point there, Scruff; especially now that Kitty Pierre has discovered the properties of water."

"Oh, my lovelies. Now, I know what you are. Feesh."

SUPER

BILLY LEIGH

Billy Leigh is a writer who, in his spare time, likes to pretend to be a Wolf on the internet. When he is not coming up with story ideas, he can be found playing guitar, going on mountain hikes, or walks in the woods with his husband Colin.

Remington Stryker by day, *Captain Doberman* by night. Browse the front page of any newspaper or tune into the news station and you'll see him rescuing people from burning buildings, saving the passengers from a sinking ferry, and even finding the time to help old ladies cross the street in-between. He's a cool-looking, tall, black and tan Doberman Pinscher with cropped ears who can fly, and wears a sleek silver outfit with green goggles and a shield with *D* for Doberman emblazoned on his chest. Girls have posters of him in their rooms, and, whenever he walks down the street, he's often asked for autographs. Even criminals love getting arrested by my father. He was once trying to stop a bank robbery, and the group of Leopards holding the place up threw down their guns and asked for a selfie with him, right before they were jumped on by the police. He is often credited with changing the public image of Dobermans from villainous canines to heroes.

Then, there's me, his son *Captain Doberman Jr.* I was smoking pot under the freeway bridge by the river where I hang out with my friend Kevin.

"Hey Spike, try some of this," Kevin encouraged. The Pit Bull handed me a joint. "It's a new stash I got my paws on."

I took the joint and inhaled deeply.

"Whoa," I breathed. "Damn, this stuff is better than the last. Where did you get it from?"

"I got the number of a new dealer," Kevin explained. "Some guy who lives down in Caldwell. Is your Dad at home, or can we crash at yours?"

"Nah, my Dad is on sabbatical being a superhero in Europe right now. He never talks to me; I don't talk to him. I don't particularly want to, either."

My father and I belong to the Federation of Canine Superheroes. All of us have powers. Like I said, his is flying. My mother could slow down time, and mine is…well, at that point, Kevin asked me to demonstrate.

"Hey Spike, you see that lady up there?" He gestured at a Vixen walking on the bridge wearing a short skirt. "Why don't you blow her skirt up?"

"No, what are you, like ten?" I retorted, shaking my head with disbelief. I might have had dubious hobbies, but I wasn't *that* trashy.

There were moments when I wished I was more responsible and a good role model. I used to think my Dad was awesome, and I wanted to emulate him as a superhero. That unintentionally started my resentment. In elementary school, we were supposed to talk to the class about what we wanted to do when we grew up. I proudly marched up to school wearing my underwear over my jeans and a table-cloth cape, but, as soon as I walked in the door, I was met with howls of laughter (including from the teacher). I guess I got a complex that my Dad was just naturally awe-inspiring, whereas I was unintentionally hilarious.

Kevin knows I'm a superhero, but I always made sure he would never hear about that story.

"Who's looking after the city?"

"Oh, I'm supposed to be," I sighed. Now, not all superheroes have telepathy. I'm given this small device that's supposed to go off every time the police, army, or government face a crisis. I have to rush to wherever the problem is when it activates. My father handed me the device before he left.

Son, I want you to take good care of things while I'm away. Honey is also staying in town, as her parents are coming with me, so she can help you.

My father patted me on the head like a cub as he handed me the device. Honey Bracewell is a dorky-looking Yellow Labrador who also comes from a family of superheroes. Her power is the ability to create whirlwinds using her paws, although I always thought it was the power to annoy people. Her superhero name is *Wind Flower*.

"It demonstrates peace and harmony," she once claimed while we were in my father's back yard, before accidentally producing a sharp gust of wind that blew an apple tree over.

Through the warning device, the police know me as Spike, which isn't my actual superhero name; it's something to cover up what's written on my birth certificate; Norman Mulberry Christmas Stryker.

Yes, really.

While my father is excellent at saving people and looking dashing, he lets himself down when it comes to social tact. My parents decided to name me after Norman Rockwell, a fruit my mother had a craving for during pregnancy, and the fact I was born on Christmas day. *He's the best gift we could have asked for,* my mother said on a home video, right before I threw up on her. My name was also the gift that kept giving to my classmates whenever they wanted to make fun of me. Unfortunately, Norman was not a common name in my school, and everyone found out my two other names during my middle school graduation.

"It's okay, Norman; at least you weren't named Papaya or Mango," Honey tried to reason.

"Oh yeah, because that's a consolation," I huffed.

"I quite like the name Norman," Honey continued, fixing a simpering expression on me with her beady eyes. "It's distinctive."

"Like having mange is distinctive. Now please just leave me alone," I growled before walking off.

When I was thirteen, my mother passed away. The doctors wondered if it was something to do with the fact her powers became too much for her. My father tried to juggle his job of saving people with being a single father, but eventually he focused on the former. I was taken to school by my grandparents, and looked after by a Border Collie nanny during the day. Psychologists would say that lacking true parent figures caused me to go, well, off the rails.

That led me to wasting my time doing drugs.

Kevin inhaled deeply and pondered something. "Hey, whatcha gonna do if someone attacks the city?"

"Pfft, probably nothing," I shrugged. "I mean why should I? Everyone here made fun of me. What do I owe them?"

"I dunno; you're like a hero. You could save a bunch of people, and everyone will love you," Kevin slurred.

As if on cue, my alarm began flashing and buzzing; a sign that there was trouble in the city. I sighed, picked it up, and walked up the riverbank to where I'd parked the car. I climbed in and tuned in to the news on the radio.

Dr. Brutus is going on a rampage through the downtown area. He has been making demands that Captain Doberman show himself, or he will keep destroying the city. Everyone is advised to stay indoors.

I rolled my eyes. *Typical.* Dr. Brutus was one of Dad's longstanding enemies. He was some kind of military scientist whose real name was Murgatroyd Smith—no surprise he changed his name to something more sinister. He had some kind of grievance with the government, so he decided to use all the weapons he had created to go around causing destruction. I saw this as another good reason not to buy into the superhero lifestyle. You establish long-standing feuds with crazy supervillains who find a way to break out of jail, go around causing mayhem, and want you to show up so they can try and kill you. I closed the car door, sat behind the wheel, and tapped my paws against it. Part of my mind screamed at me to stop Dr. Brutus. *He's evil; you should do something.* The thought was emphasized as I heard a deep *boom.* I looked up and saw a plume of flames rising up among the skyscrapers of the downtown district. But then the thoughts of being bullied and belittled as a cub came flooding back. My mind played a tug of war before I shut both thoughts out.

"Fine," I said out loud, before slamming my hind-paw on the gas pedal and speeding toward the city.

I had made my mind up.

The beer felt cool and refreshing in my paw as I sat happily at the bar. The Husky behind the counter was cowering down.

"Hey, what's the matter?" I asked. The Husky pointed with a shaking paw out the window.

"That!" he exclaimed, gesturing at a giant three-legged robot covered in missile launchers and machine guns rampaging around. It was firing rockets at cars and spraying bullets in the air as people ran away screaming and the army opened fire on it. The recognizable logo of Dr. Brutus' organization was painted on the side; a skull sitting next to a giant red *B.* I rolled my eyes. His creations were getting more and more ridiculous.

"Captain Doberman!" A voice blared from a loudspeaker on the side of the robot. "Come and fight me. I know you're out there somewhere."

I turned back to my beer as the robot rampaged past the window with a tank trundling in tow.

"Hey, aren't you Captain Doberman's son? Aren't you going to do something?" the Husky asked.

"No, I'm not," I insisted.

"Yeah, you are!" the Husky replied, before ducking back down as something exploded outside. "You gotta stop him before he kills someone. Please! I'll give you a free beer!"

That clinched it. I put down my glass and marched to the door.

I walked outside. A hatch in the top of Dr. Brutus' robot opened, and the villain himself appeared. Dr. Brutus was an albino Dalmatian with blood-red eyes. He was dressed in a dark military suit with an armband sporting his logo.

"Aha!" he cried, but his expression of satisfaction turned to confusion. "You're not Captain Doberman; you're a grungy student!"

"He's his son!" someone called, and a cheer went up.

"Oh, his son. And what do they call you?"

"He's called Norman!" another voice called before I could say *Captain Doberman Jr.* I turned and cursed as I saw Honey running toward us. "My alarm went off too, and I've come to help him stop Dr. Brutus!"

"Oh for fuck's sake," I sighed.

"Go get him, Norman Christmas!"

"My surname is *Stryker*," I growled as I thought I heard a couple of confused chuckles from onlookers.

"Christmas, pah!" Dr. Brutus tipped back his head and laughed. I felt my cropped ears grow red. "Try stopping me now," Dr. Brutus laughed. The robot bent down on its legs and scooped Honey up in a mechanical arm.

"Norman, save me!" Honey screamed.

"So, are you gonna rescue your friend?" Dr. Brutus taunted.

"Nah, just take her," I huffed, still smarting. Dr Brutus looked perplexed.

"Hold on. Aren't you supposed to fight me?"

"Nah, whatever. I can't be bothered," I replied, turning to walk away. Dr. Brutus continued to look shocked, before cackling with glee again.

"Oh well, no one to stop me. I guess I'll keep destroying stuff."

"Oh no you don't!" Honey shouted. She gestured with her paws, and suddenly a whirlwind rushed down the street, picking up leaves and litter before growing more powerful.

"What the..." Dr. Brutus began, before the wind grew to the point where onlookers began ducking for cover. The robot staggered on its legs and then keeled over. Honey leaped down before it crashed onto the road, and the wind disappeared as quickly as it had begun. The army and police rushed forward as Dr. Brutus crawled out of the hatch, coughing and spluttering. The crowd cheered, and Honey wagged her tail.

"Oh Norman, we did it!" she exclaimed. I didn't reply and slunk off back to the car.

As soon as I got home, I turned on the television to see the news report on Dr. Brutus' rampage.

"People are asking why Captain Doberman's son did not intervene. The day was eventually saved by Wind Flower," a Fox news reporter said. The image then cut to my father who was walking along a Parisian street in his superhero uniform.

"This was really unfortunate. I wish my son had helped bring Dr. Brutus to justice. I will be flying back tonight and making sure this will never happen again," my father said solemnly.

"Flying back yourself or in business class," I muttered before turning the television off. I walked upstairs, shed my clothes, and climbed into bed. I wondered what my father would have to say in the morning, but I was already used to ignoring his chastising lectures on the occasions he noticed I was there. Pushing the thoughts out of my head, I fell asleep.

I awoke the next morning as the rays of dawn touched my face. Groaning, I rolled over and checked the clock; eleven a.m. Probably time to get up. I walked into the kitchen and gave a start. A black and tan Alsatian was sitting at the breakfast bar. He had an athletic build, not unlike my Dad's, and was wearing a black varsity style shirt. His muzzle broke into a friendly grin and his tail wagged.

"Hey, Norman. It's me, Maximus Grey, although please call me Max. I don't know if you remember me or not. We were probably about ten the last time we saw each other," the Alsatian explained. His name was familiar, and I remembered he was my godcousin; another superhero called *Red Streak*. His power was the ability to shoot lasers from his eyes. *What was he doing here?*

"Your Dad invited me to stay for a week while I look for an apartment in the city, which was kind of him," Max continued, as if reading my thoughts. "I'm attending college here to study horticulture." Something about his tone was getting on my nerves already.

"Right; well, my name is Spike now as matter of fact," I explained tersely.

"Oh cool. I like it," Max smiled. I responded with a mumbled *thanks* before I began searching through the fridge for something to eat.

My paw was closing around a nice-looking mango when I sensed someone standing over me. I turned, expecting to see Max, but I almost jumped out of my fur when I saw my father. I waited for the fireworks to begin, but instead Dad merely smiled.

"Hey, Norman."

"It's Spike."

"Long time no see. I guess you've noticed we have Maximus staying with us. Norman, I'd like you to look out for him."

"It's Spike."

"And show him around the city, give him a guided tour. Also, Norman?"

"Spike."

"I'm going for a meeting with the Mayor today, so I may be home a little late. I left some takeout menus on the fridge, and you can use my Nile Fresh account to order groceries for you and Maximus. Can you remember the password, Norman?"

"Spike."

"Not quite, it's *ILoveMilkBones,* all one word, start of each word in capitals. Also, Norman, remember to keep your warning pager fully charged and make sure Maximus is feeling welcome."

"Spi—oh, you know what; just forget it."

My father patted me on the shoulder before leaving the room. I stood dumbfounded. I had expected Dad to yell or demand why I hadn't stopped Dr. Brutus. Instead, I found his usual overbearing yet indifferent attitude even more annoying.

I pulled the mango out of the fridge and huffed to myself as I peeled it.

"So, what shall we do today?" Max asked.

"I'm going to play a video game for a while. You can watch documentaries on flower-arranging or work on homework, or whatever you do in your spare time," I replied.

"I might do my daily reading of the Tao, followed by some meditation, Krav Maga practice, and watercolor painting. I'm working on a marvelous picture of the Tower of London."

"Aren't Sheps supposed to be energetic and assertive?" I muttered.

"You don't always have to conform to those traits. I find doing something creative is good for the mind and soul," Max explained. I shrugged and began shooting aliens on my game console.

Little did I know what was going to happen next.

226

My father had left the television playing in the kitchen, and I could hear one of those supposedly edgy TV shows that think they're clever by giving evil people an interview.

"And now, an exclusive interview with Murgatroyd Smith, a.k.a. *Dr. Brutus.*"

I shook my head, wondering why they'd give air time to him. *Anger at a bad guy,* that wasn't something I usually felt.

"Murgatroyd, you attempted to destroy half the city. Most people will be asking why?"

"Oh, just boredom," Dr Brutus replied.

"I see, but you were stopped by Wind Flower from the Federation of Canine Superheroes. Surely, this is a sign that you should give up on that; maybe think of something else to do?"

"Ah, but on the contrary, I've only just begun; as you'll all be finding out soon!" Dr. Brutus cackled. I shook my head and turned back to my video game. Max was working on his painting, but I ignored him.

Later that evening, Dad stepped back in through the front door. "That's fantastic, Maximus!" he exclaimed, glancing at Max's painting. "If only Norman had continued with his art classes at school."

"Thank you, Mr. Stryker," Max smiled. A vein pulsed in my temple. *Just send Dad a Valentine's card if you're that obsessed with winning his affections* I couldn't help but think, but I kept the remark to myself.

"How was the meeting with the Mayor?" Max asked. My father's ears splayed, and the smile disappeared from his muzzle.

"Dr. Brutus has escaped from prison and vanished," he explained. "All of us in the Federation have been tasked with tracking him down, including you two. We're to attend a meeting at the White House tonight. A plane has been sent to take us."

Max looked shocked while I folded my arms. *He escapes, we put him in jail, he escapes, repeat cycle.*

"Grab your outfits from upstairs. There's a car waiting outside to take us to the airport," my father continued. I sloped off to my bedroom to get my superhero outfit. To be fair, my outfit does look kinda badass, although I wouldn't admit it out loud. It's silver and almost identical to my father's with the *D* logo. My head is covered by a skin-tight hood and mask with a pair of shades similar to my father's to protect my face; only the lenses are blue instead of green. I changed and ambled back downstairs to see Max already waiting. His outfit was navy blue with two silver lightning-shaped bolts down the arms, but I shook my head disdainfully as I saw he had gone for a cape and the design that gave the impression of wearing his underwear over the top, made more flamboyant by the fact the cape and underwear were also covered in lightning bolts. Max stood proudly with his paws on his hips.

"What year do you think it is, nineteen seventy three?" I asked. Max didn't say anything, but I noticed his ears splay. I was still smarting from my father's comment about the painting and felt a hint of petty satisfaction.

"You ready?" Dad called, rushing down the stairs dressed in his outfit. We both nodded and followed him outside.

A black limousine was sitting at the end of the driveway, and we all climbed inside. We were sped straight to the airport and onto the tarmac where a helicopter was waiting. A twenty-something gray Wolf in a military uniform was waiting at the foot of the steps.

"Oh cool, Captain Doberman; I mean Captain Doberman, sir," he said, snapping into a salute. "I'm Lieutenant Wiley. Please, come this way."

"What happened to General Brandon, the usual military liaison?" my father asked.

"Came down with mange. I mean, he's off duty with an illness," Lieutenant Wiley explained, before cursing under his breath.

"I see," Dad replied, shifting uncomfortably. Lieutenant Wiley gestured for us to follow him up the steps; Dad went first while Max and I walked behind. I followed the Alsatian's gaze and saw it seemed to be in the direction of my father's behind.

"That is creepy," I growled.

"Huh?" Max replied with a bemused expression on his face. Before we could say any more, we had reached the entrance to the helicopter. I sighed as I saw Honey and her father Jeff a.k.a. *Green Ghost* (his power is invisibility) already sitting down. Both were dressed in their outfits; Honey's was a deep purple with the image of a cloud on her chest, while Green Ghost's was emerald and gold.

"Hey Norman, are you excited about going to the White House with me?" Honey simpered.

"Can't wait," I responded dryly, as the helicopter lifted into the air.

"So, who is your friend?" she asked, glancing over at Max who smiled and wagged his tail.

"He's called Max," I explained before turning away, feeling thankful that Max could talk to Honey and distract her. I could see my father talking to Green Ghost. Their worried expressions unnerved me. My father was not usually one to show fear.

It wasn't long before the helicopter reached Washington DC. I glanced out of the window and saw the famous structure of the White House below. I admit part of me was excited at the prospect of visiting despite the circumstances.

"Have you guys been to the White House before? I mean you'll be escorted straight inside," Lieutenant Wiley explained to us.

"No, I haven't been before," Max replied, wagging his tail.

"Awesome. I can show you around!" Lieutenant Wiley grinned and wagged, before cursing and muttering "Control yourself, man," under his breath. Max and Honey's tails were thumping against their seats. I found myself jiggling in my seat and realized my nub was doing its attempt at wagging.

"Aww, Norman looks so cute and funny when he tries to wag like us," Honey giggled. Everyone looked at my jigging ass and burst out laughing, including Dad and Green Ghost. Lieutenant Wiley laughed before clamping a paw over his muzzle. I growled and splayed my ears. The downside of being a docked Doberman is not having a full tail to wag, and subsequently producing the comedic results for everyone.

I was still smarting when the helicopter touched down right outside the White House and the door was opened.

"This way please," a Rottweiler in a dark suit called to us. We climbed out and followed the Rottweiler through a door and into the White House itself. Immediately, we were in a busy corridor filled with canines and felines of all breeds milling around. We pushed through and followed the Rottweiler down a set of stairs to the basement level and into what looked like a cross between a large conference room and a nuclear bunker lined with steel walls. A dozen canines were sitting in the middle, all dressed in various superhero outfits. I realized the whole Federation had assembled. I took a seat next to *Shock Wave,* an orange and red British Fox who could produce sonic waves to incapacitate people.

"Mr. President, this way please," I heard a voice say. I turned to see the President himself; a gray Fox, as he walked into the room flanked by military personnel and bodyguards. I knew the President was the first gray Fox to be elected to office.

"I voted for him," Honey whispered, nudging me in the ribs.

"No you didn't," I hissed back as the President sat down.

"General Jones, if you please," the President said to a black

Alsatian in an olive green uniform.

"Thank you, Mr. President. This evening at six a.m. Murgatroyd Smith a.k.a. Dr. Brutus escaped from a high security prison. Not long after, his men broke into a military testing facility near DC and stole a one-of-a-kind prototype weapon."

"And what is this weapon?" the President asked. General Jones shifted uncomfortably as he glanced at all the superheroes.

"It was a hand-held gun designed to sap the power from a superhero should they go rogue and pose a threat to national security."

No wonder Dad and Green Ghost were nervous.

"Only one was made, and we terminated the program," General Jones added hastily, his ears splaying with embarrassment. "Murgatroyd then released this video shortly after his escape." The Alsatian pointed a remote control at a television screen at the far end of the room. The image changed from the White House logo to show Dr. Brutus standing in front of a wall with his skull logo hastily painted on it.

Greetings heroes and Mr President! he cackled with glee. *As you can see, I have come back from my vacation behind bars and am ready to get back to work. I may have borrowed something belonging to you guys. I guess the President didn't tell you heroes that he has a gun to zap your power, but I'm going to be kind and test it out for him. Now, I'm going back to my usual hobby of causing destruction. Come and stop me if you dare...*

Murgatroyd, Murgy, who are you talking to? a voice cut in.

No one, grandma, I'm just making a video!

Okay, I was wondering if you knew where my false fangs had gone?

No I don't. Anyway, come and stop me if you dare! The Dalmatian held up what looked like a silver ray-gun from an old sci-fi B movie before the image went dead.

"That guy needs to get laid," I muttered to myself. The room was full of concerned murmuring before General Jones spoke up again.

"We do have someone here who can help to track Murgatroyd down," he explained. I knew who he was talking about; Bjorn Gunner a.k.a. *Eagle Eye.*

A young silver Elkhound stood up and waved his paw to everyone.

"I can track down Dr. Brutus' precise location," he announced in a thick Scandinavian accent. Eagle Eye had vision combined with telepathy, which enabled him to find specific people and know what they were thinking. This was great for locating kidnap victims, but bad for the times when he invited me to a party. I'd been to a few of Eagle Eye's parties before, to discover the evening consisted of eating spicy meatballs with weird ingredients ranging from cheese to liquorice that caused my stomach to explode (any we didn't eat were put in a box to take home, Eagle Eye of course knew if we'd eaten or thrown them out); and playing a tedious Mah-jongg tournament. I once claimed I was ill, having made other plans. I was going to walk to a cooler party I'd been invited to, only to find Eagle Eye standing outside the house with Shock Wave.

"Gotcha, you little bugger!" Shock Wave said triumphantly.

"Huh?"

"So, you decided another party was better?" Eagle Eye said with folded arms. "I know how to fix that."

"Wait," I began before Shock Wave chuckled and knocked me out with a sonic wave. I woke up twenty minutes later in Eagle Eye's house with gaudy schlager music playing in the background and Eagle Eye's sister offering me a plate of meatballs.

"Time to play Mah-jongg!" Eagle Eye announced.

"Noooo!" I screamed.

But I digress...

Eagle Eye was concentrating hard.

"I have him! He's still here in DC. No, wait," he stammered. "He's also in Chicago; no, wait, he's in Orlando."

"How can he be in three locations at once?" Shock Wave asked.

"Dr. Brutus hasn't zapped you with the ray already?" I asked.

"He's managed to duplicate himself somehow," Eagle Eye explained.

"He must have anticipated Eagle Eye's method of tracking," Dad mused. "He's giving us really far-off locations to send us on a wild goose chase." Being the most well-known hero in the room caused everyone to fall silent and listen to my father.

"What do you think we should do?" the President asked.

"The best way to find out is if we split into groups and search each one, Mr President," Dad suggested. The room all nodded in agreement.

"Eagle Eye, can you get us more information on each location?" Dad asked. Eagle Eye put his paws to his head and concentrated.

"If he's in DC, it's an old warehouse near Dulles airport. Orlando is his grandma's house, although I'm picking up only her in that location now. She's found her false fangs and is dancing to ABBA. If he's in Chicago, he's hiding in an old container ship called the *Adam Chamberlain* on Lake Erie."

"I guess that rules out his grandma's house, so he's either in

Chicago or here in DC."

"He's getting ready to fire missiles at civilian targets tomorrow to entice us to find him, in either DC or Chicago," Eagle Eye continued.

"Then, we have no time to lose! Eagle Eye, Shock Wave, Red Streak, and Wind Flower, come with me to Chicago. The rest of you search DC," Dad commanded.

"I support Captain Doberman's plan, and you will each have military support," the President added.

"You didn't call my name. Does that mean I can go on vacation to Spain?" I asked sarcastically.

"Don't be silly, Norman, you're coming with us," Honey laughed. "This will be fun."

"If your idea of fun is stopping a homicidal maniac who lives with his grandma, I'd hate to see your definition of horrible," I sighed as we left the room.

The helicopter was waiting outside, and Lieutenant Wiley climbed in with us.

"You guys catch up; I'll go ahead and scout out the area," Dad explained, climbing back out. Lieutenant Wiley was watching with interest while Max gazed longingly in what looked like my father's direction. I sighed. The fact that Max seemed to be crushing on Dad was getting too awkward to comment on.

"Good luck, Captain Doberman, I mean sir!" Lieutenant Wiley called as my father crouched down, took a deep breath and then launched himself into the air without saying goodbye.

"I'm afraid we go a little slower," the Wolf chuckled nervously as we took off. As we flew, I couldn't help but feel a hint of disquiet in my mind. Max was sitting with his hind-paws crossed and his eyes closed.

"Mediation helps me relax," he explained, opening one eye.

"Hmm, maybe I should try it," Lieutenant Wiley replied.

"I thought you soldiers are supposed to be tough and not afraid of anything?" I asked.

"We are. I just don't like spiders or the dark," the Wolf explained.

"Great," I muttered.

"Let's do something my family used to do," Max announced, holding out his paws. "Right, everyone hold paws in a circle."

"I think this is against regulations for me," Lieutenant Wiley sighed.

"How does this help?" I asked.

"At a time of crisis, my family would sit down, hold paws, and talk about being a happy and waggy family," Max explained.

"That's interesting. My family did something similar, except we used to talk to the spirit of grandpa," Honey replied. I rolled my eyes.

The helicopter continued flying through the night, and my nerves were beginning to grow. I had never been scared of confronting Dr. Brutus before, but the thought of him having a ray to zap my power unnerved me. Max, Honey, and Lieutenant Wiley were all holding paws (Lieutenant Wiley clearly having decided that regulations didn't count at that point). I was tempted to join in, and reached out to take Max's paw but something flashed by the window and I jumped.

"Max, get your lasers ready!" I shouted, but I felt a rush of relief as my father's face appeared outside the glass. He grinned and gestured for the door to be opened. Lieutenant Wiley complied, and the wind howled in as Dad climbed inside.

"I love night flying," he joked. "Anyway I scouted out the *Adam Chamberlain*. It looks quiet, but I didn't want to go in without backup."

I was still contemplating to myself that I had taken action in the situation, something I had never done before, unless it was to stop my father unplugging my games console when I was halfway through a game to use the socket to plug in the vacuum cleaner.

Ten minutes later, the helicopter pilot's voice crackled through the cabin to say we were coming in to land. I glanced out of the window to see we were touching down on the shore of a dark lake by a jetty. The door slid open, and we jumped out. A large hulking ship was sitting at the end of the jetty, and my nerves began jangling again.

"Dr. Brutus is in there," Eagle Eye said, placing his paws to his head.

"That looks creepy," Honey gulped, which didn't exactly boost my confidence.

"Unfortunately, villains have a habit of hiding out in creepy locations," I muttered. "If I had it my way, they'd hide out on a nice beach in Barbados."

"I try to look at the positive side of things," Max replied, gesturing to an old wooden boat sitting low on the water. "For example, there's a beautiful old motor yacht over there; probably from the thirties, I'd say."

As soon as the words had escaped his muzzle, the yacht let out a creaking, groaning sound and rolled over in the water. "Oh," Max sighed.

"Team, we won't let Dr. Brutus intimidate us. We will search that boat and find him," my father cut in. "Lieutenant Wiley, how many men are with us?"

"Me, plus three other marines," the Wolf replied.

"Eagle Eye, Shock Wave, you go with the other three. Lieutenant Wiley and the rest of you come with me."

I followed everyone toward the boat with my heart pounding in my chest.

"Um, this is really against regulations, but, in case I die in there, I want to say something," Lieutenant Wiley said solemnly to Max.

"Go on?"

"I really like your super suit, you know. I think the underwear over the top looks kinda hot and capes are underrated," the Wolf admitted.

"Oh, thanks. I specified both of those aspects to the designer when I commissioned it," Max replied.

"Do you think we should grab a drink, like coffee if we're both alive at the end?" Lieutenant Wiley added.

"Yes we should, but I like green tea," Max explained.

"Oh wow, so do I. This is against regulations again, but my first name is Isaac."

"I love that name!" Max announced with delight.

"Shut up!" I hissed as we reached the ship. "Now is not the time."

Both Lieutenant Wiley and Max splayed their ears. The hulking ship before us was making my nerves even more jumpy. I felt another emotion I rarely felt: guilt.

"I'm sorry," I whispered. "Honestly, Max, I think your suit is really cool, too. Don't listen to anyone who says otherwise. I was only joking about it earlier to be spiteful, and you two would make a cute couple." I reached out and gave both of their paws a reassuring squeeze. Max looked taken aback, but his ears perked up slightly and Lieutenant Wiley wagged his tail.

"I'm glad you were staring at Lieutenant Wiley and not my Dad," I explained.

"Well, your father does have quite a nice figure," Max replied.

"His ass looks amazing in his suit," Lieutenant Wiley added. I growled and rushed off ahead.

There was a dark hatchway at the top of a gangplank, and my father led the way up to it. Gingerly, I followed him inside. The interior of the ship was dark and dank-smelling, with rusty pipes lining the walls and paint peeling from the ceiling. We followed the corridor along until we reached a wide space open to the air, presumably where the containers would have sat when the ship was in use.

"Son," Dad said, and it took me a moment to realize he was addressing me.

"Yes?"

"I want you to know something," he began, but suddenly a beam of yellow light shot out of nowhere and hit him right in the chest. He gasped and fell to the floor.

"Dad?" I called as everyone dropped to the ground.

"I feel funny," he groaned. "Like the life has been sucked from me."

"Greetings, heroes!" Dr. Brutus' voice called. "It seems my decoys fooled you earlier, and now you have found me, but Captain Doberman has experienced the force of the ray. Who wants the next turn? Come and find me if you do."

There was the sound of footsteps clattering somewhere above.

"I don't think I can fly now," Dad gasped. "I feel weak."

Everyone turned and glanced around, trying to see where Dr Brutus had gone.

"Can you walk?" I asked.

"I think so, but I want you to take charge," Dad asserted.

"Me?" I replied. I was wracked by concern for Dad but also shocked at the suggestion I take charge. *I wouldn't trust myself to be in charge of a lemonade stand.*

"I can't leave you," I whispered, taking his paw.

"Please, stop Dr. Brutus, and, if anything, we'd probably agree that you trying to do the emotional pleading thing isn't your style," my father replied.

"You're probably right," I said, forcing a smile although the prospect of my father losing his power suddenly seemed awful despite my resenting everything he stood for in the past.

"Okay," I announced, turning to everyone else. "I could use Eagle Eye to determine where everyone is."

"Here I am!" the Elkhound called, appearing from the darkness with Shock Wave and the other marines. "I sensed you were in trouble."

"Captain Doberman got zapped of his power," Max explained.

"And if we don't find Dr. Brutus, he's gonna pick us off one by one," I added, still surprised at how authoritative I was becoming.

"Okie dokie, let's find him," Eagle Eye said, putting his paws to his head. "I'm glad I get to use my mind powers on a superhero assignment. My mother normally asks me round to track down her tortoise when it goes AWOL."

"How can a tortoise go AWOL? It moves at like one mile an hour," I sighed, before snapping myself back to attention. "Eagle Eye, do your thing."

Eagle Eye concentrated for a minute before a grin spread across his muzzle.

"He's on the bridge," the Elkhound announced.

"Stay with my father," I instructed the other marines as we ran toward the bridge.

We ran through the dark corridors of the ship as Eagle Eye guided us.

"This way," he called as we hurried up a ladder. "He's in…" but Eagle Eye didn't get to finish his sentence as a ray of light hit him in the chest. He gasped and fell down the ladder.

"Oh my. Are you alright?" Honey called.

"I feel worse than after I tried to create a recipe for gummy bear meatballs," the Elkhound groaned as he rolled around on the floor. "And my power is gone."

"Who is next?" Dr. Brutus' voice cackled. "Two down, but plenty more fun to be had."

"What a horrible man. He is what my mother would call a rotten scoundrel," Honey said.

"He's what I call a fucking cu…" I began, but I was cut off as another ray was fired down the ladder.

"We need to find a way to determine where he is upstairs without Eagle Eye," I whispered. "Honey, can you make some kind of bad weather to flush him out?"

Honey thought for a moment before smiling.

"One small tornado coming up!" she announced. She gestured with her paws, and suddenly a sharp gust of wind began blowing down the ladder. There was a yell from above followed by the sound of someone falling. Honey concentrated as the wind grew more ferocious and something clattered down the ladder. I glanced down and recognized the ray gun Dr. Brutus had brandished in the video.

"He's dropped the gun!" I announced. "Let's get him."

We scrambled up the ladder and found ourselves on the bridge of the ship. The chairs and control panels were scattered everywhere, thanks to Honey's tornado, but there was no sign of Dr. Brutus.

"Where'd he go?" Lieutenant Wiley mused. The Wolf's question was answered as a gunshot rang out, and a bullet impacted against the wall near my head. We dropped to the floor, and I glanced around, trying to find any sign of the Dalmatian.

"It seems I shall have to resort to more traditional methods," Dr Brutus called from somewhere. "But now you don't have Eagle Eye's power."

A second shot rang out, and the bullet *pinged* off the wall. Honey let out a shriek and jumped out the way, but, as soon as she stood up, she let out a gasp.

"Are you alright?" I asked.

"I feel funny," she moaned before collapsing. I looked down to see a dart poking out of her hind-paw.

"Anesthetic!" Dr. Brutus called. "I thought I'd spare the girl for now, so I can provide a more amusing death for her later in revenge for stopping me last time."

I felt trapped.

What do I do now?

My prayer was answered when a cell phone began buzzing. I glanced down, expecting to see Kevin calling me, but the sound was coming from somewhere else.

"Hello, grandma. No, I haven't seen your smelling salts anywhere. Look, I'm in the middle of something right now," Dr. Brutus' voice said. I listened out.

"I think he's over there," I whispered, pointing to a dark corner at the far end of the bridge.

"Max, shine your lasers."

Max concentrated, and two red lightning bolt-shaped beams shot out of his eyes and lit the bridge up. I could see the outline of Dr. Brutus crouching in the corner. The Dalmatian turned in our direction, threw his phone down, and aimed his gun. Instinctively, I fired a kinetic ball at him, knocking the gun from his paw.

"Cut the ceiling above his head!" I commanded, knocking Dr. Brutus off his hind paws with another kinetic ball. Max aimed his gaze upward, cutting a square from the ceiling which fell straight on top of Dr. Brutus. I stood and ran over, followed by the others. The Dalmatian growled and glared up at us. "You pesky heroes, this isn't the last you'll…"

"Meh. Shock Wave, knock him out, please," I said.

"Certainly," the Fox replied, gesturing with his paws. I felt the air reverberate through me as he launched a sonic wave. Dr. Brutus stopped mid-rant and slumped over.

"I can't stand it when villains go on a monologue. It's a tonic for insomnia," Shock Wave joked.

"Tell me about it," everyone said in chorus. However, I was already climbing back down the ladder to see my father.

Someone must have called for backup since more soldiers were storming into the ship.

"Dr. Brutus is upstairs! Also, Wind Flower and Eagle Eye need your help!" I shouted as they stormed past.

Dad was leaning against the wall; he still seemed weak, but he fixed me a smile.

"What happened to Dr. Brutus?"

"Crushed. I'd have been disappointed, too," I grinned before cringing.

I need to work on my puns; that was fucking awful.

"I'm proud of you, Spike," my father smiled. It took me a moment to realize he had used my preferred name. I smiled back, but my father suddenly let out a sigh.

"I invited Max to our house in the belief he would act as a role model for you," Dad explained. "And while I guess it worked, I realize that was a mistake; I should have just told you how I felt."

"I wish I'd been a better hero," I sighed.

"I should apologize, too," my father replied. "After your mother died, I felt I didn't have anything but my job, and now I don't even have that."

I did something I never thought I'd do; I gave my father a hug. Dad also looked taken aback, but placed his arms around me before hugging tightly and giving me a lick on the muzzle like he used to when I was a cub.

"Dad!" I shouted, feeling mortified.

I heard someone cough behind me, and I sprung away, feeling embarrassed.

Trust them to appear at that moment.

General Jones was standing there, flanked by more marines.

"We owe you and the Federation of Canine Superheroes our thanks," the Alsatian explained. I felt a sudden flash of anger.

"The only way you can repay us is by restoring my father and Eagle Eye's powers," I replied, my voice verging on a growl.

"We were in the process of working on an antidote for the ray's power," General Jones explained, holding up his paw in defense. "It was based on DNA we took from each of you, and we'll reinstate that program and return your father's and Eagle Eye's power."

"Great, but maybe not Eagle Eye. I want to escape his schlager and meatball parties," I replied.

"I heard that!" Eagle Eye called from the background. "As soon as I get my power back I'm holding a party to celebrate."

I ran from the ship's hold as fast as I could.

The following day, my father was flown by the military to the laboratory near DC with Eagle Eye to have their powers restored.

"It should take a few days to come into full effect," Dad explained over the phone. "But I'm certainly feeling a lot better. The scientists say we'll make a full recovery. Have you got your warning pager charged up?"

"Yes, Dad," I replied with a sigh. I had promised to keep watch over the city while he was away, and I guess he couldn't help but be a parent.

"How are Max and Honey doing?" my father asked.

Honey came to about an hour later, but had insisted that we pose together for the news crew that showed up. As Dr. Brutus was being removed from the ship in a strait jacket, TV network vans had pulled up with journalists demanding interviews.

"We couldn't have done it without Norman here," Honey simpered.

"Spike," I sighed.

"He was our team leader after Captain Doberman got sapped of his power," she continued. Before I could say anything, she turned and kissed me on the muzzle.

"Aww," the news crew said in unison.

"Can someone please put her in a strait jacket, too?" I growled.

Cringing as I thought back to the interview, I turned my attention back to my Dad on the phone. "She's doing fine, I think," I explained.

"Excellent. Now, I'll see you tomorrow. I love you, Norman, I mean, Spike."

"Either is fine," I smiled. "Love you too, Dad."

I hung up and turned to see Max walking down the stairs. He was wearing a button-up shirt and a pair of smart jeans.

"Are you off somewhere, Max?" I asked.

"Yes, on a date," the Alsatian replied, wagging his tail. As if on cue, a car horn sounded outside. Max jumped with joy and ran to the door.

"Have a good time," I called.

"Thanks, Spike!" Max replied before the door closed. I glanced outside to see Lieutenant Wiley sitting behind the wheel of his car. The Wolf had changed out of his uniform and was wearing a polo shirt. He smiled and waved. I waved back, feeling happy for the two of them.

I watched as Max left before parking myself in front of the TV. My phone buzzed, and I looked down to see Kevin's name on the caller ID. I was about to pick up when my pager began flashing and buzzing; there was a crisis somewhere nearby.

"Sorry, Kevin." I shrugged as I swiped to the hang-up option. "I won't be smoking weed under a bridge tonight."

My duty was calling.

My duty was calling.

Woolwertz Department Store Integrated Branch Employee Manual: Human-Furred Relations

FRANCES PAULI

Frances Pauli writes science fiction and fantasy, often with anthropomorphic characters. She eats excessive amounts of chocolate, spends far too much time online, and erroneously believes she can play the ukulele. Free stories and samples of her fiction can be found on furry social sites where she goes by MammaBear. Alternately, her list of works, newsletters, and freebies are available on her website at: francespauli.com.

Woolwertz is happy to be a diverse and fully integrated employer. We welcome all our employees, furred or human, and strive to provide a positive and cooperative environment for higher productivity, efficiency, and a pleasant and comfortable working experience for all. To this end, please read the following workplace guidelines to fully understand your part in making Woolwertz a great place to work, regardless of your species.

Section 2A: General Rules for Furred Employees.
    In order to maintain a professional and customer friendly atmosphere, the following rules will be in place at all times while you are employed at Woolwertz. We understand that some of them may seem confusing or unnecessary at first, but years of research and much trial and error in mixed employment environments have proven the need for defined behavioral standards which benefit all employees, customers,

and company property. By placing your trust in Woolwertz and adhering strictly to the rules below, we can save a great deal of time and money and prevent unnecessary personal injury or litigation.

- Clothing must be worn at all times. Special dispensation may be given for double-coated animals or for religious purposes. See HFR for application.
- Shoes are optional but encouraged. Hooves must be neatly trimmed and equipped with rubber floor-guards.
- Grooming must be done on the employee's own time. If grooming must occur during breaks, please use restroom facilities and respect fellow employees' privacy.
- Claws are to be neatly trimmed at all times.
- Antlered and hoofed employees are required to maintain a reasonably safe tine length as illustrated in *Appendix B*. Remember, safety comes first, as does company property. Keep your head clearance in mind at all times.
- Shedding and/or molting should be kept under control as much as possible. Please take all reasonable measures to keep our workplace clean and pleasant. Deodorizer is not required as per *The Act for Furred Equality in Public Spaces*, but it is polite and highly encouraged.
- Employees must be on time for shifts, and all breaks must be taken.
- Cell phones must be turned off on the sales floor. Taking pictures with or recording video of your coworkers will not be tolerated.
- Restrooms MUST BE UTILIZED. No exceptions.
- We know that, during some seasons, fleas and ticks can be difficult to avoid. For your comfort, discreet flea collars and/or pyrethrum oils are available from HFR. Your use of either will be entirely confidential.
- No scent marking or territorial pissing will be allowed on premises. This includes commission salespersons. No second warning will be given.
- Howling will not be allowed on company premises.

- If your lunch is alive, please use the appropriate container in prey storage area. (See map in *Appendix D.*) Also, it is courteous to either kill your food before joining your coworkers in the lunchroom, or to dine in the storage area. This is not required, however, as per *The Act for Furred Equality in Public Spaces.*
- Reproductive displays and reflexes such as head-bobbing, fanning the tail, strategic blushing, and/or building of nests should be kept to a minimum.
- No humping. Of anything.
- Migratory species, please inform HFR as soon as possible of your particular needs. A Woolwertz employee exchange program is available to facilitate you. Sign-ups are on a first-come, first-serve basis, however. Get your requests in early to avoid being left behind.
- If you are a member of a species which requires a hibernation schedule, alert your department manager as soon as you are placed on the schedule. Every effort will be made to accommodate a vacation schedule for *obligate hibernators* only. Abuse of this system will not be tolerated and can affect vacation privileges for all Woolwertz employees. Please, hibernate only if it is mandatory.
- Any dispute between employees, furred or human, must be brought to the attention of HFR immediately. Failure to do so will result in disciplinary action for all parties involved.

Section 2B: Conduct Toward Human Co-workers.

Part of a positive work experience is getting along with your fellow employees. At Woolwertz, that often means interacting in unfamiliar ways with humans. Many of you will already have experience working with humans, but for those of you who don't, the following guidelines will prove essential in building inter-species cooperation. Remember, your human friends are just like you! With a few minor exceptions.

- Refrain from hissing, barking, or growling at your

human coworkers. This can often be construed as aggressive and could result in unnecessary litigation and/or termination.

- If a human co-worker accidentally shows you their teeth, it is not a threat display. Do not react. Simply report the incident to HFR as soon as possible.
- Intimidating behavior or displays of dominance toward human employees will not be tolerated under any circumstances.
- Likewise, you are not required to respond to any inadvertent commands given by a human unless they are your direct supervisor.
- Restroom etiquette is of extreme importance to your human co-workers, as is their personal space. If using the restroom with humans present, please respect the average human personal space bubble as illustrated in *Appendix C*. Also, attempt to use provided toilet paper. Using your tongue is discouraged. Additionally, please refrain from sniffing human coworkers who are also using the facilities.
- Our human coworkers can smell fascinating, but sniffing should be kept to a minimum at all times on the store floor. If you must sniff a human employee, always avoid the more personal areas, which can be found in *Diagram 103* in *Appendix D*.
- Licking of human employees is prohibited at Woolwertz.
- Learn the average human personal space bubble (*Appendix C*), but understand that it does vary from individual to individual. Watch for body language that suggests you are being perceived as aggressive: cringing, trembling of the extremities, tears, and vocalizations such as, "Back," "Down," "Go Away," or "Please don't eat me."
- More information on human body language and non-verbal communication will be provided in *Training Video 1C: Humans Say What?*
- Be aware of your tail. Many inter-employee conflicts have begun with a poorly timed tail wag. A little awareness goes a long way.

Section 3A: General Rules for Human Employees

Woolwertz treasures our human employees as vital members of the company-wide family. We strive to keep them both satisfied with their employment opportunities and safe in the workplace environment. In return, we expect the highest level of professionalism and personal accountability. The following rules will remain in place at all times. Any questions or clarifications should be directed toward your store's HFR manager.

- Store dress code must be followed at all times. Inappropriate dress or lack of shoes will result in a written warning and can be grounds for eventual termination. Shirts with mascots or animal logos are strictly forbidden at Woolwertz.
- Avoid bright colors such as yellow or pink. Red clothing of any kind is forbidden. For more information, refer to *Safety Training Video 5B: The Chicago Tragedy.*
- Hair must be kept short or neatly groomed and styled at all times.
- Tattoos should be tasteful or easily covered. (Tattoos of animals can be considered offensive and must be covered at all times on company property.)
- Employees must be on time for shifts, and all breaks must be taken.
- Cell phones must be turned off on the sales floor. Taking photos with or recording video of your coworkers will not be tolerated.
- Music will be played at all times on the sales floor, in break rooms, lunchroom, or restrooms. This is for your safety. Tampering with the musical devices or speakers is grounds for termination and can put your fellow employees at risk!
- All human employees are required to watch *Safety Training Video 5A: Confident Body Language in the Mixed Employment Environment.*
- Good personal hygiene is encouraged as is the use of deodorant. Scents to avoid, however, include: fruit or food based aromas, pine, mountain or woodsy smells,

or musk of ANY kind.

- Vacation and time-off requests must be turned in a minimum of two weeks prior to the days requested. While we do our best to accommodate everyone, understand that requesting time off is no guarantee of specific dates. Requesting as early as possible is recommended.
- Any dispute between employees, furred or human, must be brought to the attention of HFR immediately. Failure to do so will result in disciplinary action for all parties involved.

Section 3B: Conduct Toward Furred Coworkers

Just as our furred coworkers will strive to accommodate our differences, so too must every human employee at Woolwertz learn to respect and safely interact with their furred counterparts. These guidelines will not only improve the working environment for all Woolwertz employees, they just might save your life. Read carefully.

- Do not smile at furred employees. Smiling shows your teeth and can be misconstrued as a hostile or threatening act. We cannot stress this enough, as smiling is a natural and often reflexive action on a human's part. Practice at home, and if you need additional training or are feeling less than confident in your ability to restrain yourself, see HFR about taking the *Non-Aggressive Body Language* extension course.
- Petting of furred coworkers will not be tolerated under any circumstances.
- Refrain from using terms such as "cute," "adorable," "fluffy," "scaly," "hideous," "nightmarish," or "creepy" when referring to your furred coworkers. (Full list of offensive terms can be found in *Appendix E*.)
- Catnip is a controlled substance and must never be brought onto company property. Anyone found in possession of catnip will be subject to immediate disciplinary action.
- Respect your furred coworkers' spatial requirements. Some furred employees require extra room for

maneuvering or have a larger than expected turn radius due to tails, antlers, horns, or bigger than average appendages. Being courteous and giving your furred fellows a wider berth can prevent conflict and injury both.

- Contrary to popular myth, fleas and ticks are very rare among our furred populace. However, if you suspect a furred coworker may be harboring parasites, please contact HFR quickly and privately.

- Some of our furred employees might have distinct and unfamiliar odors or musks. Please be respectful of your difference and avoid referencing any unpleasant smells directly. Working in an integrated environment may take some getting used to. If you believe you require assistance, nasal plugs and sachets can be obtained from the HFR office, but should be used with discretion.

- Many of our furred employees have full pelts of dense fur and/or experience regular or seasonal shedding. A single furred coworker may lose vast amounts of undercoat at certain times of the year, and learning to deal with shedding can be challenging in the mixed workplace environment. While we want our human employees to be comfortable, we demand a high level of sensitivity and professionalism when dealing with this very personal topic. The best course of action when confronted with a shedding coworker is to act as if nothing is happening. A gentle wiping of the hair from your own eyes and nose is acceptable, but do your best not to draw attention to the situation or embarrass your coworker unnecessarily. Tape rollers are available in employee break rooms and at all cash wraps, but must be used with discretion and preferably out of sight of the shedding employee.

- Never offer to brush or groom a furred coworker in any way. There are no exceptions to this rule!

- If you suffer from allergies, please notify HFR immediately for special dispensation and appropriate equipment.

- Restroom etiquette can be confusing when sharing space with our furred coworkers. Privacy stalls have been installed for your comfort, and we encourage you to use them. Understanding that different species have varying restroom culture can go a long way toward avoiding any awkward situations in the Woolwertz employee restrooms. Avoiding direct eye contact will discourage any invasion of space, as will using the locking mechanism on the privacy stalls. Promptly reporting any breach of personal privacy to HFR will assist the management staff in ensuring a safe and private restroom experience for our human employees. Using proper body language is also advisable. Remember, a tolerant and flexible attitude goes a long way in inter-species relations. Maintain your boundaries and report any questionable behavior immediately, but do not engage furred employees in a physical dispute if it can be avoided.

- This is for your safety.
- All furred Woolwertz employees will be fully trained in the concept of "human personal space" (*Appendix C*). To facilitate them learning how to apply this foreign concept, we ask that you exercise patience and clear communication skills. Should a furred employee invade your personal space or sniff you in an inappropriate area, you are encouraged to express your displeasure and redirect the attention to a more acceptable activity. It is perfectly allowable to tell a coworker that you do not enjoy such attention, to back away slowly, or to suggest an alternate form of interaction.
- Under no circumstances should you strike a furred coworker on the nose or muzzle! This form of correction is dangerous and can result in personal injury, litigation, and loss of company property.
- It is highly inappropriate to ask a furred coworker to fetch anything for you. Similarly, requesting rides on larger employees is forbidden and could result in serious bodily harm.
- Use extreme caution when closing doors, drawers, or cash registers. Many work mishaps have begun when a furred employee's tail was accidentally injured. Disaster can be easily avoided by visually assuring all doorways

are clear and by shutting things gingerly and with great caution. Additionally, watching where you place your feet, and where you sit, can avert much discomfort and incident. Respect your coworker's tail space for a happy working relationship.

- Tails can be a fantastic indicator of your coworker's mental state. Learn the signs of a happy furred employee and pay great attention to ears, tail, and vocalizations to build a strong and positive working relationship. An extensive description of furred body language and warning signs can be found in *Safety Training Video 5C: Ruffled Feathers and Workplace Peace.*
- Never approach a hissing, growling, or snarling coworker. Back away slowly and report incident to HFR immediately.

The Woolwertz family wants to welcome you and ensure that your working environment meets your needs. Together, we can make an integrated workplace the best workplace of all. With respect, communication, and a healthy dose of caution, any situation can find a happy, common sense solution, ensuring that your career at Woolwertz is satisfying, profitable, and safe. We look forward to working with you!

For further information, questions, or concerns, please contact your store's HFR office. All information in the Woolwertz Employee Manual is the property of Woolwertz Limited and fully protected under law. Copies are available from HFR and are not to be shared or taken off company premises under any circumstance.

For further assistance or to report a threatening situation or potential lawsuit, contact Woolwertz HFR Headquarters from the Corporate Directory. Copies of *The Act for Furred Equality in Public Spaces* can be obtained online or from your city's Integration Office.

No animals or humans were harmed or infringed upon during the compiling of this manual.

We welcome all our employees, furred or human, and strive to provide a positive and cooperative environment for higher productivity, efficiency, and a pleasant and comfortable working experience for all.

THE DARK END OF FURRY EROTICA

In 2016, Sofawolf editor Dark End posted on Twitter a list of things to avoid for submissions to the *HEAT* anthologies. Writer Mog Moogle decided to take it upon himself to write a story breaking as many of these rules as possible. Two other writers, Jaden Drackus and Searska GreyRaven, have also contributed stories that play off both The List and Mog's story, "The Best and Greatest Story" ("TBAGS")…talk about a high bar. So, read The List yourself to see the standards, and please read the following stories as satire, not as Mog's, Drackus', or GreyRaven's serious literary writing. Enjoy the dark end of furry erotica…

A LIST OF EROTICA CLICHÉS YOU SHOULD AVOID IN YOUR *HEAT* SUBMISSION

DARK END

Dark End is a coffee-drinking Midwesterner who is the managing editor of the Heat *and* Hot Dish *anthologies. He was also promised whisky if he allowed The List to be published here. Now where is my booze, Howl?*

1. Someone bears a secret crush for the person who turns out to have a secret crush on them too.
2. Everyone in the universe is male.
3. Every guy in the universe is gay or bi.
4. Everyone in the universe is always interested in sex.
5. Everyone in the universe wants to be with the protagonist.
6. Any combination of 2, 3, 4, and 5.
7. I'm so plain and uninteresting but everyone wants to be with me.
8. I'm so sociable and successful but no one is interested in me.
9. Characters have sex for the first time. Somehow, despite no experience or practice, they are amazing at it.
10. No one has ever heard of condoms or lube.
11. Everyone of importance is in their 20s. Anyone older than 35 exists only to be a prude.
12. Protagonist shares species and name with writer's fursona. Story is just their sexual exploits.
13. We just had a (small) fight and (quickly) forgave each other. Let's have messy sex for the remaining 3/4s of the story.
14. Love interest is only described by species, eye color, and erection/breast size.

15. He's cheated multiple times and broken trust countless more, but his SO will forgive him instantly because he's sad and (maybe) sorry.
16. Protagonist personality: alpha. Nothing more than that. Just alpha.
17. Love interest is a high school football player.
18. Gay teacher/student romance. (For whatever reason, this is really popular in the *Heat* slushpile and rarely works well.)
19. Everyone of importance in the story is atheist/agnostic. Anyone religious exists only to be a prude.
20. Writer really wanted to show that a non-standard relationship is good, so wrote a story with no conflict to emphasize the goodness.
21. Everyone has this kink and will enjoy if I talk at length about it.
22. No one really has this kink so they'll laugh if I poke fun at it
23. One of the main characters writes erotica. Author uses this to preach about the best way to write erotica.

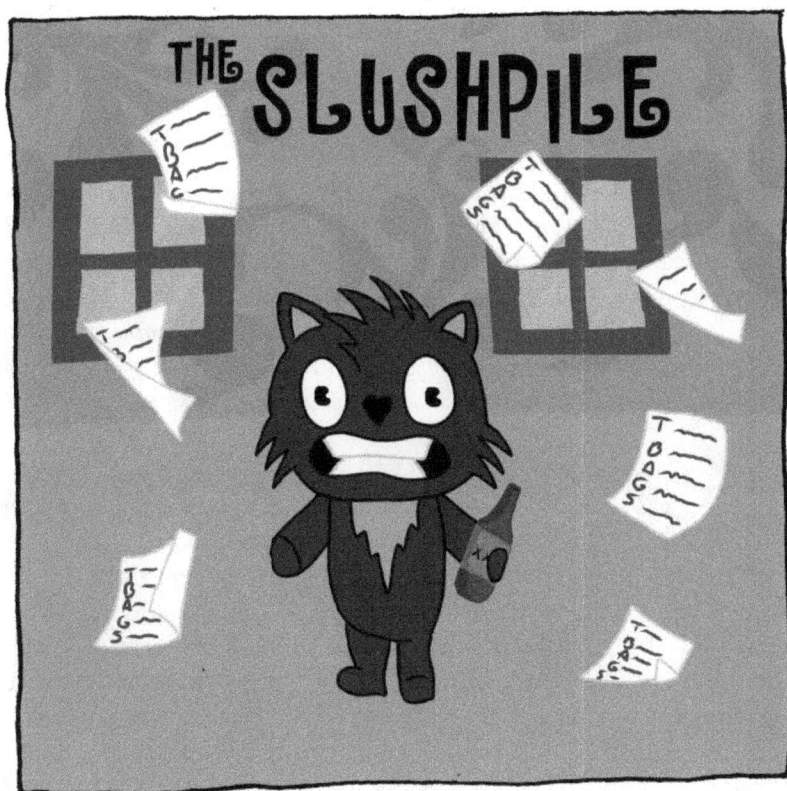

Here's your booze, Dark End! —Thurston Howl

THE BEST AND GREATEST STORY

MOG MOOGLE

Hi! I'm Mog. I write things alphaly. I'm the most alpha writer in all of the internet. You should check out my other work in things that are also really alpha.

(Mog has been writing since the early 2000s, with his first published works appearing in print in 2016. Apart from this anthology, he has been published in Weasel Press's Fragments of Life's Heart *and the free ezine* Typewriter Emergencies, *and a poem in Sofawolf's* HEAT 14 *titled "Top to Bottom." Feel free to contact him and let him know what you think of his stories, or his terrible bio.)*

Once there was a wolf that was an athlete that was good at sports and athletic things. He was big and muscular and popular. Everyone at school looked up to the wolf because he was so amazing. The only thing wrong with the wolf was that he was so popular and cool that no one wanted to be with him. He went to the Men's school for Men where everyone was manly, and all the teachers were manly too. This made him lonely because he did not have a boyfriend. He wanted a boyfriend because he was gay but did not want to tell people because he was good at sports. He was really horny because he had never had sex before and had so much manly sports testosterone. One day, he was talking to his nerd friend, a fox who was a nerd because he was good at math. The wolf, who was named Moonstar Packhowler, talked to the nerd fox who was named Twinky Yiffslut, and he said to him "Twinky, I am so popular but no one wants to be with me." But the wolf named Moonstar had a secret crush on the nerd fox named Twinky and Twinky thought to himself that he wanted to tell Moonstar that he had a crush on him but it was a secret and no one would want to be with him because he was so uninteresting. "You are so successful with sports," is what Twinky said. "I know but no one wants to be with me because they are too afraid of being with the best sports athlete in the school." "Well I want to be with you, but I keep it secret because of how plain and uninteresting I am." "That is amazing," said the sports wolf. "It's awesome because I secretly wanted to be with you. I secretly want to have a lot of gay sex with you but those good at sports are not supposed to do gay sex because others will think they are now uncool." "We can have secret sex," said Twinky, because he was smart even though he was socially awkward and uninteresting. "That way no one will think less of you for having a lot of gay sex with me." "I can't wait to put my yiffstick in your murrhole," said Moonstar and then they kissed in secret away from everyone else so no one would know. It was the best kiss they had ever had because it was the first time they had kissed anyone but Moonstar was a really good kisser because of sports. They went to the secret bedroom of Moonstar and there they took off each others' clothes. It was really awesome because it was their first time being with someone and they were having secret gay sex because they had secret gay crushes on one another. Moonstar pushed his cock in the fox's rear and humped him really hard. The fox said, "This feels so good. You are the best at fucking me there has ever been." Moonstar agreed and then he came really hard in Twinky's ass. The next day, they went back to school but they kept their relationship a secret. When class was over for Twinky, he went to his teacher, Professor Mog, who was a alpha moogle with a really big cock and said, "My boyfriend is really good at sex but I will bet you are a lot better." Mog, who was a Pee Haitch Dee despite only being 20 years old, said "We could go back to my office and have a lot of sex right now so that I can prove to you who is best. So Twinky went with Mog into the office. Twinky knew that cheating was wrong, but he had a cheating fetish. He had never been able to cheat because he was always without a boyfriend, but now that he was with a boyfriend, he could cheat with his Professor Mog like he had always wanted to. Cheating was the most exciting thing that he could ever do because it's the best fetish. He then looked at Professor Mog's big cock. It was twelve inches long and as thick as Yiffslut's forearm. "Your cock is so big professor. It will probably hurt but I want it in me because I want to cheat on my boyfriend. I have secretly always wanted to cheat on my boyfriend because cheating is hot." "It will not hurt," Proffesser Mog said as his twelve inch cock lined up with the nerdy fox's tailhole. "I am really good at sex because I get it so often, having a 12 inch cock." "Fuck me with all twelve inches of your cock, professor Mog!" And Mog pushed all 12" of his cock in Yiffslut's ass and made him cum from how awesome it felt to have the twelve inshes of cock inside of him. "Fuck my cheating slut ass, Proffessor Mog." Mog's green eyes shined with fuck lust as his twelve inch cock worked him over and over until they both cum again. It was really good because Mog was so good with his twelve inches and the nerd fox always wanted to cheat. He thought about how cheating was the best kind of sex there was. Then Moonstar wondered where his boyfriend was because classes were over. He walked around but did not see him. He was sad because he wanted to have more secret gay sex with his boyfriend, the nerd fox, Twinky Yiffslut, who was good at math. When he found his boyfriend, he saw Professor Mog in the office giving him really good cheating sex with all of his thick 12 inches. Moonstar knew he could not have as good of a cock, but it still made him sad. He waited for his boyfriend to come out of the office after he was full of cheating cum. He saw Yiffslut and profosser Mog and was like "You cheated on me because he has a big cock. I thought we were in love." Yiffslut said "We are in love and I want to have a lot of sex with you, but Professer Mog has a big twelve-inch cock and it feels really good to cheat. I hope you forgive me." And Moonstar did. They agreed to have more sex but Professor Mog said, "I will give you both extra credit if you have more cheating sex with my twelve inches." Moonstar had forgiven Yiffslut so he agreed to it. They had a threesome where Professor Mog put his twelve inches in both of them. Moonstar had never had anything put in his boy pussy before but Mog was so good at sex because of his twelve insches that it felt really good, and it was cheating sex so it felt really good. Professor Mog was a real alpha and could please even the most manly of sports wolves with his twelve inches. Yiffslut said, "Oh god, oh god," but Mog said "I am an athiest because religious people are prudes. You can worship my twelve inch cock and green eyes instead." They agreed and kept having sex until Professor Mog's office smelled like a lot of cum and secret gay cheating threesome sex. They all agreed that they should be in a relationship together and Mog would be their alpha. Mog was best suited for the job because he was really good at sex because of his twelve inches and he writes porn stories for SoFurry.com. He writes the cheating porn stories because those are the best kind of porn stories and everyone should write them because it's the best fetish. And he writes so well that people give him five stars all the time and he has so many followers that everyone agreed they should listen to him because of the twelve inch alpha 20 year old professor cock. Then Moonstar siad, "Professor mog? Didn't you have a science expereiment running for the gov't so that it would keep everyone safe?" Mog said, "There is a lot of time for sex and science, because I am so alpha that I can do all of that." Both Moonstar and Twinky agreed that Mog was alpha and his twelve inch cock was the only reason they were put on earth so that they could be his sex slaves. They had a lot more sex as the years went on and lived happily ever after. The end.

Both Moonstar and Twinky agreed that Mog was alpha and his twelve inch cock was the only reason they were put on earth so that they could be his sex slaves.

SELF-INSERTION

JADEN DRACKUS

Jaden Drackus, or Jay Dee, is a dragnox writer from Maryland. He has been writing furry stories since officially joining the fandom in 2010. A video gamer, builder of model airplanes, reader, and general smartass—Jay Dee resides with his boyfriend and 4 cats. He has recently developed a fear of ice cream scoops and a general dislike for mayonnaise as a whole, which he is sure have nothing to do with this story. In addition to comedic "masterpieces," Jay Dee also writes erotica and fantasy. Some of his "good" stories can be seen in Species: Wolves *and* Species: Foxes *from Thurston Howl Publications. He can be found on FurAffinity as JadenDrackus. His silly observations on life can be seen on Twitter:* @JadenDrakus*

"What? You can't be serious!"

The red-scaled dragon glared at his companion across the living room. The big roan stallion lounged on the couch, legs spread, meeting the dragon's gaze with an utter lack of concern. He grinned broadly and whinnied.

"Why can't I?" smirked the horse.

"Because it's a dumb idea," the dragon huffed, crossing his arms around his chest. "We're not doing it."

The giant draft horse nickered as he continued to study the dragon. His smile dropped as he tried to decide just how irate his companion was. It was a few moments of them staring at each other before he reached a conclusion. The stallion closed his legs and leaned forward.

"Look, Jayson," said the horse, glancing away, "it's not a dumb idea. It'll be fun. You know you wanna."

"And what could ever give you *that* idea?"

"Oh, I dunno, the part where you used your dragon magic to create a clone of yourself—a.k.a. me? Handsome, sexy, irresistible me."

"Yeah. To help me make deadlines by having two of me get the shit out of my head and onto paper. Not to come up with even more stupid ideas! I can come up with those on my own."

"It's not a stupid idea," the draft horse flicked his tail. "The best way to write something realistically is to experience it."

Jayson rubbed the base of his frill while his tail tip smacked the side of the chair. He'd taken to calling the clone Jack, Jack Offamann, after his first words: "If you're doing yourself, it counts as jacking off." And Jack wasn't going to let this go.

A week ago, the dragon had been surprised when the spell he'd used to clone himself had produced a stallion rather than another dragon, but after some research and hearing Jack's interests, he wasn't anymore: Jack wasn't an exact clone—instead he was the physical embodiment of Jayson's sex drive. Which, in a dragon writer of erotica, could be quite considerable and focused. Jayson's portfolio of erotic writing, and his toy collection, was extensive and varied. The stallion was into all of it. In the week the horse had existed, he had constantly pressured the dragon for sex. When Jack had realized that Jayson was focused on writing, he suggested sex while writing as a compromise. Jayson wasn't convinced it was much of one.

He studied the big draft horse. Much of his reddish-brown hide was exposed as he often insisted on wearing nothing but shorts around the house; Jayson's shorts, which on Jack amounted to boxer briefs. Tight boxer briefs that left nothing to the imagination. The stallion had blue eyes similar to Jayson's and a light brown mane. But the worst part of him was his personality. Jayson hated the term "alpha," but if it applied to anyone, it applied to Jack: the stallion was loud, brash, and completely obsessed with sex.

The dragon sighed and finished the soda he'd been drinking. He still didn't fully comprehend why a dragon's sex drive would manifest *as a stallion*. Jack would suggest it was because only a horse could be such a stud—but Jayson was tired of this debate.

"If you think it's such a good idea, how about you try writing while I'm railing you in the rear?" Jayson huffed. With that, the dragon stood up and headed out into the kitchen leaving the draft horse looking defeated.

That specific subject didn't come up again for the rest of the day, and the cloned horse managed to write up a few hundred words. Jayson was impressed, despite the fact that Jack had frequently interrupted the dragon's own writing by rubbing his crotch or rear against Jayson's wings.

"Jack! Off!" Jayson yelled when he'd had enough of the horse leaning against him. He shoved the stallion away.

"Well, that's one thing we could do," he replied with a grin.

Jayson stared at him blankly for several seconds, and then realized what he'd just said. Jack's smile grew wider as the dragon's muzzle dropped in shock as he wrapped his wings around himself in embarrassment.

The next morning brought the usual round of annoyances at suddenly having a roommate of a different species—the biggest being how much time Jack took in the shower. It was kind of hard to fault him for that, though; after all, Jayson didn't have a long mane or tail to wash and brush. While waiting for Jack to finish, Jayson fixed his morning breakfast sausage. As he was eating, the horse came into the kitchen stating that the shower drain was clogged again. The dragon sighed and slammed his head into the table, knocking over his meal.

"You're wasting your weanies, man." Jack commented. "But you know I've got another one for you."

Jayson pointedly ignored the comment as he cleaned up the mess.

It was the middle of the afternoon when things finally came to a head. The horse was complaining about the lack of green foods available in a dragon household, when Jayson had had enough.

"Look, I'm sorry, but this isn't easy! I was expecting you to be a dragon."

"It's not like it's been easy for me," Jack whinnied. "None of your clothes fit me. Your tail is so much thicker than mine, so it's like my ass is just hanging out. That's fine most of the time, cuz it's a great ass," he went on with a grin. "But it gets drafty back there. Same with your shirts. With the slots for your wings, it's like they don't have a back at all!"

Jayson sighed and glared at the stallion, trying to decide if it was worth reiterating that he'd been wishing for a dragon. The clothing stores he went to didn't exactly cater to non-winged individuals, so he had to order clothes for the horse online. Jack's blue eyes met his gaze with equal determination. The silence continued for several moments as they stared at each other. Finally, Jack stuck his tongue out, causing the dragon to jerk back and snort a small jet of flame.

"Really?" he asked, glaring at the stallion.

"What? Were we just going to stare at each other all day?"

"I'm considering it," Jayson growled.

The dragon tapped his claws on the table as he considered the horse. He couldn't really blame the clone for his fixation on sex. After all, he was just doing what his instincts told him. It wasn't exactly his fault that he'd been created as the physical embodiment of someone else's libido. For the millionth time since he'd done it, Jayson asked himself what he'd been thinking trying to clone himself.

He knew, of course. It just hadn't worked out the way he'd wanted—instead of his creativity, he'd gotten his libido. None of that was the draft horse's fault: he hadn't asked to be aggressive, horny, and sex obsessed—he'd been made that way. If anyone was at fault, it was Jayson for failing to read the fucking manual. Now, he had to live with someone whose idea of "a fucking manual" was a guidebook on sexual positions. The dragon sighed again. Maybe if he gave the horse what he wanted, it would help Jack focus on what they were supposed to be doing.

"Alright, fine. We can do it."

"What?" the stallion asked, stunned.

"I said we can do it," the dragon said. "We can try your fucking idea of having sex while writing a story. Goddamn. I know I'm not going to get anything of real use out of you until we at least try it. So fine. Let's do it. What's the worst that can happen?"

"Well, if 'the worst that can happen' is you getting laid," Jack said with a huge grin. His tail was a blur behind him. "You're doing pretty good in life."

The dragon sighed and shook his head. "I'm going to go get ready. You set up the office for this nonsense."

"Lube and elbow padding, got it."

"And the laptop," Jayson reminded him as he stood to leave. "It's the whole point of this exercise."

"Right, right."

The dragon snorted, sending a little tongue of flame into the air as he headed upstairs.

Half an hour later, Jayson went into his office dressed in a t-shirt and gym shorts. The room was spartan: a desk, a chair, a bookcase, and a futon that allowed the office to double as a guest room. Jack slouched on the futon, grinning at him as he entered. The stallion was dressed in only a t-shirt and boxers, which were doing a terrible job of hiding what the horse was packing. Jayson had to admit that he was impressed by the horse's equipment and could feel his own shorts tightening a little bit in response. Jack grinned and licked his lips as he looked the dragon up and down.

"Looking good," the stallion neighed. "You ready to do this?"

"Hold on," Jayson snorted. "There's still a couple things to figure out before we get started."

"What things?" Jack cocked his head and looked genuinely puzzled as he sat up.

"Like the entire point of this exercise," the dragon snorted. "You do remember why you suggested this in the first place, right?"

"Yeah, yeah!" Jack hopped to his hooves. "But that's the easy part."

"When has anything with you been easy?"

"I'm easy," the horse protested as he rose. He grinned and reached down to cup his bulge, leaving no doubt to his meaning.

"That's not the way I mean it," the dragon muttered.

Jack strode across the room and put an arm around the dragon. He pulled him into a hug and held him tight, letting his bulge press against the dragon's.

"I think you'll enjoy taking it *this* way."

"Maybe," Jayson admitted with a sigh. "But we still haven't figured out what we're going to be writing about."

"I told you. Just write about what we're doing. That's not any different from what you usually write."

"I don't typically write sex scenes while actively participating in them!"

"Hey, the best way to come up with ideas is to experience them."

The dragon closed his eyes, groaned, and rubbed his crest. Jack whinnied and nuzzled between his ears. Jayson finally opened his eyes and looked up at the underside of the taller horse's muzzle.

"So, you think I should write about an erotic author writing while he's having sex with his boyfriend?"

"Yup yup," the stallion agreed with a flick of his ears and a swish of his tail. "It'll be the best and greatest story ever written."

"I highly doubt that," the dragon said, his crest flattening in displeasure. "But whatever. I'm ready when you are."

"Alright then," Jack replied as he kissed the dragon's head and gave his ear a lick. "Want me to blow you a little first?"

"I'm good," Jayson said. "I just want to get on with this. I'll let you lead."

"Gladly," the horse soothed.

With that, Jack ran a paw down Jayson's shorts. The horse nickered in pleasure as he discovered that the dragon wasn't wearing any underwear. In spite of his annoyance with his clone and the situation, the dragon giggled as the massive horse mitt took hold of his junk and the bulge poking his rear got firmer. The stallion wiggled his hips and rubbed Jayson's belly as he continued to hold on to the dragon's maleness. He sighed as he relaxed. Jack gently pushed him in the direction of the desk and the laptop on it. The draft horse had helpfully opened the word processor, so everything was ready. He pressed his elbows on the pad and mentally prepared himself.

Jack neighed and pulled Jayson's shorts off. The dragon carefully stepped out of them, spread his legs, and helpfully raised his tail. The stallion pulled his own boxers off as Jayson stared at the white screen and tried to figure out just what exactly he was going to write during this nonsense.

"You should make it about a horse and a dragon," Jack put in.

Jayson began to type as the stallion massaged his rear, caressing his rump and relaxing him for what was to come. "With the horse as the top?"

"Of course. It's how things work," he whinnied. "And young guys. In their twenties. Older guys are just prudes."

"I'm thirty-three!"

"Oh. Right. Well, thirty-five is the prude cut-off. They should still be in their twenties."

Jayson sighed and kept typing as Jack's weight left him. He heard the snap of a lube bottle opening and misspelled "dragon" as "dragggggooon" when the stallion stuck a lubed finger into his tailhole. The dragon moaned and somehow managed to keep going as Jack worked the finger back and forth, loosening him.

"There you go. Don't forget to talk about how amazing it is to have something under your tail."

"You're not...helping...with the story."

"Sounds to me like I am," the draft horse chuckled as he withdrew his finger and stood up. "Oh, it should be their first time, but because the dragon's an erotic writer, he's amazing already."

"It doesn't work like that," Jayson muttered.

Jack ignored him. He leaned forward, flopping fourteen inches of horse cock on Jayson's rump and back and cutting off any reply from the exasperated dragon. He worked his hips, rubbing the massive rod against the dragon's scales. "No cock like horse cock," he sang.

"Still not helping."

"And still sounds like I am. All these ideas I'm giving you. Not to mention all of this stallion sausage I'm about to give you. Ooo. Put that in. That's a great line."

The dragon wasn't so sure of that, but added it in anyway, if only to stop the horse from asking about it any further. Maybe the story stallion worked as a line cook or something. He'd figure it out later.

Jayson kept writing, going through the foreplay ("ferplaie") and prep while the horse did the same, lubing him more, and using two fingers to make sure the dragon was properly stretched. Jack kept humming that adult toy company jingle to himself, causing Jayson to switch between exasperated sighs and moans of pleasure. After a few more moments, the horse seemed satisfied and withdrew from Jayson's rear.

As he typed, Jayson heard a lube bottle click open again and caught the slick sounds of stallion shaft being greased. He wrote it that way, keeping the cooking metaphor going. Stallion paws landed on his hips, and he stopped typing to brace himself as Jack lined up his tip with his tail hole.

"Hey, com'on. I thought you were being serious about this."

Jayson glared over his shoulder as best as he could. "Next time, *you* can write while I fuck you."

"Heh. Sure, I guess. It'll be trash though—I'm just an idea stud. Still don't get what you're making such a show about. You've taken stuff like it before, no prob. I'd swear you're part fox."

Jayson was about to snap back some sort of reply, but it was cut off by the horse's abrupt entry into his rear. His tail spines and wings shot to full extension.

"Ffffuuuccck!"

"Duh. That's what we're doing. Now relax, Scales. I'm trying to please you, not drill a hole."

The dragon muttered under his breath as he attempted to do as the stallion requested, folding his wings and settling his tail as he did so. He couldn't help but clench a little as the horse worked his way further, but he relaxed enough to resume the story.

Somehow, he managed to keep up with what was happening to type it as it happened. He described how the horse whinnied and nickered as he began thrusting in earnest, his bulk pressing against the dragon's rump as he went. Jayson did his best to chronicle his little gasps and moans as the dragon in the story, but it was difficult to keep his attention on his screen. Jayson was actually rather proud of himself for typing anything at all. Part of him was amazed this was actually working. Maybe it wasn't such a bad idea after all. Jack, as was his way, picked that moment to annoy the dragon.

"That's it," the stallion grunted. "Keep it up. Remember the emotions. Not just the physical."

"Yeah, yeah," Jayson moaned as he became aware of the *thunk thunk* of his horns against the wall. He hadn't even noticed that he'd been pushed that far forward as the stallion plowed him.

"Don't forget their eye color and how big their cock is."

"Do...You...Mind?"

"Com'on, it's important to know that the dragon can take an exactly fourteen-inch cock."

"I'm sure that violates some list out there of what not to do in erotic writing," Jayson grumped.

Jack's only reply was to slam his hips into the dragon even faster. Jayson groaned as well, but kept his fingers moving. He briefly caught that the stallion in the story had a "furrtein inshes cwak." He slapped the draft horse with his tail to try and slow him down, but the stallion trapped it under his arm as he kept going. He smacked the dragon's leg with his own tail. Jayson growled as Jack snorted.

"This is the best way to write sex," the stallion panted. "To have it while you write."

"Are you preaching at me?" the dragon moaned.

The stallion picked up his pace again. Jayson lost track of where his fingers were going, but kept typing. He let out a yip as his own member slapped the edge of the desk. Jack repositioned him, but not enough to stop his horns from hitting the wall. The dragon wondered for a moment how big of a mess they were making on the carpet—he hadn't looked to see if Jack put a towel down. But the worry was driven from his mind: he was panting as well—like the dragon in the story who was "aprorchin hys klimex."

"Oh yeah. Get ready for my stud mayo, Scales," Jack yelled in his ears.

"What the fuck?"

The only answer he got was the stallion slamming his hips against his rear. The motion rocked the dragon forward, slamming his head into the wall. He growled in pain as his head hit the wall again with a final thrust from the horse, sticking his horns fast into the wall.

"I'm cumming!" Jack ejaculated.

A moment later, Jayson felt the clone shudder and then collapse against him. He couldn't look back, as his horns stuck in the wall. All he could do with Jack's full weight against him was hold himself up off the desk and whimper as he hovered just on the edge of fulfillment.

"Mmm. That was amazing," Jack sighed as he withdrew.

"Yeah, great. A little help here? I'm not done over here yet." Jayson's cock throbbed uncomfortably as the massive shaft slipped out of him. He groaned at the feeling of being so close, but unfulfilled as warm stallion spunk started running down his leg.

It was no use. From behind him, the dragon heard the sounds of snoring. Jack had fallen asleep. The dragon sighed. He moved to brace himself to pull his head free when the white laptop screen caught his eye. Nothing he'd written on the screen made any sense.

"This is absolute shit..."

"Oh yeah. Get ready for my stud mayo, Scales," Jack yelled in his ears.

"What the fuck?"

THE BEST AND GREATEST SEQUEL: PRON HARDER DAMNIT!

SOME GUY WHO IS DEFINITELY NOT THE MAIN CHARACTER

Once upon a time, there was a super-awesome sparkledog sergal with neon purple and green eyes named Amethyst Twilight Tw'inkle. He—

"Wait wait wait. That's not right. I'm a girl!"

Shut up. You're guy. There are no girls in this story. No one will read gay porn with a girl in it. They ALL have to be guys!

"Dude, I'm pretty sure I'm a chick."

He was not a chick. He was totally an alpha dude with a twenty-inch cock that could DESTROY any yiffhole in its way.

"But I don't even have a—"

PENIS!!!

"Gah!! How do I even walk with this thing?!"

Not my problem.

Ahem.

One day, Amethyst Twilight Tw'inkle started at a new school. He was the most alpha of all the sparkledog sergals, until he met his first professor, Professor Mog, who was a moogle.

He had never seen anyone more alpha in his life and he was instantly and madly in love with Professor Mog, who was alpha and moogle and hot. So very, very alpha, as was his bulge. After spending all day watching Professor Mog, Amethyst Twilight Tw'inkle couldn't take it anymore and had to have this most alpha moogle.

Amethyst Twilight Tw'inkle confronted Professor Mog one day before class.

"I see you have a bulge," he said, thrusting out his own considerable package.

Professor Mog's eyes roved down Amethyst Twilight Tw'inkle's body and settled on his own ample bulge. His eyes bulged at the sight of it.

"What's this?" he said, alphaly.

"You're the most alpha moogle I've ever met," Amethyst Twilight Tw'inkle said. "We should have gay sex, to see who is more alpha. And because I secretly have a crush on you."

"I also have a crush on you, my student," Professor Mog said, his green eyes twinkling.

"Aren't you afraid of cheating on your foxy boyfriend, Twinky Yifflut the fox or Moonstar Packhowler the wolf?" Amethyst Twilight Tw'inkle siad as he pulled out his cock that was bigger than any porn star EVER and aimed it at Professor Mog.

"They will forgive me. They always forgive me when I cheat after we have a little fight, because cheating is their fetish and the best fetish. We make up and then have even more sex with my awesome twelve inches," he said. "But enough talk! Show me how alpha you are, Amethyst Twilight Tw'inkle!"

Amethyst Twilight Tw'inkle looked around. "Wait, don't we need lube or a condom or—"

ALPHAS DON'T USE LUBE OMG!! SHUT UP AND FUCK!!!

"Prepare your cuckhole for my ass-blaster, Professor Mog!!" Amethyst howled, spitting wetly into his paw and smearing it up and down the twenty inches of his studly lap rocket.

"Murr," Professor Mog said, stroking his own jizz stick.

But even with twenty inches on studly man loaf, Amethyst Twilight Tw'inkle was no match for Professor Mog's alpha alphaness or his throbbing python of lust.

"Oh God, Professor Mog, shove your twelve inches into my pink taco. I mean my boy pussy, because I'm totally a guy. Fill me with your moogle mayo!" he said, because he's totally a guy with a twenty inch meat henge.

And Professor Mog filled Amethyst Twilight Tw'inkle's buttcunt with all twelve inches of his passion pump, and it was amazing, the most amazing sex in the histry of sex. "I'm an atheist!" he moaned as he came six times in Amethyst Twlight Tw'inkle's tight sparkledog skin ditch.

"I'm going to write a story about this," Professor Mog said as he readied his pork steeple for another go at Amethyst Twilight Tw'inkle's mudslide. "I can do it while I'm waiting for my extrememly dangerous and important science experiments are running."

"Isn't that dangerous?" Amethyst Twilight Tw'inkle said, stroking his own cocktapuss.

"I'm alpha," Professor Mog said. "Wait, are those tentacles?"

They were totally tentacles, because no porn is complete without tentacles, because they are the best damned fetish EVER and anyone who tells you otherwise is a lying squid-hater.

Amethyst Twilight Tw'inkle's twenty inch pork sword became twenty phallic tentacles, which grabbed Professor Mog and started probing his murrhole.

"Feel the alpha in my noodly appendages!!" Amethyst Twlight Tw'inkle crowed, plunging one squirmy cream cannon into Professor Mog's moogle rosebud.

Amethyst Twilight Tw'inkle made Professor Mog cum so hard that his stud butter splattered across the ceiling.

"I didn't know you were so good with tentacles, Amethyst Twlight Twinkle," Professor Mog said.

"It's the first time I've ever had tentacle sex, but I knew I'd be awesome at it because I'm as alpha as you, Professor Mog, even though I'm only 20!!" Amethyst Twlight Tw'inkle said.

And Amethyst Twilight Tw'inkle agreed to be in Professor Mog's harem, and they had much more gay sex with their spooge sticks and lived happily ever after.

PENIS!!!

"Isn't that dangerous?" Amethyst Twilight Tw'inkle said, stroking his own cocktapuss.

JOKES

Thurston Howl asked the writers of this anthology to come up with their favorite furry jokes as a fun conclusion for you the reader. So, please enjoy these last laughs.

SCOTT BRADSHAW

"Circus dogs jump when the trainer cracks the whip. But the really well-trained dog is the one that turns somersaults when there is no whip..." –George Orwell

JENNIE BRASS

What did one of the three-blind-mice say at his brother's wake? "He didn't see that coming."

JALETA CLEGG

Why won't they let elephants on the beach? Because they won't keep their trunks up.

DARK END

What do you call a story about a snow leopard in a spaceship? Snep-ulative fiction.

JADEN DRACKUS

When narrator Savrin Drake was recording the audiobooks for Kyell
Gold's *Out of Position* series, he would privately refer to the main
characters Dev and Lee by nicknames he claimed they gave to each
other. Dev called Lee "Cocksleeve" and Lee called Dev "Wallet."
"Shut up so I can fuck you, Cocksleeve."
"Yeah, sure. Buy me a house, Wallet."
I laughed so hard the first time I heard this on Savrin's audiobook, I
almost drove off the road.

SHAWN FRAZIER

How did the politician win the election?
He promised to balance the budget, lower taxes, and put a Unicorn in
everyone's backyard.

SEARSKA GREYRAVEN

A lion comes across two people, one reading and one writing. The lion
pounces and devours the person reading and ignores the person
writing. Why?
Because we all know a writer cramps while a reader digests!

JAMES HUDSON

Why was a dog made king of Denmark?
Because he was a Great Dane.

MADISON KELLER

A lady goes into a restaurant and sits down. As the waiter approaches, he sees a Chihuahua stick its head out of the woman's purse. "Ma'am, we don't allow dogs in here." "Oh, it's fine. I have a concealed weapon permit."

BILLY LEIGH

Furry—the one place where you can be a Wolf and date a Dragon, and no one will question what your kids will look like.

MARY E. LOWD

"Outside of a dog, a book is a man's best friend. Inside of a dog, it's too dark to read." —Groucho Marx

MIKASIWOLF

How would you react after waking up to a wereanimal transformation? Non-Furry: Argh! What's happening to me? Furry: YES! FINALLY!

MOG MOOGLE

I was asked to think of a joke for this. I thought about it, and I think I have come up with a good furry joke. Please turn to "The Best and Greatest Story Ever" and reflect on the fact that this story is in print.

BanWynn Oakshadow

You can teach a cat to do anything that it wants to do.

Lisa Pais

There was a papa mole, a momma mole, and a baby mole. They lived in a hole out in the country near a farmhouse. One morning Papa mole poked his head out of the hole and said, "Mmmm, I smell sausage!" Momma mole poked her head outside the hole and said, "Mmmm, I smell pancakes!" Baby mole tried to stick his head outside but couldn't get past his parents. Baby mole said, "The only thing I smell is molasses."

Fred Patten

The dog thinks of his master, "He feeds me, takes care of me, and loves me. He must be a god."
The cat thinks, "He feeds me, takes care of me, and loves me. I must be a god." —paraphrased from *The Portable Atheist*, edited by Christopher Hitchens

Frances Pauli

Why did the chicken cross the road?
To prove to the opossum it could be done.

Nidhi Singh

Hell hath no furry like a she-wabbit scorned.

SKUNKBOMB

How do you stop a skunk from smelling?
Hold his nose!

SOFOX

Why should you never play poker with a group of lions?
In case one of them is a cheetah!

TELEVASSI

"In ancient times cats were worshipped as gods; they have not
forgotten this." —Terry Pratchett

MAGGIE VENESS

There was this donkey who couldn't seem to make any friends and was
very sad and lonely, even though he had an IQ of 186. Just goes to
show, even in the animal world: nobody likes a smart ass.

TYSON WEST

A lion, a leopard, and a coyote were called into a CIA office to interview for a secret mission. The bureaucratic beaver and buffalo sat still-faced in cheap suits behind a desk. They asked the lion, who stood broad-chested at attention in front of them, "How much is two and two?" The lion looked puzzled and replied, "Why, four, of course!"

They thanked the lion, then called in their next candidate, the leopard. The leopard slunk in, chewing on a toothpick, and leaned against the desk with his eyes closed. They asked him the same question. The leopard barely opened his eyes and mumbled, "Well, during the day it's four. At night who knows what it can be?" The buffalo and beaver thanked him, then called in the last candidate, the coyote.

The coyote furtively looked around and stood by the door as if ready to escape. The two bureaucrats asked the coyote the same question.

The coyote immediately began checking for electronic bugs, looked around to make sure there was no one else in the room, got close to the two and whispered, "How much do you want it to be?"

They decided the coyote was the perfect candidate for the job.

RECOMMENDED READING

FRED PATTEN

Furry humor is rare outside of juvenile fantasies, such as the seven *Bunnicula* books by James Howe (*Bunnicula: A Rabbit-Tale of Mystery* (1979), *Howliday Inn, The Celery Stalks at Midnight, Nighty-Nightmare*, etc.). Adult furry humor does exist, although it is mostly outside the literature of furry fandom. Here are some titles that you may find enjoyable reading.

This bibliography lists first editions. Some of these books are easier to find in reprints.

Anderson, Poul, & Dickson, Gordon R. The Hoka series. *Earthman's Burden*. Illustrated by Edd Cartier. Gnome Press, July 1957, 185 pages.

The first six s-f stories about Alex Jones, the harried human ambassador to Toka, the planet whose teddybear-like Hoka natives have gone crazy over Earth culture. They remodel themselves, depending upon the Tokan country, into small, furry cowboys, Mozart's *Don Giovanni*, a juvenile TV "Space Patrol", "arr matey" pirates, Victorian London with a Sherlock Holmes, and the French Foreign Legion.

—. *The Sound & the Furry: The Complete Hoka Stories*. Science Fiction Book Club/SFBC, March 2001, 399 pages.

All ten Hoka short stories and novelettes plus the one novel.

Bradfield, Scott. *Animal Planet*. Picador USA, October 1995, 231 pages.

A satiric capitalistic rewrite of George Orwell's *Animal Farm* in pop-media language. Humans force "equal rights" on all animals to turn them into a new lower-class consumer market; penguins drinking cocktails, and so on. The animals revolt, but soon succumb to creating their own commercialism, meaningless TV talk shows, etc.

Cook, Kenneth. *Play Little Victims.* Illustrated by Megan Gressor. Pergamon Press, September 1978, 87 pages.

A bleak comedy. God wipes out life on Earth, but misses two mice, Adamus and Evemus, in a small valley. They breed so fast that they are forced to adopt man's customs of warfare, reckless traffic accidents, alcoholism, drug addiction, etc., as desperate attempts at population control. (Birth control? Don't be silly!)

Freer, Dave, & Flint, Eric. *Rats, Bats & Vats.* Maps by Randy Asplund. Baen Books, September 2000, 388 pages.

—. *The Rats, the Bats & the Ugly.* Map. Baen Books, September 2004, 391 pages.

A science-fiction duology. Note that the authors' names are reversed on the second book. When alien space armies attack the human colony planet Harmony And Reason, its inept military leaders create an expendable army of vat-cloned humans and cyber-enhanced intelligent bats and rats (actually elephant-shrews). The bats and rat/shrews have names and personalities based on famous human anarchists like Michaela Bronstein and Eamon Dzhugashvilli. Cloned human soldier Chip Connolly and aristocratic heiress Virginia Shaw find themselves leading a raunchy team of seven talking rats and five bats against the aliens. Another character is Fluff, a galago with the programmed personality of Don Quixote.

Gray, Pat. *The Cat.* [British edition] Dedalus Ltd., March 1997, 124 pages. [U.S. edition] The Ecco Press, November 1998, 124 [+ 1] pages.

"A dark comedy with universal appeal, THE CAT is the ANIMAL FARM of the post-communist 1990s," says the American dust-jacket blurb, while a review of the British edition says that, "Gray's reworking of the ANIMAL FARM concept brings in a post-Thatcherite twist." A cat, rat, and mouse are best friends in a typical British suburban home. The cat is the man's pampered pet, while the rat and mouse feast on food he leaves out. When the man dies of a coronary from overeating and his widow moves away, the animals get hungry and their friendship dissolves. The cat represents Capitalism and consumerism, while the rat is a Socialist labor leader who tries to organize the local small wildlife, and the mouse, his friend, stands for ineffectual intellectuals.

Magrs, Paul. *Mad Dogs and Englishmen*. (BBC *Doctor Who* Novels, 100) BBC Worldwide Ltd., January 2002, 250 pages.

One of many authorized *Doctor Who* novels; this was advertised as #100 in the series. It is less serious than most. The Doctor and his two companions (Fitz Kreiner and Anji Kapoor, this time) get involved in a civil war between futuristic-gun-waving poodles dyed bright scarlet, orange, green, and other neon colors. One of the poodles, Fritter, joins them. Other characters include a boar British-vacation hotelier; Professor Alid Jag, an aphid master criminal; and dozens of Nöel Cowards. Anji says, "'It's like [...] some mad version of Planet of the Apes... with, um, poodles instead of monkeys...'"

Maguire, Gregory. *Leaping Beauty: And Other Animal Fairy Tales*. Illustrated by Chris L. Demarest. HarperCollins, August 2004, 197 [+ 1] pages.

A collection of eight classic fairy tales, rewritten in the style of Jay Ward's "Fractured Fairy Tales" and with animal characters. "Leaping Beauty" features a bullfrog king and queen whose polliwog daughter is cursed by an evil hornet fairy. She grows up and demands that the fairy remove her curse, or she will use her bullfrog voice to make Dame Hornet miserable. "Rumplesnakeskin" features Norma Jean, a sheep who dreams of becoming a movie star, and a stag horror movie director who wants her golden fleece to finance his next movie. Other tales are "Little Red Robin Hood", "So What and the Seven Giraffes", "The Three Little Penguins and the Big Bad Walrus", "Goldiefox and the Three Chickens", "Hamster and Gerbil", and "Cinder-Elephant".

O'Neil, Russell. *Jonathan*. Based on an idea by Ann Noyes Guettel. Frontispiece by Doug Anderson. Appleton-Century-Crofts, March 1959, 214 pages.

A movie company is shooting a Western in northern Mexico. Jonathan Cartwright, an often-drunken scriptwriter and practical joker, is required by his contract to be present. He loathes Bruce Gentry, the egotistical cowboy hero star. When a Mexican witch turns Jonathan temporarily into a horse, he takes advantage of the transformation to embarrass Gentry and play jokes as a horse on the movie crew.

Pratt, Theodore. *Mr. Limpet*. Drawings by Garrett Price. Knopf, January 1942, 144 pages.

A World War II fantasy. Meek, henpecked Henry Limpet falls off the Coney Island pier and turns into a handsome but unique fish. He gradually adjusts to his piscine form and finds a mate, Ladyfish. He diplomatically declines to help Adolf Hitler sink Allied shipping in the North Atlantic (this was written when the U.S. was still neutral). He foretells that mankind will kill itself off through warfare, and the future will belong to the fishes. The basis for the movie *The Incredible Mr. Limpet*, which was made long after the war with a U.S. Navy vs. Nazi U-boats theme.

Smith, Thorne. *The Stray Lamb*. Doubleday, November 1929, vi + 303 pages.

The only bawdy animal fantasy written during the Prohibition Era. T. Lawrence Lamb, a rich but bored investment banker, wishes he wasn't so inhibited; that he was free like the animals. A little russet man who may be Budai, the Chinese god of humor, nods and Lamb begins turning into a series of animals (usually drunken), one week for each -- horse, seagull, dog, kangaroo, goldfish, etc. Some are handsome and mischievous, others are miserable and may not live until he becomes human again. Sapho, his social-climbing wife, is mortified, but Hebe, his unembarrassed flapper daughter, and Melville Long, her lounge-lizard fiancé, are delighted. Some of Lamb's transformations like into a lion help Hebe and Melville when they become bootleggers; but Sapho wants to get rid of Lamb while keeping his fortune, and realizes it isn't murder to kill an animal.

Stern, David. *Francis*. Illustrated by Garrett Price. Farrar, Straus and Co., October 1946, x + 216 pages.

A fix-up novel from 15 World War II magazine short stories. The narrator, an unnamed young 2nd lieutenant in Burma, discovers that Francis, an Army mule, can talk and fly. Francis does not want publicity and uses the lieutenant as a figurehead to warn the Army about some Japanese sabotage or pending attack on Burma GHQ; but the lieutenant's insistence on giving Francis credit always ends with the lieutenant being sent to the neuropsychiatric ward. The lieutenant's superiors finally cannot find any other source for the information, and try to catch Francis in action. Francis must fake his death to escape notoriety. The novel that the "Francis the Talking Mule" movies of the 1950s are based upon.

Varhaug, R. N. *Pongo and Jeeves*. Xlibris Corp., May 2000, 168 pages.

Blurb: "A mutation gave two chimpanzees above average human brains. They made the best of it, living full lives that included impersonating aliens, writing speeches for a presidential candidate, driving expensive cars into swimming pools and more." Two experimental chimpanzees with human intelligence adopt the names and mannerisms of British comical twits and play tricks on the lab staff. When the head scientist plans to dissect their brains, they reveal their intelligence to two sympathetic lab assistants, Patricia and Thor, who smuggle them out and hide them. After Pat and Thor get married and Thor inherits a ranch, the four move there. Some of Pongo and Jeeves' humorous pranks occur during the cross-country drive there; others take place by phone and mail from the ranch.

Wolf, Gary K. The Roger Rabbit books. *Who Censored Roger Rabbit?* St. Martin's Press, October 1981, 214 pages.

'Toon Roger Rabbit hires human private eye Eddie Valliant to learn why the DeGreasy newspaper comic-strip syndicate won't let him out of his contract. Toons have the ability to make temporary doppelgangers of themselves. When Rocco DeGreasy is murdered, Roger is the main suspect. Then Roger himself is murdered. Eddie must solve the case(s), with the aid of Roger's doppelganger before it fades. The novel that the 1988 Disney/Touchstone movie is based upon. Wolf wrote two sequels, *Who P-P-P-Plugged Roger Rabbit?* (1991) and *Who Wacked Roger Rabbit?* (2014), not as funny.

Zelazny, Roger. *A Night in the Lonesome October*. Illustrated by Gahan Wilson. William Morrow/AvoNova, August 1993, 280 pages.

In October of a late-Victorian year, an evil group of 31 supernatural villains (Baba Yaga, Count Dracula, Jack the Ripper, Dr. Frankenstein, the Wolfman, "the Mad Monk", the two grave robbers, etc.), one for each day of the month, plus The Great Detective gathers near London for a demonic contest to determine the fate of the world. Each player has an animal familiar. The story, written in the style of H. P. Lovecraft, is seen through the eyes of Snuff the hound, Graymalk the cat, Bubo the rat, Needle the bat, Nightwind the owl, Tekela the raven, Quicklime the snake, and the others.

LETTER FROM THE ARTISTS

Hello everyone,

Thank you so much for reading through this collection of stories and looking through our art. We thoroughly hope you enjoyed it; it was certainly a fun and unique project for both of us!

For a lot of these stories, we based the illustration off a general sense of the plot, so we apologize if specific body details were not followed. As the prefatory footnote suggests, a big part of our project was to take these stories, their supplementary styles, and have fun with it.

Tabsley's art has appeared on the covers of *The Auraless, Furries Among Us 2, Passing Through,* and more. He's also had artwork published in *Wolf Warriors III: Winter Wolves,* and he was the illustrator for *Curious Things.* He is a panda and enjoys chewing bamboo in his spare time. Jeqon, on the other paw, is a cyan and magenta deer-horse hybrid who is just beginning his art career. This is his "debut."

Between the two of us, the entire project took about three months. Jeqon did a lot of the planning and designing. Both Jeqon and Tabsley drew. And Tabsley did all the coloring.

Below, we include a list of the illustrations, the styles they were based on, and who drew each piece.

Again, we hope you enjoyed! Feel free to check out our FAs at user/Tabsley and user/Jeqon.

Yours,
Tabsley and Jeqon

Preface, The Simpsons – Jeqon
FAPD, Dr. Seuss – Jeqon
Perfect Harmony, Bojack Horseman – Jeqon
Counter-Curlture, The Regular Show – Jeqon
The Carrot is Mightier Than the Sword, Winnie the Pooh – Tabsley
A Web of Truths, Courage the Cowardly Dog – Jeqon
Suddenly, Chihuahua, Hayao Miyazaki – Tabsley
Kenyak's Saga, Thundercats – Tabsley

Rapscallions, Don Bluth – Tabsley
Dazzle Joins the Screenwriters' Guild, Dilbert – Jeqon
A Late Lunch, Disney – Tabsley
Riddles in the Road, Tim Burton – Tabsley
The Lost Unicorn, My Little Pony – Tabsley
Boomsday, Steamboat Willy – Jeqon
Oh! What a Night!, Okami – Tabsley
Moral for Dogs, Calvin & Hobbes – Tabsley
Broadstripe, Virginia Smells Like Skunk, Roald Dahl – Tabsley
A Legend In His Own Time, Looney Tunes – Tabsley
The Cat's Meow, Garfield – Jeqon
Woolwertz Department Store Integrated Branch Employee Manual: Human-Furred Relations, Peanuts – Jeqon
A List of Erotica Clichés You Should Avoid in Your Heat Submission, Happy Tree Friends – Jeqon
The Best and Greatest Story Ever, Spongebob Squarepants – Tabsley
Self-Insertion, Pokemon manga – Jeqon
The Best and Greatest Sequel: Pron Harder Damnit!, South Park – Tabsley
Jokes, Family Guy – Tabsley
Recommended Reading, Sonic the Hedgehog – Tabsley
Letter from the Artists, Cyanide & Happiness – Jeqon

CREDITS

www.ingramcontent.com/pod-product-compliance
Lightning Source LLC
Chambersburg PA
CBHW062151080426
42734CB00010B/1647